# SHAME

Connie,
Now watch it sell a million and we'll really be shocked.

Cousin,
Bob

# SHAME

**THE WAY OF REDIRECTION UNTO *THE PERSON* WITHIN**

*R.J. Chuck*

SERAPHINA PRESS   *MINNEAPOLIS*

Copyright © 2012 by R.J. Chuck

Seraphina Press
212 3rd Avenue North, Suite 290
Minneapolis, MN 55401
612.455.2293
www.SeraphinaPress.com

All rights reserved. No part of this publication may be reproduced, stored in a retrieval system, or transmitted, in any form or by any means, electronic, mechanical, photocopying, recording, or otherwise, without the prior written permission of the author.

Quotations from the Bible are taken from:
The Holy Bible, New International Version® (NIV), copyright © 1973, 1978, 1984, 2010 by Biblica, Inc.™ Used by permission. All rights reserved worldwide.

Holy Bible, New Living Translation (NLT), copyright © 1996, 2004, 2007 by Tyndale House Foundation. Used by permission of Tyndale House Publishers Inc., Carol Stream, Illinois 60188. All rights reserved.

The Holy Bible, New King James Version® (NKJV), copyright © 1982 by Thomas Nelson, Inc. All rights reserved.

Quotations from *Shame: The Power of Caring* are taken from Gershen Kaufman, *Shame: The Power of Caring*, 3rd Edition, Schenkman Books, Incorporated, 1992. All rights reserved.

ISBN-13: 978-0-9846204-9-4
LCCN: 2011944883

Distributed by Itasca Books

Cover illustration by Ann L. Brennan
Cover Design by Becky Kent
Typeset by Kristeen Ott

*Printed in the United States of America*

SERAPHINA
PRESS

Here's your book, Gee!

In memory of Patty Kay

# TABLE OF CONTENTS

Contents / vii
Acknowledgments / ix
Introduction / xiii

**Part 1: Emotional and Psychological Mechanisms of Shame**

Chapter 1   Something Old, Something New / 1
Chapter 2   Shame, the Family, and Society / 19
Chapter 3   The Enemy inside the Gate: Internalizing Shame / 33
Chapter 4   The Intimate Adversary: Defending Ourselves from Shame / 51
Chapter 5   When Shame Destroys a Human Being / 64

**Part 2: Shame, God, and the Bible**

Chapter 6   How Did Shame Get Mixed up with Religion? / 90
Chapter 7   Shame and the Chosen People / 105
Chapter 8   When Shame Defines a Nation / 120
Chapter 9   Shame on the King / 140
Chapter 10  David, the "Man after God's Own Heart" / 152
Chapter 11  Solomon and the Golden Age of Israel / 168
Chapter 12  A Kingdom (Self) Divided, a Prophet's Voice / 183
Chapter 13  Jesus—Sent to Show Us the Way / 204
Chapter 14  Paul the Apostle and His Long Journey toward Understanding / 225

**Part 3: Finding the Way of Redirection**

Chapter 15  So . . . Now What? / 272
Chapter 16  The End of the Journey . . . and the Beginning / 292

# ACKNOWLEDGMENTS

I must first acknowledge my great debt to Albert J. Randall, without whose encouraging comments on the first one hundred typed pages, this book would probably have never been published. Whenever I had a doubt about the book or became weary with the work, I would read his comments. I wouldn't be at all surprised if I read them fifty times since he sent them to me in July of '09.

I must equally acknowledge the great debt I owe Dr. Gershen Kaufman, without whose book on shame I would never have had the opportunity to take this most incredible journey.

I am also grateful to Reverend David McShane, who provided needed encouragement and also graciously read much of the edited manuscript.

I appreciate the efforts of Matthew Pall, a senior psychology/neuroscience major at Ursinus College, who read and reviewed the manuscript and provided helpful perspectives.

Many thanks also go to my editor, Thom Lemmons, who went well beyond the requirements of the contract. He brought increased clarity and many pertinent additions to this work.

Finally, and most importantly, I want to thank my family, most particularly my mother, Anna, who is probably as shocked by this, and as tired of this, as I.

# SHAME

**THE WAY OF REDIRECTION UNTO *THE PERSON* WITHIN**

# INTRODUCTION

If I told you that everyone in the world—every single human being who has ever lived, in fact—suffers from the effects of a deadly emotion; and that minimization of the effects of this emotion is not only the most important issue of human existence, but also that a complete elimination of this emotion is possible for every person on the planet; and if I told you that a complete eradication of this emotion requires—demands, in fact—that you *do* absolutely nothing . . . you'd probably think I was some kind of nut case.

And yet, that is precisely the claim I am making.

Perhaps I should explain. The potentially deadly emotion that strikes us all is called shame. Shame causes us to view ourselves as flawed and defective human beings. Shame makes us mentally and emotionally ill; it seduces us into behaviors like addiction, greed, lust, and victimization of other human beings. Shame causes people who love each other to sometimes behave as though they hate each other. It leaves children with scars—both physical and emotional—inflicted by parents who are trying to escape their own shame, and these scars, in turn, become the breeding ground for the shame that is inflicted on a whole new generation. Shame fills the population of our prisons . . . and our executive suites. Both the convicted criminal and Fortune 500 CEO are tortured, in various ways and to varying degrees, by the effects of shame. And both have adopted their particular behaviors in an attempt to escape—an attempt that is doomed to failure.

To some, especially those of you with some sort of religious background, it may sound like I'm describing the effects of sin. But I'm not. As a matter of fact, one of the central points that I will make in this book is that the *mistaken* association of shame with sin—misbehavior, transgression, violation of the social compact, or any other religious or humanistic metaphor that has been devised through the centuries—is one of the principal obstacles to the extermination of shame that we so desperately desire. (And now, my religious readers are even more certain that I'm a heretic or a whack job. But bear with me—this isn't headed where you may think!)

When I speak of the devastating effects of shame, I can assure you that I have been there and done that and have the actual scars to prove it. I am unfortunate enough to possess an earned doctorate in the many ways shame can torment the soul and suck the life from a human psyche. Without going into too much detail at the moment, I'll just say that my journey to the depths of shame included a one-way ticket on the Meth Express and other assorted conveyances that were just as unpleasantly captivating. It wasn't until I was in a jail cell in Hopkinsville, Kentucky, doing time—again!—for a third drug conviction, that I finally started to gain—actually, I should say it was presented to me as a gift—an understanding of the cure for the universal disease of shame . . . but I'm starting to get ahead of myself.

Right now, I'd like you to imagine two young boys, playing in the backyard.

**Finding the Key**
"Quick, you go up first," Billy commands.

Tommy grabs the higher climbing spike with his left hand, while placing his right foot on the lower one, and heaves himself upward. Within seconds he traverses nearly half of the strategically placed pins toward the tree house above.

## *Introduction*

Billy starts climbing as well.

In less than a minute the two boys are safely tucked within their shadowy hideaway, high in the old oak.

"Where'd you put that other piece?" Tommy asks.

A moment later Billy returns to where his friend is kneeling on the floor with the more recently found object lying before him.

"There is no way they fit together," explains Tommy. "This one looks really, really old, but that other one looks brand new."

"But didn't you notice their shapes?"

"Nah, the only thing I noticed was that one was dull and old and the other looked shiny and new."

At that moment the two pieces in Billy's hands snap together with a loud click.

"Wow," Billy yells as he drops the stone globe. "They came together like magnets!"

The two friends sit spellbound as the softball-sized sphere begins to glow brightly and chase the shadows from their gloomy hideaway above the backyard . . .


**The Pieces Come Together**

Like Billy and Tommy, I found two pieces that seemed, at first glance, to be unrelated. And yet, when I placed them in proximity to each other, they came together with an irresistible force and began to shed light on the confusing and frustrating aspects of my life that I had despaired of ever understanding, much less changing. One ancient and one relatively modern, these two "puzzle pieces" soon proved to provide a key for understanding life and its true purpose with a clarity that I would never have imagined myself capable of.

# SHAME

As I have indicated, this journey toward understanding came at a point in my life when I was, in the words of an early teacher, "out of looking places." I was at a dead end—literally. And at that point of utter despair and hopelessness, I had decided that something had to change. I could not go on any longer the way I was. There had to be something I was missing, and if there wasn't, I was out of here.

I remember thinking something along the lines of, "Okay God, this is your time. If you exist, then you somehow need to prove it. If a truth exists, then you need to show it to me!"

I started reading on all the major religions. I was already familiar with Buddhism, and I also evaluated a number of the philosophical schools of thought, including existentialism and humanism. I looked at psychology and sociology. I was somewhat familiar with such concepts as cognitive restructuring and many of the other more widely used mental health therapies of the last thirty years. Because of my choices in life, I was already very familiar with the "Twelve Steps." I started reading the Bible for the first time. And, at about this same time, I began reading a book by renowned psychologist and author Gershen Kaufman, a book titled *Shame: The Power of Caring.* And that was when the pieces clicked together.

In fact, the image of pieces coming together is a very apt way to describe the state of my search for meaning during this time. It was as if each book or subject I read about was a picture puzzle. It was then as if I put each puzzle into a much larger box and started mixing all the pieces together. Finally, when the box was full, it was then as if I heaved the box of pieces skyward and shouted out to God, "Now, let me see you make a picture out of that!" This book is a description of the picture that formed when the pieces came down.

## Introduction

**God and Shame**

And speaking of God and the big picture, I should also state at the outset that one of the things that has become clear to me—a conclusion that will be troubling to those of you with Judeo-Christian religious backgrounds—is that rather than being a tool of some malevolent evil force intent upon our destruction, shame is actually God's idea. Yes, you read me correctly: This newly revealed understanding tells us that rather than being a consequence of wrong or sinful actions, shame is really a mechanism of interpersonal redirection. For over five thousand years it has been perceived by many of the world's religions that shame has an action cause, but this has now been revealed to clearly not be the case. As we'll see in the following pages, shame actually occurs from the violation of the interpersonal expectations stemming from a universal human need for which I've coined the term "primary interpersonal need." It is the *unsatisfied* primary interpersonal need that creates the interpersonal expectations that, when violated, cause the self to feel shame and then view itself as wrong, deficient, defective, sinful, or worse. These perceptions of an action cause have led the world's religions to propose that adherents could act their way out of shame through obedience to some do/don't action plan. However, the subsequent failure to defeat shame using such effort then led these same adherents to perceive themselves as hopeless sinners in need of a savior.

## The Plan of This Book

Have you ever wondered:

- Why are our most important relationships sometimes so damned difficult?
- Why are our most important relationships also the ones that cause the most pain?
- Why do *we* suffer when someone important to us tells us a lie?
- Why is it that when we get stung by a bee, bitten by a dog, or mauled by a bear, we are only hurt physically, but when similar things are done to us by people, we are often emotionally hurt as well?

The answer to these and many other fundamental questions begins in contemplating that strange object made up of two pieces, one old, and one new: the Bible and Kaufman's *Shame: The Power of Caring*. Like Billy and Tommy in the tree house, the light emanating from these two connected pieces will illuminate the deep connections between shame and the history of humanity's spiritual strivings. By juxtaposing the Bible with the emerging understanding of how shame has the capability to permeate almost every aspect of human psyches and relationships, we'll come to a greater understanding of the mechanism of shame and how it affects us, moment to moment.

Next, we'll embark on a lightning tour of the history of humanity's failed attempts to overcome shame as that history is presented in one of the world's oldest sacred texts, the Bible. Along the way, we'll discover that shame, our most ancient enemy and our most basic malady, has become *mistakenly* associated with behaviors, both "good" and "bad." I will make

## Introduction

the point that it is largely only by ceasing our striving to *earn* our way out of shame—by discontinuing our trying to be "good"—can we then begin to be released from its effects. But, as it turns out, we humans are inclined—by our senses, by our bodily needs, by our ways of living in the physical world—to believe that we should be able to completely free ourselves from the effects of shame through effort and action. The spiritual history of the world—not just the Judeo-Christian tradition, but all the world's religions—is a tale of repeated failures to understand our inability to solve our shame problem on our own power.

Finally, we will explore the idea of "relational union"—another term that I've coined—and show how it alone can completely satisfy our primary interpersonal need, thus completely removing the experience of shame. The problem—whether we consciously realize it or not—is that humans are stubbornly predisposed to look to people for satisfaction of the primary interpersonal need. God actually invented shame as a mechanism of redirection to assure relational union with himself!

That will be the end of our journey: to arrive at the place where our union with God—undeserved, unearned, and freely given—is a present reality. Yes, I believe it is not only possible, but necessary for each human being to be joined to God in relational union, not in the "Sweet By-and-By," but right now! Once we have recognized that reality in our lives, we will be ready to live each day, each moment in a world where shame has lost its power to diminish, alienate, and wound us. In that blessed state, we are free to be everything that God intended for us to be.

But first, we must gain an understanding of how shame works and of the subtle lies it tries to tell us. We need to spend some time basking in the glow of that strange key that is made up of two parts.

# PART 1

## *Emotional and Psychological Mechanisms of Shame*

# CHAPTER 1:

## *Something Old, Something New*

*I* no longer believe it a matter of mere chance that my first reading of *Shame: The Power of Caring* just happened to coincide with my beginning to read the Bible. I may be feeling this way because I can no longer imagine my life without having read the two books at the same time, or it may have something to do with the startling impression deep within that told me the two books were somehow vitally connected. Actually, it felt like more than an "inner indication"; it was more like getting smacked in the head with a two-by-four!

As I read, I was continually surprised to find passages in one book that seemed to illuminate, restate, or explain passages in the other. Here are a few examples:

> **THE OLD:** At that moment their eyes were opened, and they suddenly felt shame at their nakedness. So they sewed fig leaves together to cover themselves (Genesis 3:7, NLT).

> **THE NEW:** The urge to hide, to disappear from view, follows quickly in the wake of

# SHAME

shame. Reducing that often agonizing scrutiny is critical, and all hiding behavior therefore originates in the necessity of covering the self (*Shame: The Power of Caring*, 3rd ed., p. 196).

**THE OLD:** When the cool evening breezes were blowing, the man and his wife heard the Lord God walking about in the garden. So they hid from the Lord God among the trees (Genesis 3:8, NLT).

**THE NEW:** To feel shame is to feel *seen* in a painfully diminished sense. The self feels exposed both to itself and to anyone else present (*Shame: The Power of Caring*, p. 8).

**THE OLD:** The man replied, "It was the woman you gave me who gave me the fruit, and I ate it" (Genesis 3:12, NLT).

**THE NEW:** Strategies of transfer, in contrast, are aroused only after some shame has begun to be felt. Such strategies of transfer aim at making someone else feel shame in order to reduce our own shame. For example, if I feel humiliated, I can reduce this affect by blaming someone else. The blaming directly transfers shame to that other person, enabling me to feel better about myself (*Shame: The Power of Caring*, p. 81).

## Something Old, Something New

**THE OLD:** Then the Lord God asked the woman, "What have you done?"
"The serpent deceived me," she replied. "That's why I ate it" (Genesis 3:13, NLT).

**THE NEW:** This interpersonal transfer of shame usually follows the lines of the familiar pecking order, or dominance hierarchy which emerges in social groups. Whether it is in the *family*, the *peer group*, the *school setting* or the *work setting* a dominance hierarchy will have emerged based on either actual or perceived power. Shame will transfer right down the line, from stronger to weaker (*Shame: The Power of Caring*, pp. 81, 82; emphasis in original).

As I read, I was struck dumb by the similarity of these two phenomenological descriptions. After all, millennia separate the two writings. Not only that, but they are written for two completely different purposes: one religious and the other scientific. And yet, the almost innumerable points of congruence between them made it increasingly difficult for me to deny that there was something monumentally significant in this unexpected parallelism between two texts that, by rights, should have been wildly divergent.

What I first thought to be a line connecting two points in time has actually turned out to be an arc connecting one and the same point. Indeed, the circumference of *the circle* has now been joined, and *the circle* has now been closed. With stunning clarity, I realized that the events in the Garden of Eden were perfectly planned and executed; there were no

# SHAME

mistakes, accidents, or surprises. The serpent was *selected* because it was the most "cunning"—prudent, shrewd, subtle, wise and crafty—"of all God's creatures." The part that God needed the serpent to play was critically important; it had to somehow convince Adam and Eve to eat the fruit of the tree, even after God had told them not to eat. Why? Because they had to experience shame. *The whole purpose of the garden was for the inducement of a shame experience—essentially, the introduction of God's mechanism of interpersonal redirection unto Himself.*

I've already mentioned how shame becomes manifest because of our looking externally to satisfy all our interpersonal needs. It is therefore significant for us to realize that Adam and Eve perceived God as an external, localized, and physical presence. The Bible even speaks of God "walking in the garden in the cool of the day!"

So, the lesson that God has always been trying to teach the human race about shame is that it cannot be relieved by the usual, physical means. In order to start humanity on the long road toward learning the correct way to be healed from shame, God first placed Adam and Eve in a situation where every physical need was perfectly supplied: they had all the food and water they needed; they were in no danger from predators or the environment; they had each other for the satisfaction of sexual needs; and they had each other for the satisfaction of their more basic interpersonal needs. And then, with the help of the dear serpent, God confronted them with a need that could not be met by any of the usual methods. Thus began the first of God's numerous attempts to educate, and these lessons have been ongoing for all the millennia since: teaching us the who, what, where, and why's of shame generation and the way to the satisfaction of the primary interpersonal need. I'll return to the Garden of Eden for further discussion once we look at shame through the eyes of Gershen Kaufman and his predecessor and colleague Silvan Tomkins.

For now, though, it's important to realize that our biggest problem with shame is that we are predisposed to attempt to avoid it by means that work for our other needs, thinking that by avoiding it we will satisfy our primary interpersonal need. When we are hungry, we find food and eat it. When we are cold, we cover our bodies or build a fire. When we feel the biological urge toward procreation, we seek out a suitable mate. But none of these "seeing and doing" means work for the total destruction of shame. What further exacerbates the problem of shame is the deeper taking of action toward the satisfaction of this foremost interpersonal need. The more intensely we seek to satisfy this need through action, the more intense our expectation of success. And, as we will see, when these interpersonal expectations are then ultimately violated, the intensity of shame—in all its multiplicity of varieties—is proportionally increased as well.

So, in exactly the same way that physical pain is implemented to prevent us from taking a hammer to our toe, shame has also been implemented to redirect us from hammering our souls. However, because the discomfort that accompanies shame does not emanate from a tangible source (a very important factor that I'll spend a big part of the book explaining), it is harder for us to learn the cause-and-effect lessons we need to learn for avoiding shame than it is for us to learn to stop hammering our toes.

That means that our first order of business is to understand what shame is—and isn't—and then to understand how it operates in the human psyche. Finally, we need to learn what doesn't work in getting rid of shame so that we can finally discover the cure for this malady that has afflicted humankind for its entire history.

Fortunately, we have access to an extensive record of humanity's failed attempts at dealing effectively with shame—the Bible! When we read it through the lens provided by a better understanding of shame, we can more quickly quit trying methods that humanity has already proven unworkable.

But first, let's take a look at some modern, scientific descriptions of what shame is and how it operates in the human mind and emotions.

**A Modern Understanding of Shame**

There was evidently a major change in traditional mental health treatment during the decade of the '80s. This shift in paradigm was initiated and facilitated by the explosion of drug usage that had occurred in the '70s. It was becoming clear to some of the practitioners within the mental health field that the little known emotion called shame was playing a significant role in the development of addiction. This renewed interest in shame just happened to coincide with the pioneering study of emotion by Dr. Silvan Tomkins.

Tomkins' pioneering study of emotions provides us with the missing key: a new theory, a new imaginative grouping, a radical rearrangement of experience (p. xi).

One of the primary reasons why shame had remained so uninvestigated by the mind sciences was because of the nature of shame itself. Whenever we experience shame there is a sense of feeling exposed: we want to hide, we want to run, we want to cover ourselves. We are also extremely reluctant to approach someone else whenever they experience shame. But shame had to be looked at because of the tidal wave of addiction now being confronted by the mental health profession. In the introduction to Dr. Kaufman's *Shame: The Power of Caring*, Sylvan Tomkins writes:

> The paradox about shame is that there is shame about shame. It is much easier to admit one is happy or sad than one feels ashamed. In part this is because of the close association between shame and inferiority. One is ashamed to announce shame as one is ashamed to announce the fact of one's inferiority. . . . This is particularly amplified in a culture which values achievement and success.

Kaufman writes that Tomkins was the first to design a psychological model that gave emotion primacy over drives, thoughts, and language: an arrangement that was a direct challenge to both classical psychoanalysis and cognitive behaviorism. Cognitive behaviorism positions emotions as derivatives of thought. Classical psychoanalysis views emotions as derivatives of drives. Interpersonal theory, object-relations theory, and self-psychological theory all view emotion as a consequence of something else. Tomkins' innovation of placing emotions as primary to thoughts and drives provided an entirely new way of viewing the human experience.

This arrangement by Tomkins makes a lot of sense. When I think about it, emotions do indeed seem to spontaneously occur in response to an activator, which is most often something externally perceived. Emotions seem to pretty much happen on their own without any real ability on my part to stop or create them. Sure, I can attempt to suppress them and keep them from showing, but it's impossible to keep them from happening. Nor do I seem able to change them. "Don't worry, be happy . . ." Yeah, right!

Kaufman says of a new perspective regarding shame revealed by Tomkins' theory of affect,

> Viewing shame from the perspective of affect theory means that, first of all, shame is an affect—an emotion or feeling—not a thought, drive, or interpersonal phenomenon per se. While shame may of course include self-evaluative thoughts or become expressed interpersonally, it begins and remains an affect. As such, shame functions to amplify our awareness, connecting whatever event activated shame with any responses that follow it, including constructed thoughts, motor actions, and retrieved memories (p. xi).

When shame was viewed through affect theory as proposed by Tomkins, certain implications revealed themselves:

1. Shame is not only the product of dysfunctional families.
2. Shame is not only the result of disturbed relationships.
3. Our identity and sense of dignity are greatly affected by shame.
4. Shame plays a pivotal role in the development of self-esteem.

5. Shame greatly affects our pursuit of intimacy with others.
6. Shame occurs throughout the life cycle.
7. The endless debate concerning shame vs. guilt is now rendered pointless.
8. Shame is much more important than only its relationship to addiction and abuse.

These implications pertaining to affect theory in general and shame in particular reveal a number of false assumptions that continue to distort our understandings, many of which still concern the relationship between guilt and shame. We are still widely held by other perspectives that still view shame and guilt as two entirely different emotional states. Another implication of affect theory is that shame is not the necessary cause of addiction, though addiction can certainly create shame. Likewise, dysfunctional families are not needed for the creation and amplification of shame; such families do indeed provide a breeding ground for shame, but they aren't required for the birth and growth of shame. In other words, dysfunctional families can generate shame and shame can lead to addiction, but shame doesn't directly cause addiction or familial dysfunction. Shame can thrive when relationships are healthy, and addiction can develop when relationships are flourishing.

### The Genesis of Shame

So, where in the human psyche do the roots of shame lie? It appears that we begin to experience shame at the same point in our existence when we begin—however unconsciously or simplistically—to answer two of the most fundamental questions

# SHAME

of human existence: "Who am I?" and "Where do I belong?" The answers to these questions seem vitally connected to each other—that who I am seems defined and constrained by how well I first try to gain a sense of belonging. It also appears that figuring out who I am and where I belong is linked to my sense of feeling complete: if I can't define myself and find a place where I feel that I belong, then I'll never feel whole. But it is my looking for a sense of wholeness via my interpersonal interactions with others which then lays me open for the feeling that I don't belong, in turn negatively affecting "Who am I?" In fact, according to Kaufman:

> Shame itself is an *entrance* to the self. It is the affect of indignity, of defeat, of transgression, of inferiority, and of alienation. No other affect is closer to the experienced self. None is more central for the sense of identity. Shame is felt as an inner torment, a sickness of the soul, in the words of Silvan Tomkins. It is the most poignant experience of the self by the self, whether felt in the humiliation of cowardice, or in the sense of failure to cope successfully with a challenge. Shame is a wound made from the inside, dividing us both from ourselves and from one another. Shame is the *affect* which is the source of many complex and disturbing inner states: depression, alienation, self-doubt, isolating loneliness, paranoid and schizoid phenomena, compulsive disorders, splitting of the self, perfectionism, a deep sense of inferiority, inadequacy or failure, the

so-called borderline conditions and disorders of narcissism. These are all phenomena which are rooted in shame (pp. xix–xx, *Shame: The Power of Caring*).

According to Tomkins, the experience of shame becomes internalized through shame-colored event memories that begin to link with one another and then begin enhancing one another. These scenes create meanings for the self that can then cause shame to be entirely generated from within—without the need for an external shame-generating event.

Without any clear indication when it starts, we begin questioning our worth and potential. When we begin such wonderings, we secretly begin asking ourselves if the problem lies with us. These periodic bouts of self-doubt, accompanied by fear and distress, are shame. To feel shame is to feel or believe you are seen as less than: as inadequate or defective. Feeling shame can sometimes cause us to believe that all eyes are on us and are witnessing our deficiency. This, in turn, results in our urge to run and hide—just like Adam and Eve in the garden!

Shame is a significant factor in both our personal development and our personal relationships; it plays a role equally as important as anxiety and suffering. However, though the last hundred years have seen significant progress in developing a psycho-scientific language for fear and pain, there has been no such progress with understanding shame.

## Shame and the Self

Shame is manifested during our interactions with others, and *the more significant the relationship, the more severe the shaming potential* (this principle will be important throughout the book). Shame, though initially experienced as a passing emotion, later becomes internalized, and once shame becomes internalized it becomes autonomous: it no longer needs an interpersonal activator. Once internalized, shame can spread throughout the self and shape our developing identity, which, as we've already seen, is the self's answer to the question, "Who am I?"

Identity is the self's relationship with the self, sometimes evidenced by the inner conversations known as "self-talk." This matters deeply, because self-talk is colored by perceptions of worth and adequacy, both of which are called into question by the experience of shame. Thus, shame becomes central to the self's experience with, and identification of, itself. Our worth and adequacy "can be obliterated through protracted shame, leaving us feeling naked, defeated as a person, and intolerably alone" (Kaufman, p. 8).

The sense of exposure that accompanies a shame experience can cause painful inner scrutiny. It can seem that the people around us are seeing into our very souls and seeing our deficiency. The perception of deficiency, the fear that there might be something *wrong* with us, can then keep us from approaching others.

### The Range of Shame-Expression

Shame has the ability to occur in an incredibly wide range of manifestations. Embarrassment, humiliation, guilt, and shyness are all varied forms of shame. The factors that contribute to the intensity of shame can also vary significantly. Public shame is almost always more severe than shame in private. The shame we suffer at the hands of a stranger is almost always less severe than the shame involving a parent, teacher, spouse, or friend (remember: the more significant the relationship, the greater its shaming intensity potential). Further, our ability to cope with the sources of shame, to endure shaming experiences and the repetitiveness of shaming, are all factors that contribute to defining the scope and effect of a shaming experience. In other words, some people are more resistant than others to certain types of shaming. I believe we commonly refer to this as being either thick- or thin-skinned.

The shaming experience, as such, is not always easy to observe in others. In fact, the three primary naturally occurring outward reactions to shame are fear, distress, and rage. On most occasions it is one of these three emotions that we see portrayed by others in response to a shame experience.

I believe road rage is a perfect example of the rage response to a shaming experience, for to feel disrespected is to also feel shame. When we are disrespected—by being cut off in traffic, let's say—we essentially first call into question our own worthiness of respect, that we are also unworthy of belonging. But then at the next instant of recognition that someone else was at fault we feel rage—we are expressing a defensive emotional response to being shoved face-to-face with such unsettling uncertainties regarding our worthiness of belonging and value as a person. The paradox of the rage response to shame, of course, is that it keeps others away, even though what the self really wants is to be comforted in response to inner fracturing.

## Shame and Others

The mechanism by which shame is generated is through the breaking of an interpersonal bridge. An interpersonal bridge is established with someone when they become important to us. The more deeply I connect with someone—the more deeply I believe they are a possible source for my achievement of a sense of interpersonal wholeness, when their mattering comes to matter more—the greater the intensity of possible shaming occurrences. For example, a cursing from a friend carries much more weight—shame intensity—than being cursed by a stranger. Simply, the expectations I have for how my friend should or shouldn't treat me are not necessarily different than my expectations for a stranger, but they are stronger and more clearly defined. We could equally say that my interpersonal expectations have increased with my friend. The cursing from my friend causes me to momentarily question my worthiness of friendship; this causes me to feel exposed, unworthy—ashamed. In Kaufman's words,

> We stand revealed as lesser, painfully diminished in our own eyes and the eyes of others as well. Such loss of face is inherent to shame. Binding self-consciousness along with deepening self doubt follow quickly as products of shame, immersing the self further into despair. To live with shame is to feel alienated and defeated, never quite good enough to belong. And secretly we feel to blame. The deficiency lies within ourselves alone (p.12).

Kaufman addresses interpersonal expectations in the phrase "mutuality of response," especially in reference to our more important relationships. According to Kaufman,

## Something Old, Something New

> Needing a relationship with someone else translates into needing to *feel* that that other person who has now become significant also wants a relationship with us. *Mutuality of response* is indispensable to feeling that one is in a real relationship with another, in a word, to feel wanted for oneself (p. 13).

While it is certainly true that the establishment of an interpersonal relationship is primarily fueled by the need for a sense of intimacy, the desire to forever lose that sometimes subtle and sometimes not so subtle sense of aloneness and separateness—a quality that we usually attach to our most significant relationships—I think the problem extends even farther. I believe that any and all of what we commonly refer to as "people" needs—the needs to identify, to belong, and to have a relationship—require the establishment of an interpersonal bridge of sorts. I believe that it is the very act of delineating someone as a human being that allows another human to potentially cause me shame. Though the interpersonal bridge may only be slight, it still exists because of certain expectations I hold for how a person—any person—should act towards me, from my spouse to the person who takes my order at the drive-through. Whenever these interpersonal expectations are violated, I feel shame.

Our interpersonal expectations have developed from the perception that if we can get everyone to always treat us as we want—they never do or say anything that causes us to question or doubt our sense of worth—we might then find interpersonal wholeness at last. It is only when we are in an environment where we generally feel that we belong, that we feel safe and accepted, that we then move on to find something deeper. (A sense of belonging seems largely a prerequisite to our subsequent finding of a primary intimate relationship.) My point here is that my interpersonal expectations are a key to susceptibility to the production of shame. The higher my expectations for the relationship, the higher the intensity of potential shame it carries.

I also believe that any human interaction can be loosely qualified as relational, even the momentary one we have with the clerk at the drive-through. I agree with Kaufman that it is a deep relationship that is our ultimate goal, but we can't lose sight of the fact that anybody we come in contact with has the potential for causing us to feel disrespected. We don't really expect the clerk at the drive-through to "want us for ourselves." However, any relationship, however casual, contains a degree of expectation of "mutuality of response"; we expect the clerk to treat us with the same degree of respect that we treat him or her. No matter whether the other person is a loved one or a stranger, we automatically have opinions about how he or she should act toward us.

Thus, the shame that occurs upon violation of interpersonal expectations can occur at a multitude of intensities along a continuum ranging from slight to severe, depending on the depth of the relationship. Remember, too, that we all have the core need for deep intimacy. We are ultimately driven to find someone with whom we can unite, can commune, and whom we can know intimately in order to forever escape our sense of loneliness and separation. Being respected is but a prelude to finding a deeper relationship. The problem is that once we find it, we then only seem to eventually *expect more and more.*

**No Way Out**

In other words, *we cannot avoid holding expectations of our relationships*—and even "upping the ante" on those expectations. I am possessed by an interpersonal need that at first drives me to belong, and then drives me toward deeper relationship, accompanied by higher expectations—and correspondingly higher potential for more intensely experiencing shame. The harder I try to fulfill this need, the more I seem to expect from the other person in the relationship. No matter where I look, I look with interpersonal expectation. And at the same time, others are looking at me the same way. No wonder shame seems inevitable!

> Experiencing a need and expecting a response can be viewed as two sides of the one and same phenomenological event (p.14).

When I look toward a particular person for the satisfaction of my deepest interpersonal need, my expectations of others may seem to diminish some, but with regard to the individual from whom I am seeking relational completion, my expectations seem to rise, along with the potential to experience shame more intensely. It can thus seem that it is my very looking which is afoul—I should just stop looking, so as to avoid all risk of feeling shame. But how am I not to look? After all, finding the place where I feel interpersonally whole is one of my most fundamental human needs. And since I cannot *keep* from looking, I cannot keep from experiencing shame.

It seems that we human beings are in a rather serious bind! We must either seek to satisfy our primary interpersonal need, suffer failure sooner or later (usually sooner), along with

# SHAME

the consequential shame, and start defending ourselves from it, or else seek to mask our need by immersing ourselves into some distraction—some interest, excitement, enjoyment, or pleasure—that often carries consequences that are harmful to our health or our societal standing, thus paradoxically causing shame to escalate even more. What a predicament!

In short, we seem condemned to live in a world where we each will forever be causing each other shame. This, of course, is part of The Plan . . . but more on that later.

Next, let's consider some of the ways shame plays out in some of the most significant of human relationships—those in the family.

# CHAPTER 2

## *Shame, the Family, and Society*

No relationship has more capacity for deep shaming than that between a child and parent. Four factors contribute to this potential:

1. The child's physical dependence;
2. The child's lack of maturity;
3. The child's lack of interpersonal skill;
4. The child's lack of power.

As previously implied, shame can and does occur in preverbal children. However, shame cannot become internalized until the child has learned to conceptualize oneself as separate from the parents and developed the verbal ability to label these concepts.

The parents' expression of anger is unquestionably the most common method of inducing shame in the young child. Not only can expressions of anger sever the interpersonal bridge, but they can also disrupt a child's sense of security. It is not really clear where interpersonal needs end and safety/security needs begin; what is clear, however, is that anger can produce shame in the child and cause a rupture in the relationship with the parent. If the interpersonal bridge between them is not restored, the child may feel stuck in shame and will also often face a rising sense of insecurity. Kaufman does not suggest that parents avoid expressing anger, but he does suggest that parents stay alert for signs of increased anxiety, shame, and insecurity.

> Without language, the only reparative means available to the young child is through physical contact. The rupture in the relationship will very likely be followed by the child's spontaneous, nonverbal request for holding (p. 18).

Kaufman suggests that the parent should hold the child while still expressing displeasure. The physical touching allows the child to feel reunited and secure, even while hearing the parent's displeasure.

Whenever young children are not allowed to regain their sense of security they may come to experience shame as abandonment. Feelings of abandonment can also occur in a child whose parent becomes emotionally unavailable or silently withdraws.

Kaufman clearly specifies that one or even multiple shame-inducing experiences will not necessarily drive a child toward a shame-based identity. In fact, minor shame experiences can actually be constructive in teaching the child how to cope with the shame experiences that will surely occur in later years:

> Avoiding necessary encounters with shame will only breed an individual lacking

those essential resources, for shame is inevitable in life. It is the pattern of experiences within significant relationships over time that carries deepest and lasting impact (p. 20).

However, it is a pattern of shame experiences over time that can lead to the internalization of shame.

When children begin getting a little older, the parents will often resort to intentional shaming in order to achieve certain behaviors. By the time parents adopt shaming as a method to control behavior, it is very likely that shaming has become routine. Unfortunately, parents generally have no clue how tumultuous intentional shaming can be for the self. Two examples of intentional shaming presented by Kaufman are "Shame on you!" and "You should be ashamed of yourself!"

A much more public and intentional shaming commonly used by parents is, "Stop that, you're embarrassing me!" Such expressions in public cause the child to feel judged and exposed. This is also an example of a shame transfer, as we discussed in chapter 1: the parent first experiences shame because of the child's public behavior and then passes it on to the child.

Another category of intentional shame inducement occurs when a parent expresses disappointment. Whenever a parent yells "You disappoint me!" or "How could you do that?" the child will undoubtedly feel exposed and defective. Other widely used shame-inducing methods used intentionally by parents are disparagement and belittlement.

When a parent openly compares one child's *good* behavior with another child's *not-so-good* behavior, the latter child will obviously feel less than, if not worse. This sort of comparison-making by a parent may set up certain self-evaluative mechanics

# SHAME

that predispose the child to constantly be comparing themselves to others. Such judgments of self versus others can be a means of perpetual self-shame inducement. Whenever we have adopted the habit of comparing ourselves—our appearance, our performance, our accomplishments—to others, we have surely entered the realm of perpetually shaming ourselves.

Blaming is another fairly common method whereby parents induce shame in their children. A parent's facial expressions of contempt or disgust are very powerful inducers of shame. Indeed, I've read elsewhere that many prominent child development and parenting experts caution parents against facial displays of disgust when changing the infant's soiled diaper, lest the child come to associate shame with normal bodily functions.

Parents who are highly critical of others are very likely to subject their own children to continual feelings of shame. Also, the performance expectations developed later by parents for older children can become a source of shame. Parents often attempt to compel their aging children to live up to extremely high standards of performance, including expectations far above and beyond those deemed reasonable:

1. Personal cleanliness
2. Respect for others' property
3. Respect for others' privacy
4. Respect for the rights, feelings and needs of others
5. Peace ability

Some of the worst performance-related shaming occurs when parents drive their children towards excellence and perfection. Such high parental expectations can create disabling degrees of self-consciousness in children. The paradox of performance expectations is that instead of enhancing performance, they can actually hinder it. According to Kaufman, "It is only to the degree to which however we do is *good enough* that we become free to do our best and thereby maximize chances of success" (p. 25).

Conversely, the anticipation of possible failure to meet these parental expectations arouses fears of being seen as deficient, defective, or worse, and therefore not worthy of being cared for and loved. Such fears are not conducive to optimal performance, whatever the effort at hand.

### Shame and Peers

Not all shaming of children occurs at the hands of parents. A child's own peer group can present an environment for some of the most destructive shaming of all. The child may actually have his or her first shame experiences at school. For a child who has never experienced shame at home, ridicule and mockery by peers can be especially devastating.

Perhaps even worse, however, is open humiliation by a school bully. This can invite a type of feeding frenzy, such as when classmates join in and start calling the victim a sissy for not fighting back (indeed, the classmates are engaging in classic shame-avoidance behavior by concentrating the shaming on the victim and thus avoiding it themselves). Matters can even worsen when the bruised child goes home and is then punished—physically, emotionally, or both—by the father for not "standing up for himself" and being battered by the bully.

As Kaufman says,

# SHAME

> There is no more humiliating experience than to have another person who is clearly the stronger and more powerful take advantage of that power and give us a beating (p. 24).

Such humiliation can cause the child to be consumed by rage and create ideal conditions for the seeking of revenge. It can also lay the groundwork for the victim becoming the tormentor of others later in life.

A child's move into adolescence can be a particularly poignant time of shame experience. Adolescence is a period of great physical change. The changes themselves (or the lack of changes as compared with peers who are maturing at a different rate) give cause for positive or negative evaluation by others. There is probably no part of human development with more wide-ranging susceptibility to shame than adolescence, much of which is centered around the reactions, real or perceived, of a peer group. Kaufman rightly asks,

> Why does the peer group carry such weight with us? Why is the family able to affect what ails us? Where comes their power? That is a question of profound significance, for with it rests an understanding of development itself. It is in the honest looking to others for our most essential human needs that we give over to those others the power of which I spoke. We are needing creatures to begin with. And that is a source of strength as well as a potential source of shame (p. 30).

## Shame and Culture

The culture into which we are born and in which we live shapes our personalities in much the same way as the family and peer group (both of which are, in turn, shaped by the culture).

Along with the home and school settings, the workplace is an equally powerful instrument of culture for teaching and enforcing values and taboos, and also for the production of shame. It seems that we never outgrow this capability; even for adults, the perception or belief that one is powerless in the world may cause feelings of shame. To the degree that one feels powerless, one may feel deficient, defective, or worse. Conversely, to the degree that we have power in the world we are less likely to be subjected to the disrespects, inattentions, and slights of others. In other words, power and influence—however a given society measures these attributes—can confer a perception of belonging due to the absence of shame. This principle operates especially powerfully in the workplace.

Work environments are hierarchical by design. Since hierarchical arrangements in the workplace—from wage structures to the authority conferred by the organization flowchart—also mirror stratifications in power, shame has the strong tendency to flow downward from those with more power onto those with less power (and remember that since the primary interpersonal need is still at play in the work setting, shame generation cannot be avoided). Whenever something occurs at work that causes us to question our worth, purpose, or place, we may ultimately feel disconnected, that we don't belong—ashamed.

But no matter who we are, the president or the packager on the assembly line, we will all suffer shame equally because of our own efforts toward interpersonal wholeness. Fame and power in the world do not translate to that ultimate sense of interpersonal completion.

Nobody likes the feeling of shame, including those at the top of power structures. Further, because of the hierarchical nature of blame-placing as a shame defense, these structures are particularly efficient arrangements for those at the top to transfer their shame without having to be subjected to someone else's shame. While it is true that there is often only one person at the top of every company, even that powerful president or CEO must often answer to the stockholders or a board of directors. The truth of the matter is that *nobody* can fully escape the effects of shame by using sight, effort, or action . . . no matter how powerful or tyrannical they are.

Another source of shame in the workplace is comparison making. This is a method whereby we can create our own shame without any interpersonal interactions with others. We first learn to compare ourselves with others in school, if not earlier. The academic grading system handily creates an environment that fuels comparison making along with the fear of being viewed by others as "less than." It is nearly impossible for a student to avoid comparing his or her grades with those of classmates. In fact, as discussed earlier in the section on shame and the family, when we develop the habit of comparison making, we embark upon a path where we continually subject ourselves to self-shaming; whenever a comparison results in somebody else being perceived as better than we are, we cannot help but to then view ourselves as *less than*. By the same standards that we judge, criticize, or condemn others, we will also judge, criticize, or condemn ourselves.

Shame and honor are the guideposts, the boundaries at opposite ends of the acceptable range within which we must remain in order to belong. Kaufman informs us that there are three predominant cultural scripts in America to which we are expected to be obedient, and each of these pathways toward favor—toward relative freedom from cultural shaming—are reinforced through shaming.

**Success Ethic**

There is probably no culture on the planet that emphasizes success quite like America. We idolize success; we revere it. Not only that, we bestow cultural favor on those who gain it. The contemporary American mantra might be summed up as, "Be successful, or else."

The problem with success is that there is no clear definition of what it really is. Furthermore, success, however it is defined, does not lie entirely within our control. Another conflict arises from the fact that in order to succeed we must compete, but competition is antithetic to our efforts to belong. Indeed, competition often breeds hostility and fear.

We are taught as children to view our achievements as a measure of personal worth and that accomplishment is a measure of success. The implicit message is that we must compete and achieve so as to succeed, or else we'll be *thrown into the night*. Thus, competition for success can engender deep anxiety, especially in the form of fear of failure. To not be successful usually generates feelings of deficiency and defectiveness.

There is a difference between the competition necessary for survival and competition in order to belong and avoid shame. When our efforts to succeed are tied to our efforts to belong— especially if we or others perceive those efforts as insufficient— we may begin questioning both our worthiness to belong *and*

# SHAME

our worthiness to be in a relationship.

### *Independence and Self-Sufficiency*
Here in America we are also urged—commanded, practically—to stand tall, to take care of ourselves, and to never need anybody for anything. Needing something—anything!—is seen as deficient, defective, weak, or worse. To need is shameful; it is equated with unworthiness for belonging or relationship.

For those who devoutly adhere to this injunction, there is often a tendency to look upon those who have needs as less than, inferior, or lazy. Some may even look upon the needy with scorn and contempt. I was astounded by the realization that the American male gender script, the psychological concept of differentiation (as opposed to identification), and the Republican Party (conservative) ideology all align themselves rather nicely to this injunction to be independent and self-sufficient. I don't believe this is a coincidence.

### *Conformity and Popularity*
The final primary injunction in America is the expectation to conform and be popular. To be seen as separate, different, or independent is to be neither praised nor recognized. In order to conform and be popular we have to be a part of; we have to identify. To be popular is to be praised, adored, revered, recognized, and esteemed—favored. To not be popular is to feel deficient, defective, or worse. I believe this injunction conversely emphasizes that we *are* our brother's keeper; this injunction also seems to match up nicely with the female gender script, the Democratic Party (progressive) ideology, and the psychological

concept of identification.

## The Cultural Bind

Kaufman notes that the paradox with these conflicting cultural imperatives, of course, is that we cannot be popular and independent at the same time. We cannot compete and belong at the same time. And as we'll see later, we also cannot identify and differentiate at the same time. Trying to do so causes shame.

It appears to me that it is the underlying need for relational union which manifests as an impulse toward identification, belonging, and relationship, that provides the motivation for the adherence to these injunctions. Simply, we pursue the lesser-shamed paths towards the satisfaction of this need. Where goes shame we don't go. Though being independent and self-sufficient can't satisfy an interpersonal need per se, we still try to go this way, particularly we men, because we have wrongly perceived that our obedience to these injunctions will ultimately lead us to a state of interpersonal completion and wholeness.

## Shame and Gender Roles

Our behaviors as men and women have been profoundly influenced by shame. All cultures have been constructed with their own sets of rules to which each sex must be obedient. Though these scripts may vary widely from culture to culture, the primary method of enforcement shared by them all is cultural shaming.

Gender scripts are developed through gender shaming. The process of gender script development has produced vastly different psychologies in men and women. While it is true that modern neuroscience has revealed startling differences in the brains of men and women (it was Tomkins who theorized that the autonomic differences may have originally developed in response to the differential gender shaming), it is also true that the shamed behaviors of men and women have changed dramatically over the last forty years—perhaps more so for women than for men, when we consider the shifts in behavioral "norms" for women that have come about as a result of the women's rights and women's liberation movements of the late nineteenth and twentieth centuries. I doubt very much that changes in women's brains have produced these relatively recent behavioral changes. What has changed, however, is the cultural shaming that has historically been bestowed upon women by men.

It would have been unimaginable a few decades ago, for example, to predict that by the early decades of the twenty-first century there would be just as many women as men taking upper-level math courses in high school—and yet this behavior on the part of women is now hardly considered unusual at all. Again: *This surely hasn't resulted because of recent changes in women's brain chemistry.* What this shift has resulted from is a change in the ways that women have been shamed by men (and, in some cases, by each other).

Not only has shame controlled how men and women act, it has equally controlled how we think. In 1958 it would have been all but unthinkable for a woman to realistically imagine herself as president of the United States. If a woman—or for that matter, a black man—were to openly express a desire to become president, the individual would have been patronized, mocked, ridiculed, belittled, or worse.

Kaufman verbalizes the "cultural norm–enforcing" function of shame by stating,

> From this perspective, the role of shame is crucial in the partitioning of affects/drives/needs/purposes deemed acceptable versus those deemed unacceptable (p. 203).

For example, American men have traditionally been shamed—and still largely are—for the expression of fear and distress. American women were once heavily shamed for expressing anger or excitement. And though these emotions are no longer as rigidly restricted as they once were, we still have a long way to go in allowing both men and women the free expression of the full range of emotions.

Not only are emotional expressions scripted and enforced through shaming, but needs and drives are also differentially shamed as well. Women were once implicitly told to express only their needs to nurture, touch, and hold. Further, they were allowed to express their needs for self-definition only in relationships with men. Women were supposed to be popular and conform—they were not supposed to be independent and self-sufficient.

The masculine gender script influenced men to give preference to expressions of contempt, disgust, anger, and excitement. Men were told to express the need for power, and they were expected to be independent, self-sufficient—to compete and succeed.

Such gender scripts—largely unspoken but undeniably powerful—assure the development of gender personalities and gender roles. Furthermore, gender scripts are primary over other scripts, including racial, religious, cultural, or national/political scripts; we are first told to be men or women and then we are told to be something else. Gender scripts determine the

# SHAME

primary path we must follow in order to satisfy, or attempt to satisfy, our need to identify. Gender scripts actually determine the *look* of all our relationships with others; they are the genesis of gender ideologies.

Now that we have briefly explored the beginnings of the shame experience in the human soul and have looked at ways that the family and society reinforce or contribute to the experience of shame, let's examine how shame becomes internalized. For when this occurs—as I believe it does for everyone—shame can arise from within, with no outside event or interaction required to stimulate it. Shame, in other words, becomes a part of us. How this occurs is the first topic of the next chapter.

# CHAPTER 3

## The Enemy inside the Gate—Internalizing Shame

*E*ven though the sense of exposure that results from the severing of an interpersonal bridge can pass rather quickly, this relatively momentary aspect of shame cannot account for the way it can eventually come to play such a significant role in human development and interpersonal relationships. In order for us to come to grips with the horrendous havoc shame can wreak upon the self, we need to understand how shame is internalized.

**When Shame Moves in to Stay**

As mentioned previously, whenever shame becomes internalized we are able to activate it without any interaction with another person. It is at this point that shame has become autonomous, entrenched, and resistant to change. Through the process of internalization we gradually move along the continuum from "I *feel* defective" to "I *am* defective." When shame comes to lie at the core of the self, our identity becomes fused with shame in such a way that we then begin defining ourselves as a defect: a failure, a convict, a sinner, an addict . . . the list is almost endless. But how does this happen? One important place to look is in the process of identification, which nearly begins at the moment of our birth.

### *The Identification Need*

The timeless questions of "Who am I?" and "Where do I belong?" never seem truly answerable. And though we may find a dozen labels with which we personally identify ourselves—a son, a daughter, a husband, a wife, an American, a doctor, a white man, an athlete, a Christian, a Protestant, an Eagles fan—we never seem able to reach a place where with conviction we can say, "This is who I am; this is where I belong." I believe that we mostly seek an identification label as a prerequisite to the more interpersonally based sense of belonging. The urge to identify ourselves as this or that is a prelude to the hope of then losing our sense of separateness. It is through our identification with a like kind that we believe we can then fully and forever escape our sense of separateness. But it is this very desire to completely and forever lose our sense of aloneness that then opens us up to shame's onslaught and its potential internalization. Kaufman says of our need to identify:

> Identification is a human process. By this I mean it is an inevitable occurrence in human affairs, universally experienced, and life long. We never outgrow the need to identify, though the need may become evermore differentiated as one proceeds through life (p. 40).

## *The Enemy inside the Gate—Internalizing Shame*

The first person with whom a child seeks to identify—to unite with and lose the sense of aloneness and separateness—is the parent. Through a behavioral process called modeling, the child observationally learns how to function and behave. It's not difficult to conclude that there is a survival component to modeling; even in the animal world, we can observe predators and prey alike learning the necessary skills for survival by imitating the behaviors of their parents.

Indeed, the identification need is of immense importance; it has a direct bearing on the process by which shame becomes internalized. When we identify with someone who is important to us, we learn to treat ourselves in much the same way that they treat us. Whenever a child identifies with a parent who suffers some degree of internalized shame, the child will often take into itself the parent's own perceptions of deficiency, defectiveness, sinfulness, or worse. The child will essentially learn to see and treat him- or herself in much the same way as the parent perceives and treats him- or herself.

With Kaufman, we may ask, "Why identify with a shaming or contemptuous parent?" A couple of answers suggest themselves. In the very early and intensely formative years, a child's world is unlikely to contain other alternatives for modeling. Further, because of the child's inability to survive on his own, he is largely unable to free himself from subjection to a shaming parent. Indeed, studies and life experience seem to demonstrate conclusively that a child will continue to identify with a parent even though he or she may be physically or emotionally abusive. This appears to indicate that the child's will to survive—or at least her perception of her ability to survive—is even more powerful than the experiences of severe emotional and physical pain. Additionally, the child's need to identify appears to be of equal influence to his need to survive. Consequently, mirrored by the parent's abuse, distancing, or neglect, a shame-based identity will develop in the child.

We have already mentioned how the beginnings of the shaming experience lie at the same place in our development as the point at which we become verbal and self-aware enough to begin asking the questions "Who am I?" and "Where do I belong?" Thus, at the point when our internal questioning of our worth and potential begins, as mentioned in chapter one, we begin, through the process of identification, to treat ourselves as we are treated by those most significant to us (typically for children, the parent or parents). Kaufman says, "This forms the beginning basis for our relationship with ourselves, another important dimension of identity" (p.41).

Finally, we internalize the images we receive through visual, verbal, and emotional interaction with the objects of our identification. The spoken and implied messages we receive about ourselves from those who are most important to us in our most impressionable and malleable years combine with our own self-questioning to confirm and solidify the way we view ourselves. The identity that is shaped through internalization thus becomes our conscious experience of the self with the self.

### *Emotions, Memory, and Behavior*

I hope that we have now established internalization as a *nearly* natural consequence of identification (or at least a natural consequence of the seeking of identification in that which is seen and perceived). Internal transfer is primarily mediated by visual images—though the auditory can play an equally significant role. However, this still does not explain the process

## The Enemy inside the Gate—Internalizing Shame

whereby shame specifically becomes internalized. In order for us to come to an understanding of how such a devastating emotion can take up such permanent residence within the self, we must first briefly talk about the formulation of affect theory as developed by Sylvan Tomkins.

According to Tomkins, there are nine basic affects (emotions):

1. Interest/Excitement
2. Enjoyment/Joy
3. Surprise/Startle
4. Distress/Anguish
5. Fear/Terror
6. Anger/Rage
7. Shame/Humiliation
8. Dissmell (a term Tomkins coined to indicate the negative reaction to a bad smell)
9. Disgust

These emotions can be even more powerful motivators than the biological drives or physical pain. Some people would actually choose physical pain over some great embarrassment or humiliation!

According to Tomkins, these affects and their combinations are the primary motivating mechanisms for all human beings. Indeed, the corresponding facial responses for each affect have been observed within every culture on the planet. Furthermore, emotions amplify experience, whether positive or negative.

The experiences we have in connection with these affects, both positive and negative, are stored as memories.

# SHAME

Kaufman writes, "Affective experience becomes stored in memory in the form of scenes" (p. 193). In some cases, according to Tomkins, a process of psychological magnification takes place, in which emotionally laden scenes become interconnected and then magnified by other affective scenes. Over time, we evolve a set of rules for responding to and interpreting the scenes—a sort of "script" that we follow in response to the emotional "cues" generated by a given situation, memory, or feeling. Kaufman explains,

> The scenes next give rise to scripts which embody specific rules for interpreting, responding to, controlling, and predicting any magnified set of scenes. Whereas the scene is a happening, perceived with a beginning and an end, the script encompasses the individual's developing rules for dealing with scenes. . . . While initially scenes determine scripts, those *scripts increasingly determine future scenes. Scripts comprise rules for action, for cognition, and for decision (my emphasis, p. 193).*

In other words, at some point our scripts take on an interpretive life of their own; they start to affect the way we perceive and understand what is happening to us. Our responses to certain emotionally laden events become, in effect, hardwired into us! Shame defense strategies—which we will discuss a bit later—are one type of such a reactive script that we develop in response to shame inducements.

Remembered scenes—and the emotional responses they trigger in us—are constructed and reactivated using three

## The Enemy inside the Gate—Internalizing Shame

components: emotions, sight, and language. A memory thus becomes imprinted with emotional features, visual features (people present, facial looks, actions performed), and language features (spoken words). In other words, our memories contain auditory, visual, and kinesthetic features.

Research indicates that for a large percentage of the population, memories are accessed almost solely through the language component. These individuals experience an inner voice whenever they recall a memory. This voice can be either the actual voice of a specific person or an auditory linguistic signifier connected to the scene. For these people, the language channel is the means to retrieve and re-experience the memory, with or without an accompanying emotion.

Another significant percentage of the population will hear no inner voice. Instead, they will fully experience their memories visually, but will not possess a language or emotional component to their scene.

A third and smaller group of individuals will not have any auditory or visual components to their scene. For them, these channels are disconnected from the memory. Instead, they will often become overwhelmed by emotion for no apparent reason. For these people the reactivation of a memory is silent, blind, and emotional.

These differences, by the way, help us understand why the goal of psychotherapy is often the full recall of all three channels to a scene. The therapist must first determine which of the three channels remains open and then work through it to open the others.

Perhaps now it is easier to see why a child who is characterized by a persecuting parent to be less than, defective, sinful, or worse will, because of the identification need that we discussed at the beginning of this chapter, take into himself these identification images. If a child is repeatedly called stupid, selfish, sinful, or evil, she will often internalize these labels as core affect beliefs—they become part of her script. The child will come to identify herself as a stupid, selfish, sinful, or evil person. These words in and of themselves can trigger memories with whatever pertinent verbal, visual, and emotional components were in the original scene. Not only may the child now forever see himself as sinful, but he then may learn to treat himself as a sinful person. This process then has a high likelihood of being repeated with his own children.

**Shame Binds**

Because our responses to situations become scripted, we can become almost inextricably bound to certain reactions in a given situation. When shame becomes associated with a particular affect (emotion), drive, or need, the result is a "shame bind": we experience shame any time that affect, drive, or need surfaces in our lives. Kaufman explains it this way:

> Whenever the expression of a particular affect, whether it be anger, fear, even enjoyment, is followed by some parental response which induces shame, an internalized affect-shame bind can result. The parental response may be direct and intentional shaming, or it may be unintentional. The impact is what matters. The development of an affect-shame bind then functions to control the latter expression of the particular affect involved (p. 45).

## The Enemy inside the Gate—Internalizing Shame

As you can probably imagine without too much difficulty, this can become a particularly crippling experience. Let's look at a few examples.

### Affect-Shame Binds

Almost any affect (emotion) can become linked with shame, given the necessary circumstances. For example, fear or feeling afraid can itself become shameful. A fear-shame bind can actually cause me to feel defective or sinful for *feeling or responding to* fear. By the way, this is a perfect example that seems to clearly discount any inherent biological or evolutionary justification for the development of shame: When it becomes shameful to experience or show fear I may actually develop a reluctance to step out of the path of a charging rhinoceros!

Seriously, how could fear possibly be construed as sinful? Fear is an essential component for life itself. Indeed, men have been dying on battlefields for thousands of years for no other reason than to *not* experience shame—and that *is* a shame. Once fear becomes tied to shame in a fear-shame bind we often develop a fear of fear itself. When this occurs, the mere thought of a fear-producing event—an impending battle, let's say—can itself induce shame; the very experience of fear itself has now become sinful. It is at this point where shame can spontaneously occur without an interpersonal activator. (There is no longer the need for the severance of an interpersonal bridge.) Shame has now become internalized, hence, autonomous. It is here where not only our behaviors, but our personalities themselves, can then become heavily influenced by shame.

Not only can fear become bound to shame, but so, of

course, can any of the other affects or affect blends. Male and female gender scripts, which we discussed in chapter two, are perfect examples of certain emotions being silenced through shaming. Women were once heavily shamed for expressing anger. The experience of anger for women could thus produce feelings of guilt and cause them to question their worthiness to belong and be in a relationship—to have the chance to lose their sense of aloneness and separateness. The experience of a shame-bound emotion is then only consciously felt as feeling exposed, less than, defective, sinful, or worse. As Kaufman states, ". . . whenever that feeling but creeps into awareness, shame is spontaneously activated, and the feeling becomes bound, controlled and now silenced internally as well" (p.46). In other words, we lose our capacity to experience the emotion itself, be it fear, anger, distress . . . or even happiness and excitement! In its place, we only feel the shame—the feeling of less-than-ness, of deficiency, of defectiveness—to which it has become bound.

### *Drive-Shame Binds*

A drive is an innate, biologically determined urge. Of the many biological urges, the one that has been the most profoundly bound to shame is the sex drive. In a similar vein as fear, sex is an essential element for life itself. I find it further astounding that a function so necessary for life itself has now become regarded as shameful, immoral, and sinful. And though I agree that what is currently occurring in our culture may appear pretty *intense*, it is a vitally needed process for the destruction of the shame binds which have strangled the sex drive for ages. Because of the sin/shame tie, and the fact that the sex drive is so imbued with shaming inducements, a multitude of activities—homosexuality

## The Enemy inside the Gate—Internalizing Shame

(primarily between men), premarital sex, and so on—even the sex drive itself was eventually viewed as sinful, immoral. In fact, the cultural use of shame has *never* been a facilitator toward a place of freedom, but actually a barrier preventing that freedom! Later in the book, we'll discuss in more detail how and why sex-shame binds developed.

Any and all of a child's developmental sexual activities can be bound to shame. Whenever a certain behavior is repeatedly remarked upon or directly shamed by the parent, a drive-shame bind can be created. Whenever a specific sexual activity becomes bound to shame, the sexual urge itself can become similarly involved. Once that happens, the shame-bound sexual urge will often follow a child into adulthood. It is then here where this most natural biological urge will cause the self to view itself as bad, nasty, dirty, sinful, or worse whenever the individual experiences sexual desire.

The drive to succeed dominates our culture, compelling us to excel in everything from bedroom to boardroom. To *not be perfect* in any activity or pursuit is unthinkable. Not surprisingly, holding a performance expectation offers a near-guarantee of shaming oneself, sometimes known as "performance anxiety." Ask any golfer who suffers from "paralysis by analysis" what happens when an insistence upon success is tied to every effort.

Conversely, it is only to the degree that *however we do is good enough* that we become completely free to explore and participate in all that life has to offer. The difference between the pursuit of excellence as an avenue toward respect, acclaim, recognition, and belonging and the pursuit of excellence as an avenue toward basic survival is both subtle and vast. The pursuit of excellence does in fact reduce the rapidity of shame, but when it does occur its intensity is increased. And though we may have the impression that *excellence* is the way to interpersonal completion, excellence doesn't satisfy the primary interpersonal need. Nevertheless, it is difficult to pursue excellence without expecting people to treat us differently. As long as the primary interpersonal need is still unsatisfied, we can hardly do anything without developing the expectation that they *should* now treat us differently because we did what we did. It is only from within relational union that we can pursue excellence without interpersonal expectation. Actually, relational union reveals that the motivation for the pursuit of excellence has disappeared. We are now no longer driven toward something as a means to gaining respect. We are now completely free to do without any interpersonal expectation and whatever we do is exactly to the degree that we are supposed to do it.

### *Need-Shame Binds*

Another group of motivators that can become bound to shame are the needs. Indeed, the internalization of shame is fundamentally facilitated through interpersonal needs. Our seemingly unbreakable tendency to look to other humans for interpersonal completion and satisfaction of these needs provides the primary opening for shame to wreak havoc upon the self.

*Identification-shame bind.* It appears that the identification need lies along a continuum from general to specific: we start by looking at people in general—to find a like kind—then we look to a particular kind of person, and finally we settle on a particular individual as "the one" with whom we must find interpersonal completion. Of course, the prerequisite for this deeper relationship is finding another who feels the same about me as I feel about him or her. As infants, we thought our

## *The Enemy inside the Gate—Internalizing Shame*

parents could satisfy this need; we later thought it was one of our friends. We then thought that the answer must surely lie with someone to whom we were sexually attracted. Oh, how wrong we were, time and time again!

The whole process begins with observation. As we conduct our search for those with whom we can identify, we see something in the eyes of our fellow human beings that we clearly don't see in a cat, a dog, or a horse. It is this act of *recognition* that then creates the environment where shame can occur. After all, dogs don't shame us; cats don't shame us; horses don't shame us. It is only people that are able shame us.

The need for deep intimacy requires, then, that we gradually lay ourselves open to a human with whom we seek to identify. This process involves trust and risk and it progresses slowly, in a setting where we feel that we belong, one that is relatively free of shame. An interpersonal bridge is built upon a mutuality of response characterized by trust. As the trust goes, so goes the interpersonal bridge. As soon as anybody causes us to feel less than—causes us to experience shame—there goes the bridge. Basically, whenever we aren't treated as expected, we feel slighted, disrespected, disparaged, unimportant, or worse. And if the shaming is intense enough over time, the need for relationship itself can now form a shame bind. We can then become fearful, distressed, or angry whenever we get the feeling of needing anybody.

*Differentiation-shame bind.* The mind sciences have long ago determined that just as powerful as our need of identification (for relational union) is the need for differentiation (to separate from, to self-manifest). As with identification, the need to differentiate can also be bound to shame. Children have long been shamed by parents for trying to differentiate themselves from their parents along the lines of religion and career. A parent can also induce shame in a differentiating child whenever she pursues a personal interest or enjoyment. Most of us know stories of children who held a passion for pursuing a career in the arts, for example, but whose parents browbeat them with their insistence on the child studying for "a real job": usually, a career in the sciences, business, or industry.

The problem, of course, is that differentiation is essential for us to become fully independent individuals and achieve a sense of identity that is separate from the family into which we were born. When this essential process becomes associated with shame, however, we are handicapped in our pursuit of the appropriate level of autonomy and self-efficacy.

Two methods whereby the family can unintentionally inhibit differentiation in a child are when it is overprotective and overly possessive. A more direct and intentional shaming occurs when the son or daughter is shamed for expressing a preference—any preference—which is different than the parent's. This attempt at parental control can leave the child feeling powerless, exposed, less than, and possibly defective or sinful—merely for attempting to be a separate individual! Kaufman states,

> The salient point is that differentiation, whether expressed through separation or mastery, is vulnerable to shame. One can emerge feeling either strong or weak, autonomous or dependent, competent or inadequate in the world. The failure to actively encourage and support differentiation, as well as a tendency to punish, shame, or otherwise

interfere with it, is most apt to foster a dependent adaptation to life (p.66).

**Need-Shame Binds and Culture**
I mentioned earlier how closely these two needs seem to align themselves with the cultural injunctions of conformity and independence. And like the two cultural injunctions we discussed in chapter two (conformity vs. independence), we also cannot identify and differentiate at the same time. Dr. Kaufman informs us that shame can result when we try to satisfy both these personal needs simultaneously. He also writes that these two needs are often referred to as the twin poles of our natures. This analogy highlights the significance of these needs appearing almost as opposing phenomena. It is perhaps indicative that when the identification need has become heavily bound to shame, the result is often a raging conservative. Conversely, when the differentiation need has become shame-bound, we often see a militant liberal.

Historically, women have not only been heavily shamed for trying to differentiate themselves from their parents, but were also shamed for trying to differentiate themselves from their relationships with men. Indeed, the notion of a woman remaining unmarried by her own choice was considered unthinkable for most of our history—and still is, in many quarters.

Other interpersonal needs that can be tied to shame include the need to touch and hold, the need to nurture, and the need for affirmation. And though any of the needs can be shamed, I believe it is the underlying unsatisfied relational union need which is fundamental to the development of *all* shame binds.

# SHAME

In summary, any and all of the affects, needs, or drives can be bound to shame. In each such case, the result is that shame becomes internalized. When shame thus comes to lie at the core of the self, the self can come to experience itself as deficient, defective, sinful, or worse. This view of the self then forms the perspective from which all of life is experienced. And even though this affect-belief of the self may recede from consciousness, it still forms the ground upon which our identity ultimately stands.

**"We Have Met the Enemy, and He Is Us"**
The above well-known quote from the *Pogo* comic strip pretty well sums up how shame, once it is internalized by the processes introduced in this chapter, makes us feel about ourselves. By various means, most of us have acquired emotionally laden memory-scripts that predispose us to react to certain experiences, words, or feelings with certain responses that have become almost indelibly programmed into our psyches. Though each of us expresses and understands these experiences differently, they all have a common denominator: shame. Kaufman says,

> While the underlying affect is the same, the conscious experience of internalized shame differs widely. For example, feelings of inadequacy, rejection or self-doubt, feeling guilt-ridden or unlovable as a person, and pervasive loneliness are all conscious or semi-conscious expressions of internalized shame.

## *The Enemy inside the Gate—Internalizing Shame*

Furthermore,

> Internalization also means that the self can now autonomously activate and experience shame in isolation. Conscious awareness of limitations, failures, or simply awareness of not achieving a prescribed goal can activate shame. There need no longer be any interpersonal shame-inducing event (p.74).

An outgrowth of the internalization process is a phenomenon Kaufman calls the "internal shame spiral." Say, for example, you are having a conversation with a significant other: a friend, a spouse, a girlfriend, a boyfriend, a parent, or whomever. In an instant you realize that you've been deceived—lied to!—about something important. The instant recognition of the lie from someone significant in your life causes you to feel less than, defective, not worthy of relationship.

You then find yourself in a spiraling flow of related thoughts and feelings: each one begins triggering another in a deepening vortex of all-consuming shame. This experience can last for a few seconds or for days. Other names for this phenomenon are "tail-spinning" and "snowballing."

There seem to be similarities between such a shame spiral and a depressive episode. I myself have experienced these shame spirals, and they're no fun. In my experience, they are characterized by a general sense of unlovableness, defectiveness, deficiency, insignificance, and unworthiness of respect. As we will see in the next chapter, some of us will react to the shame with anger, even rage—particularly when we have determined that we were shamed without cause. We may then stay angry for days, even years. This, of course, is the birthplace for deeply held resentments.

Once shame becomes internalized, the sense of exposure that accompanies a shaming experience can become incredibly acute. To be exposed now means having our defectiveness exposed. As we have seen already and as Kaufman has remarked, "To be seen is to be seen as irreparably and unspeakably bad."

Given the toxic, unpleasant feelings about ourselves that shame usually generates, is it any wonder that humans have developed a number of strategies for mitigating or defending against the feelings of shame? It is to these shame-defending behaviors and strategies that we turn in the next chapter.

# CHAPTER 4

## *The Intimate Adversary: Defending Ourselves from Shame*

*T*here is no particular point when we begin learning to defend ourselves against shame, but a number of factors can contribute to when, where, and how individuals begin defending themselves. For one thing, shame defenses are significantly influenced by whether one is predisposed to either an introverted or extroverted personality. An extroverted person will be much more inclined to respond to shame with expressed anger, while an introverted person will have a tendency to withdraw.

Kaufman states,

> Adaptation is what defenses are all about. Defenses are learned because they are the best means available to the child for survival. Defending strategies are adaptive and have survival value. That is the natural reason they come about. If they were not necessary or did not work at all, we would be most unlikely to develop them (p. 80).

Defenses can remain either flexible and temporary or else become internalized and rigid. The more positive defenses remain conscious and controllable, while the more negative ones are internalized, becoming unconscious or instinctive, and therefore largely uncontrollable. Note that shame need not have become internalized before the self sets up permanent defenses to deal with future shame occurrences. But once shame does become internalized the self then becomes particularly desperate in its search for some mechanism to restore inner peace.

**Shame Defenses: Prevention and Transference**
Defenses also can be divided into two broad categories as to their intent. First, there are defenses that aim to prevent shame from being experienced at all. These strategies of defense are forward-looking and aim at protecting the self from any future potential slights, disrespects, non-attentions, inconsideration, blaming, or judgments from others. For example, I may strive to become so wealthy, powerful, or otherwise indispensable that no one would dare to treat me in any way that could cause me shame.

The second broad category, strategies of transfer, aim, as the name implies, to transfer shame once it is felt. For example, if I begin to feel embarrassed, I can humiliate someone else and thereby alleviate my own sense of wrongness or sinfulness by transferring it to someone else. Interpersonal transfers of shame almost always proceed from someone with more power to someone of less power, from stronger to weaker. Thus, we tend to employ shame transference strategies in settings where we have more power, since in one interpersonal setting we may have a lot of power, while in another we may have little or none. Another fundamental requirement is that there must be another human being to serve as the object of the transfer; trying to transfer shame to our car, a tree, or our pets just doesn't seem to work so well.

With these two broad categories in mind, let's take a look at some of the specific strategies intended to prevent the experience of shame.

### Shame Prevention: Striving for Power

When someone pursues power as a defending strategy against shame, the goal is to essentially occupy such an elevated rung of the social, political, or corporate ladder that nobody would dare be disrespectful, inattentive, inconsiderate, discourteous, or rude. The point of the pursuit of power—though it's seldom consciously realized—is to decrease the potential for the occurrence of any events that could cause one to feel less than, defective, worthless, or worse. The more power one achieves over others, the less one becomes subjected to not only the potential for intentional shaming but to any inadvertent slights as well. Since adoration, acclaim, applause, celebrity, reverence, fame, wealth, and the perception of having wisdom are all forms of having power, any determined pursuit of these in and of themselves is an attempt to free the self from the potential for any future shame occurrences.

### Shame Prevention: Pursuing Perfection

In much the same vein as striving for power, pursuing perfection is a direct attempt by the self to compensate for an internal sense of defectiveness. This effort can also be an attempt of the self to head off the possibilities for any future unfavorable attention from others. We live in a culture that reveres perfection and excellence (though what constitutes these qualities is often ill-defined). We are all expected to be perfect in some special way. Of course, if we were all perfect, the pursuit of perfection would then be completely meaningless. The point is, we believe that to be perfect at something ultimately means being respected, idolized, honored, and favored. Furthermore, achieving perfection would seem to prove conclusively that we're not deficient, defective, or worse. Inevitably, however, none of us will be able to become "perfect enough" to completely destroy the occurrence of shame.

The profile of one who adopts the pursuit of perfection as a pathway toward the elimination of the sense of aloneness and separateness usually involves a perception of self as never quite good enough to be worthy of relationship and belonging. Every effort or achievement is somehow lacking: it could have been better, quicker, or more accurate.

Another attribute of the striving for perfection that can generate shame is the comparison making that accompanies the pursuit. A perfectionist will always be comparing his or her performances and accomplishments to the performances and accomplishments of others. Through the continual comparison of themselves to others, they will always be looking for the ways in which they feel they are better. However, comparison making by its very nature also causes us to see all the ways in which we fall short and are imperfect. Ironically, we hardly ever consciously recognize our own inadequacies but only see the real or imagined imperfections of the person with whom we are comparing ourselves. Subconsciously, it's entirely another story, however. In other words, our conscious minds tell us one thing, but our shame tells us something entirely different.

Closely related to the pursuit of perfection are the strivings for excellence and success. Our culture bids us to be perfect, to be excellent, to be successful . . . or else! And though the "or else" is never openly stated, the implementation of favor, praise, acclaim, and adoration on those deemed to have achieved excellence heavily imply that opposite consequences will befall those who fall short. The "excellent" and "successful" are much less likely to then be slighted, shunned, discounted, or inconvenienced.

The paradox of all our strivings in order to achieve a sense of belonging and relationship—toward a place where we believe we will no longer feel alone and separate—is that they are not only doomed to fail, but their pursuit always compels us to compete with and compare ourselves to others. Competition paradoxically works against our efforts to feel that we do belong. No matter how well we try to isolate ourselves within a segment of society where we can be "king of the world," we ultimately encounter another segment of the culture—or in the world more broadly—where we are held—or believe we are held—to be insufficient, inadequate, less than, defective, sinful, or worse. The volume or frequency of shame may decrease as we become successful, but shame's intensity only increases. Ironically, the higher we ascend in our efforts, the more we ratchet up our expectations, and the higher the expectations, the more intense the shame experience when it occurs—and it will inevitably occur. This, incidentally, may explain why people of power often go postal over relatively minor occurrences of perceived disrespect.

# SHAME

### *Shame Prevention: Withdrawal*

Another final strategy for preventing the occurrence of shame—or, more properly, for attempting the avoidance of shaming circumstances—is internal withdrawal. This defense is often adopted by people with introverted temperaments. Introvertedness is determined by the amount of time an individual lives within himself and apart from interpersonal interactions with others. Kaufman defines the dichotomy succinctly: "The introvert lives more often and more of the time inside while the extrovert does the opposite" (p. 95).

Whenever an introverted personality is exposed to intense shame, the self will usually withdraw inside of itself in an attempt to escape the sense of exposure as unworthy, sinful, and so forth. The paradox of internal withdrawal, of course, is that it distances the self even more deeply from being reunited with those it believes are critical for a sense of belonging, relationship, and interpersonal completion.


### **Shame Transference: Getting Rid of the Hot Potato**

An interesting thing about shame transfers is that there is seldom any conscious recognition by the initiator that a shame transfer is actually taking place. The specifics by which a transfer does take place can vary significantly: a derogatory or belittling comment, a verbal judgment, a criticism, blaming—each can serve as a vehicle of shame transfer. All that seems to matter in a transfer is that we either induce shame directly or say or do something that activates the other person's own pre-existing sense of deficiency, defectiveness, sinfulness, or worse. We may indeed be aware of what we actually say or do, but we generally have no recognition of the underlying shame transfer that is taking place by means of our words or actions. We may even have what appears to be a rational justification for what we said or did, but the true underlying motivation is often really only about a shame transfer, or at least about a shame inducement. Simply put, we want to hurt someone else the way we've been hurt, or we want to hurt them so that they will behave the way we *want* them to behave or the way we believe they *should* behave.

One interesting implication of this may be that those who label others as immoral, sinful, or evil possibly feel that way about themselves; the act of denouncing others as sinners transfers the shame of the denouncers, thus consoling the self that already views itself as such.

The developed concepts of *sin*, *sinning*, and *sinners* have actually caused the production of shame to escalate. The mere verbal expression of the word "sinner" toward someone can be a powerful shame inducer; whenever we even hear the word *sinner* said by someone, particularly someone important to us, it nearly always induces a feeling of defectiveness.

### Shame Transfer Strategies: Rage

We've already mentioned rage as one of three naturally occurring secondary responses to shame. It is one thing when we do something to cause ourselves shame, but when it is somebody else who causes us shame—particularly when we perceive it as being done without cause—we are much more likely to react with rage. Similarly, it is one thing when we ourselves do something that causes us to question our worthiness, but another matter entirely when someone else says or does something that causes us to question our worthiness to belong and be in a relationship—especially when we believe that it was done without cause.

Rage has two general purposes relevant to shame. First, it serves as a self-protective mechanism by keeping others away. Second, it is a means of shame transfer. In other words, rage can either be used defensively or offensively in response to shame. It is also more often expressed by extroverted personalities, while introverted personalities tend to hold it inside.

Whenever we see someone who has adopted rage as a general defense against shame, we usually conclude that the individual is either hostile towards everyone or always bitter. Kaufman informs us that when anger is internalized—much like shame—it becomes entrenched, creating a toxic, deadening environment for the personality.

> There is no more certain poison for the self than internalizing rage and thereby fomenting bitterness within the self. Bitterness can kill, can so wither the self inside the person that it becomes like dead wood, dried up, old and withered. Coming in contact with an embittered individual usually will leave us with a bad feeling (p. 84).

### *Shame Transfer Strategies: Contempt*

Unlike rage, which occurs almost instinctively, the adoption of contempt as a defending strategy has to be learned; this usually occurs by means of having been modeled by a parent. Contempt is an affect blend consisting of anger and dissmell (the reaction to a bad odor). When people use contempt they are seldom even aware of the emotion—they are only aware of the object of their contempt. In some cases, the object of contempt might be the self itself: "I'm such a disgusting, wretched, dirty, sinful, evil person . . ." Whenever contempt develops as a defending style, the personality often becomes judgmental, fault-finding, or condescending. Kaufman explains,

> To the degree that others are looked down upon, found lacking, or seen as somehow lesser or inferior beings, a once-wounded self becomes more securely insulated against further shame, but only at the expense of distorted relationships with others. . . .
>
> While rage keeps others away and contempt both distances the self from others and elevates the self above others, the striving for power is a direct attempt to compensate for the sense of defectiveness which underlies internalized shame (p. 85).

### Shame Transfer Strategies: Blaming

It seems like such a rare event in our culture to hear anybody admit failures or mistakes. Often, such admissions seem to have ulterior motives—the one making the admission appears to gain some personal advantage by the appearance of penitence and acceptance of responsibility.

Such reluctance to be forthcoming about accepting blame is, in a twisted sort of way, understandable: not only is the admission of mistakes a personal recognition of imperfection, but an admission of failure also seems to confirm one's unworthiness for belonging and relationship. (Personally, I completely understand the willingness to do anything to avoid feeling shame. What I don't understand is why one person is praised for her defenses while another is mocked, ridiculed, or condemned.)

What we do hear most often in our culture is excuse-making and people blaming people. It seems that everybody is blaming somebody else or something else as the cause.

Most of us believe there is an external cause for our continuing lack of inner peace: "It's got to be somebody else's fault," we think, whether consciously or not. But in truth, we are actually doing nothing more than finding someone to blame and thereby transferring our shame.

There are still white men blaming the black man and black men blaming the white man. The same with Democrats and Republicans, rich and poor, Christians, Jews, and Muslims, husbands and wives, gays and straights . . . Wherever there is a perceived ill, mistake, incongruence, injustice, or immorality, there will always be somebody there blaming others as the cause in an attempt to transfer shame.

I find it truly amazing that even after these many eons of finding people to blame, we have still not yet found the solution. Could it be possible that we're continuing to look in the wrong places? Though my thinking about shame is only a few years old, it has become absolutely apparent that blaming—finger-pointing included—is unquestionably the foremost shame-transfer method used by man. Criticism of someone is often but a veiled method of affixing blame in order to transfer one's own shame in order to feel better about oneself.

Kaufman informs us that blaming is largely a behavior

# *The Intimate Adversary: Defending Ourselves from Shame*

learned from parents who are themselves experienced at fixing blame. Like shame that has become internalized and unconscious, blaming can also become internalized and unconscious. Much like the objects of contempt, the objects of blame are often all that the blaming person is aware of; the people who use blame to transfer shame are often not even aware that they are blaming and attempting to find the causes for their continuing lack of inner peace and wholeness.

We most often blame in order to transfer the shame we receive from others. We will either counter-blame the person who blamed us, depending on our relative power, or look for somebody else with relatively less power to blame. In instances of equal power or perceived equal power, we may see shame batted back and forth like a lengthy game of tennis. These "arguments" or "blame games" can last for hours, days, weeks, months, or years. Sometimes in the international arena, the shame-and-blame game goes on for decades—or centuries! For either nation to accept the blame would be equal to accepting the resulting shame and thereby validating that nation's wrongness, weakness, defectiveness, or worse. Once shame becomes internalized—or nationalized—it becomes nearly impossible to accept more shame. Remember, the self will do almost anything to prevent more exposure to shame. For a nation, like a self, there is no deeper torment to its soul than feeling unworthy of existence.

Kaufman's analysis is telling:

> And when blaming becomes sufficiently directed outside oneself, that is, externalized, we may see an individual who perceives the source of all that goes wrong to lie outside the

self, and, paradoxically, beyond internal control. And though that individual resents the resulting feeling of powerlessness, a powerlessness to affect and change what ails him, he never recognizes that he has colluded in the very process of creating that powerlessness. . . .

While the blaming individual escapes culpability for wrongdoing or mistakes and hence avoids shame, he reaps a harvest of discontent derived from perceived powerlessness. If the source of what goes wrong in life becomes external to the self, one has also relinquished the power to affect or alter what happens (p. 92).

With blaming, as with many of the previously mentioned shame-defending strategies, the external expression of the defense may be significantly influenced by whether one tends towards introversion or extroversion. An extroverted personality will tend to blame others, while an introverted personality will tend to blame herself. The extrovert's blaming of others can actually hinder the internalization of shame, but only at the cost of personal power, as Kaufman states above. For many such people the apocalypse is "right around the corner and there is nothing we can do to prevent it!" The introverted personality, on the other hand, will more often tend to see evil as lying within.

There can even be occasions where an individual will learn to blame himself in order to preempt any blaming by others. This self-proclaimed scapegoat thereby gains a degree of control within an environment that is often totally out of control. The problem with this tactic is that it creates a situation

## The Intimate Adversary: Defending Ourselves from Shame

where the self consistently shames itself. And that can lead to pathologies of a dark and pernicious nature, as we will see.

**Shame Defenses: Summary**

When we use shame defenses they become a part of us. They're a lot like a suit of armor that protects us from the outer, interpersonal world. We keep these defenses ready for even the slightest hint of a shame encounter. The threats we encounter may rarely be of a physical nature, but rather interpersonal. But we perceive them as real, and we employ our defenses in an attempt to avoid feelings of unworthiness.

As mentioned previously, an individual's defenses may eventually be turned inwardly against the self, or more specifically, be turned against a part of the self the individual views as bad, nasty, defective, sinful, or worse. This phenomenon can bring about some of the most harmful pathologies we can inflict on ourselves. And coming to grips with the role of shame in bringing these dark consequences about is the topic of the next chapter.

# CHAPTER 5

## When Shame Destroys a Human Being

We have now spent a fair amount of time discussing three important process dimensions pertaining to shame and its effects on the self. We first spoke about the inducement of shame and how it manifests itself through our interactions with others. We then discussed how shame becomes internalized through the process of identification and how internalization causes shame to become autonomous, no longer needing an interpersonal activator. In the previous chapter we discussed the ways in which the self attempts to defend itself against shame's onslaught. This now brings us to the developmental process where the self begins disowning parts of itself, thus creating splits within the self. The internal havoc that disowning plays within the self creates conditions ripe for the development of many of humankind's most devastating psychological ailments.

**Disowning the Self**
Though it can use defenses to combat external shame exposures, the self must now also deal with an enemy

## When Shame Destroys a Human Being

increasingly seen as lying within. Thus, by turning its defenses upon itself, it begins to dissociate from those aspects of itself it perceives as inadequate, diseased, broken, sinful, or worse. It begins a frantic search for some method or means whereby it can restore inner peace, balance, wholeness, or holiness. But it is impossible for the self to achieve this calm as long as it is actively engaged in a war against a part of itself it continues to see as *wrong*. Kaufman explains,

> We learn to shame ourselves, hold ourselves in contempt, blame ourselves, hate ourselves, terrorize ourselves, and even disown a part of ourselves that had been rejected and consistently enough cast away . . . (p. 102).

It doesn't matter if the teaching or conditioning was done intentionally or not; all that matters is the self's perception of itself. Unfortunately, as we have already seen, what many of us concluded or were taught is that there is clearly something *wrong* with us. We were further told or encouraged to believe that if we "did this" and "didn't do that" we'd no longer feel the wrongness, that we'd eventually find favor and interpersonal wholeness. However, since we're not finding that which we were told or led to believe that we could achieve—that which we believe would give us interpersonal completion—then the cause, we assume, must surely lie with us (or with *them* or *it*, if you're more externally inclined). The problem with any action-oriented, do/don't plan believed to lead to a sense of interpersonal wholeness is that it is not only doomed to fail, but the plan itself will always increase shame's intensity because of the heightened expectations from effort and action.

# SHAME

These internal machinations within the self may come to be eventually mediated by an internal representative. This identification image can be based on one or both parents or anybody else with whom the child attempted to identify: Aunt Betty, Grandpa, Pastor Tom. Kaufman says that the identification image

> Serves as the watchdog of the inner life, the gatekeeper of the unconscious, the self-appointed guardian scrutinizing all that happens inside the self and dispensing shame, contempt, hatred, or fear as warranted (p. 102).

Consequently, we learn to speak to ourselves in much the same ways we were either spoken to or spoken about by the figure on whom the identification image is based. Unfortunately,

> If we were treated in critical, judgmental, belittling, or otherwise disrespectful ways, what other model have we on which to base our beginning relationship with ourselves *and with which to combat the parent's internal representative? (p. 102).*

Any of the naturally occurring emotions, needs, or drives can be rejected and cut off by the self as it seeks to dissociate from that part of itself it views as wrong, deficient, sinful. Because the parent models what is to be expressed and what is not to be expressed—the need to's, musts, oughts, and shoulds—a young girl who never sees her mother get mad concludes (subconsciously) that it is wrong for her not only to

## When Shame Destroys a Human Being

express anger, but also to even experience it herself.

The self can similarly disown any of the affect blends: hate, jealousy, contempt, guilt, and so forth. Any of the emotions can be rejected by the self as well. This same blanket of rejection can also be applied to all of the interpersonal needs. For example, when needing in general is perceived to be rejected by the parents, the result is often a person who idolizes self-sufficiency and independence (examples could include the male gender script, the ideology of the Republican Party, and other behavioral and belief systems that highlight the differentiation need). For such a person, the need for anybody—or anything—may come to be seen as wrong, defective, sinful, or worse. Such a person may even look upon others who express the need for others as weak, burdensome, deficient, or sinful. They may even go as far as to express contempt or ridicule toward anybody who expresses a need of any kind.

Conversely, whenever independence and differentiation are rejected by the identification model, a person often results who is totally dependent on others (examples could include the female gender script, the ideological platform of the Democratic Party, and other behavioral and belief systems that highlight the identification need).

Through the years, the disowned part of the self can become effectively isolated from the conscious mind. The "bad" parts of the self are increasingly pushed deeper and deeper into the subconscious, but they can never be pushed deep enough to bury them completely.

Remember that because the child has looked at her parents and significant others as both perfect and all-powerful, she cannot help but conclude that the problem somehow lies with her. The process of disowning is thus an attempt of the self to destroy any and all traces of perceived defectiveness. It is also an attempt to lessen the criticism of the internal representative. When disowning becomes consistent enough and pervasive enough, a part of the self may be split off and become independent. When this occurs, the self may begin using the same defending strategies once employed against external sources of shame against the part of itself that has now become separated. The voice of the self toward this part of the self may be judgmental, contemptuous, prosecutorial, or possibly even terroristic. The use of such emotionally laden language by the self toward a part of itself can have a devastating impact on the individual's inner peace, self-confidence, and even ability to function in society.

### The Shame-Based Identity

By the time the self begins to disown a part of its self and split apart, it has fully evolved an ability to perpetually generate shame on its own. The final destination of shame internalization is the development of a shamed-based identity. Kaufman vividly describes the painful predicament faced by those who have arrived at this state:

> In such an event, defeats, failures, or rejections need no longer be actual, but only perceived as such. Simple awareness of a limitation may be sufficient to count as a mortal wounding of the self, a new confirmation of inherent defectiveness. Such an individual may experience himself as an inherent failure as a human being. Mistakes, which ought to be expected in the course of daily functioning,

## When Shame Destroys a Human Being

become occasions of agonizing self-torture.

The internal shame process has become painful, punishing, and enduring beyond what the simple feeling of shame might produce. The internalization of shame has produced an identity, a way of relating to oneself, which absorbs, maintains, and spreads shame even further. And the internalized relationship between owned and disowned parts of the self re-creates directly within the inner life the very same shame-inducing qualities which were first encountered in interpersonal living. That internalized relationship becomes expressed and maintained through the active use of defenses directly against disowned parts of the self (pp. 115–116).

This final destination of shame internalization results in what Tomkins referred to as "postures", a posture then developing into and revealing itself as a psychological syndrome. The prerequisites necessary for any particular syndrome to develop can vary immensely, many based on the temperament of the individual. Temperament, in fact, continues to play a significant role in both the qualification of shame defenses and the development of psychological syndromes. We have already mentioned that when an introverted personality is subjected to shame he is likely to withdraw. When he is then pushed ever deeper into shame, he is likely to develop a schizoid posture. This schizoid posture creates confusion in his relationships with others. He enters "an oscillating pattern of going in and out of relationships," according to Kaufman.

# SHAME

Schizoid individuals will periodically forfeit having relationships altogether. Since introverted personalities are primarily inwardly focused, it becomes relatively easy for schizoids to do without any human interaction.

However, this same kind of isolation is nearly impossible for someone more externally focused. It makes a lot of sense that the people who live more externally will also tend to do something more external with their shame. When an extroverted person is subjected to prolonged shame inducement, the tendency towards cyclic mood swings can lead to the emergence of the depressive posture.

A depressive episode is a continuing mood characterized by disappointment in oneself. It is here where shame has begun to perpetually generate itself. These spiraling episodes of shame generation often result in periods of depression.

A third posture, paranoia, is, according to Kaufman, "the third fundamental stance which an individual may be pushed to adopt in an effort to adapt to the exigencies of shame." Kaufman informs us that either the introvert or the extrovert may develop a paranoid posture in response to excessive shame. "In such an event, the individual becomes vigilant and watchful, always waiting for the humiliation, betrayal, or blaming he knows is coming" (p. 119).

This posture reveals itself in someone who has learned to interpret relatively innocuous events as personally malevolent: "Somebody is always out to get me." Such people will also remain forever watchful for somebody they can blame.

Wrongdoings, mistakes, and other instances of personal failure cannot be honestly owned by the paranoid-prone individual and so must be disowned but then *transferred from the self to others (p. 119)*.

I believe that the widespread selling of conspiracy theories is just such a response of a largely paranoid culture that is now drowning in shame. The bogeyman is very much alive in twenty-first–century America. Many have observed that a paranoid outlook is a feature of both the radical left and the radical right.

For someone with internalized shame, the search for causes seems a natural response to the wrongness that is now perceived to lie within. The self is compelled to look for the causes of its lack of inner peace and happiness, for the cause of its ungodliness. Since it is perceived that some action caused the shame in the first place, then obviously there *has* to be an effort plan toward its elimination. This search for causes can also then be utilized as a place to transfer shame. As we'll see later when we examine the Bible, God was initially blamed as the cause of internal unrest caused by the shame sending, but this tactic was later changed, for it was determined that if God was the sender of shame, it was not appropriate to send it back to him.

Persons exhibiting paranoid behavior often have extreme difficulty admitting any part they may have played in how they feel; it becomes nearly impossible for them to admit their mistakes or transgressions. As the "galloping paranoid" (in Kaufman's terminology) becomes evermore successful in transferring shame, he may come to invent a malevolent system of beliefs that provides an always-ready target for his blame. I believe that the many conceptualizations of "evil" are just such outcomes of paranoid minds. Karma is another. And after all:

# SHAME

isn't the best object for blame one that can't blame you back?

This emerging belief system may ultimately integrate the conscious self of the paranoid around a self-righteous "holy war" if he then decides to persecute his perceived persecutors. In this eventuality the paranoid believes he has found his true calling in life, which in turn provides him, though in a distorted way, with that vital sense of meaning for which we all search (p.120).

Three decades have now passed since the first release of Kaufman's book. A great deal of what he presented—much of which was built upon the work of Tomkins—has now become household knowledge. The shame basis of abuse, violence, and addiction has now largely become accepted fact. We even see on our television programs that in many cases of sexual and serial violence, the perpetrators were themselves abused as children. The generational transfer of shame is now almost as predictable as gravity. Since so much of this has now become common knowledge, I will be especially brief in the discussion of the following shame-based syndromes.

**Physical and Sexual Abuse**

Physical abuse, sexual abuse, emotional abuse, and the addictions, which will be discussed more fully below, are all members of a category of shame-based syndromes called compulsive disorders. Compulsive disorders are characterized by attempts of the self to reduce the feelings of shame that paradoxically result in the intensification of shame. Basically, anything that causes the self to feel ever more powerless only causes the self to feel ever more defective. The specific actions that the self adopts in its effort to cleanse itself of shame will vary from one compulsive disorder to another. However, the similarity between all these disorders is the self's attempt to put out the fire of shame by using gasoline.

In order to understand why abused persons so often become abusers themselves, we need to remember that inherent to the humiliation received at the hands of another is powerlessness to prevent the humiliation. Children who are subjected to repetitive beatings are the defenseless recipients of horrendous shame inducement. Such inducement of shame is accompanied by governing scenes that then often become reactivated with their own children. As Kaufman says, "Like a magnet, these scenes compel reenactment" (p. 182). He further states,

> Incest and rape are two distinct types of sexual abuse which activate intense inner states of powerlessness, personal violation, and humiliation. In the midst of shame, one feels to blame. Childhood incest generates intense and crippling shame, which can and all too often does culminate in a profound splitting of self (p. 182).

The childhood victim's subsequent acts of abuse are attempts to gain power, attempts born of having experienced utter powerlessness at the hands of another. The rapist is often tormented by memories of intense humiliation and becomes driven to reenact those scenes, only with the roles reversed. The rapist is momentarily freed of shame through defeating and humiliating his victim, just as a murderer may achieve this result through the killing of a hated enemy. But the shame will

# SHAME

inevitably return and worsen. Because of the cyclic nature of this phenomenon, police psychologists can predict fairly accurately when a serial rapist or murderer will strike again.

When a triggering event occurs and reactivates the scene of origin, the abused person, perhaps now a parent, can actually begin reliving the original experience, only now with the roles reversed. The act of abuse thereby causes shame in the abuser, which in turn causes the abuse to increase. In other words, uninterrupted abuse hardly ever decreases but almost always gets worse.

**Addiction**
Addiction is another broad class of shame-based disorders. While addictions to drugs and alcohol are the most widely recognized, many have increasingly realized that we can develop a compulsive and obsessive desire for nearly any object or experience. Along with specific substance addictions, there are over six hundred recovery programs based on the twelve-step recovery model. These groups address addictions involving everything from hoarding and porn to work, gambling, video games, sex, food, relationships, and shopping; there is even a recognized addiction to exercise.

Characteristics of all addictions include:

1. compulsive and repetitive behavior;
2. resistance to change;
3. the addict's rising sense of powerlessness;
4. the addict's increasing humiliation (due to being controlled).

Similar to those characterizing abuse, the acts leading to addiction are the attempts of the self to change the way it *emotionally* feels—most often caused by shame. After all, "We feel defeated by our addiction. We grow to hate ourselves, disgusted at our helplessness, our lack of resolve, our lack of inner strength" (p. 184).

**The Guilt/Shame Dynamic**
As we transition from a psycho-scientific discussion of shame into considering its spiritual implications, a couple of additional points are worth mentioning. First, let's take a look at the distinction that some would draw between shame and guilt. Are they really two different qualities, or merely two different expressions of shame?

I earlier mentioned Dr. Kaufman's observation—a recognition held by Dr. Tomkins as well—that shame had essentially remained hidden from investigation until fairly recently. There were two reasons given for this. First, the speech-binding effects inherent to shame resist attempts to describe it verbally. Simply put, to admit feeling shame is to admit feeling unworthy of belonging and relationship. Second, we all have the tendency to want to hide our own shame from others; we also have extreme reluctance to approach anybody else's shame. It has now been over thirty years since Tomkins determined that guilt, embarrassment, humiliation, and shyness were, at their core, simply shame wearing different sets of clothes (though shyness is more about the fear of a possible future shame occurrence). Tomkins was the first to announce that guilt, shyness, self-consciousness, embarrassment, inferiority, inadequacy, and humiliation all contained one and the same core experience—shame.

Self-consciousness at talking before a large group, shame at failing to measure up to one's basic expectations of oneself, feeling embarrassed at having come inappropriately dressed to an important social gathering, shyness in the presence of a stranger, and guilt for an immorality or transgression are phenomenologically felt as distinctly different experiences. Yet the underlying *affect* in each experience is the same, as Sylvan Tomkins convincingly argues. This is the affect termed shame, the root of which is the feeling of exposure of the self in a painful or diminished sense (p. 121).

Previous to Tomkins, it had long been assumed, thought, and theorized that guilt and shame were two distinctly different emotional states. It was thought that shame was largely about the self that was seen and public. To be publicly disgraced was to be shamed. However, guilt was perceived as much more private; it was perceived as resulting from the actions of the self done in private. There had even been attempts to classify cultures as either shame- or guilt-based. More recently there were attempts to classify people as either shame- or guilt-prone. Kaufman writes that this had been "the traditionally accepted view of things that no one really questioned" (p. 125).

Kaufman also writes that it was through his discovery of Tomkins' work that provided him with

## When Shame Destroys a Human Being

> A more precise language to differentiate the basic affects that could be identified and clearly distinguished from one another.
>
> Tomkins then made the critical observation that shyness in the presence of a stranger, shame at a failure, and guilt for a transgression or immorality were, *at the level of affect, phenomenologically one and the same affect. Different components in the three experiences along with shame are what make them feel so distinctly different. Here, guilt can be understood as feeling disappointed in oneself for violating an important internal value or code of behavior. Shame over a failure also feels like a disappointment in self. But here no value has been violated; one has simply failed to cope with a challenge. The meaning of the two experiences is as different as feeling inadequate is from feeling immoral. But in each experience one feels bad as a person; the head hangs low* (p. 125).

Please notice how all of these manifestations are related to our efforts to identify, belong, and find relational union in the world. All shame-based occurrences cause us to essentially question or doubt our worthiness to belong and have relationships with others—in other words, they call into question our worthiness or ability to satisfy the need for a sense of interpersonal wholeness. With each incidence of shame there has either been a violation (or the fear of a violation) in

## SHAME

our behavioral expectation of another person or a violation (or the fear of a violation) in a behavioral expectation of ourselves.

From the perspective of inner experience, it becomes almost pointless to try and differentiate shame from guilt, for the affect is the same with either experience. Kaufman notes that not only is inner experience the realm of emotions, but it is also the domain of identifications, defenses, impulses, fantasy, and the unconscious.

> The critical differentiation is not between shame and guilt but between *shame as affect and internalized shame. It is this developmental event which becomes the precursor for the development of defenses aimed inside as well as outside and, later, the actual disowning of parts of the self (p. 126).*

Whenever the shame-defending strategies of blame and contempt are generally adopted, they are directed toward that which has aroused the blame and contempt. We can even hold contempt for, or blame, the self. As Kaufman explains:

> Tomkins broke with tradition in suggesting that much that has been traditionally labeled as guilt is on closer inspection, internalized contempt [an affect blend of anger and dissmell]. Intuitively I knew he was right . . . The internal image of the contemptuous, fault finding, brutally critical parent becomes the model for the self's engaging in like action (p. 126).

Thus, the guilty, contemptuous self is now likely to engage in an internal dialogue telling itself just how "deficient," "incapable," "defective," "disgusting," "nasty," "wretched," "sinful," or "evil" it is!

Another form of what has been labeled as guilt is internalized blame or self-blame. We already discussed how blame is an attempt to transfer shame elsewhere. When blaming oneself becomes relentless, shame has likely become internalized. The self may then adopt blaming itself as a method of defense against the feel of shame. When self-contempt or self-blame becomes a dynamic within the self, pain becomes continuous. This punishment of the self towards a part of itself lies far beyond the simple occurrence of shame as a passing emotion:

> Guilt now becomes a descriptive symbol referring to one particular manifestation of the affect termed shame, much as self-consciousness, embarrassment, and shyness are other such forms, each also encompassing its own special activators of shame. Guilt refers to shame which is about clearly moral matters, a poignant disappointment in self owing to a sudden break with one's own most cherished values in living (p. 127).

### Shame and the Primary Interpersonal Need

The final point to consider and reinforce before beginning our survey of the spiritual "history" of shame and the human race

# SHAME

is how shame impacts each human being's ability to satisfy the primary interpersonal need that dwells in each of us. Recall from the earlier chapters that the presence of another person is essential for the initial implementation of shame, but once shame has become internalized, the self is then able to generate its own shame. In other words, if you were to wake up and suddenly find yourself the only person left on the planet, there would never again be an interpersonal event that caused you to feel disrespected, insignificant, less than, inferior, or deficient. Also, you would never again feel shy or have any other social fears, for that matter; the animals and plants surely aren't going to humiliate or embarrass you. You would undoubtedly feel lonely—possibly very, very lonely—but in some subtle way you might not feel any lonelier than the day before when you were surrounded by a million people. However, if you had already internalized shame, you might still feel its sting, even though there wasn't another human available to instigate a shaming event.

Remember, too, that unlike hunger, the need for relief from our sense of separateness and aloneness doesn't seem to be one that is entirely within our control to satisfy. We can't simply go out and *pick a bunch of love.*

I'm at an age in my life where I've had a few instances of thinking, *I've found her at last*: my *completeness*, my *soul mate*, my *life partner*, someone with whom I'll feel, as Tom Cruise's character said in *Jerry Maguire*, "You complete me." As a result, we all put our best foot forward, but the other foot doesn't account for what often soon follows. Why do I still feel dissatisfied with this incredible other person? Is she not what I really thought she was? Is the problem my fault or was I possibly deceived? Yes, there may have been *some* misrepresentation—on both our parts—but deception alone can't be claimed when it's our third, fourth, or fifth significant—and failed—relationship.

Many of us who have found ourselves in this situation have used mischaracterization as a cause and justification for moving on and looking elsewhere. But these rationalizations can only be used so long. Eventually, we come to the end of the road of looking for causes and have to face the fact that the cause just might lie with us. Indeed, the cause *is* with us, but it is with *each of us*.

Some of us may have stayed in the relationship for various reasons: the children, the church, the refusal to admit defeat. What often happens in this case is that we then go off in pursuit of our own set of interests, excitements, enjoyments, and pleasures. At best, we now have a partner to assist us in much the same pursuit that we had before we met him or her. Where once the mere presence of this other person was all we needed to feel complete, this is no longer the case—and hasn't been in quite some time. Some of us may have "made it work" by entering into contractual arrangements where we each agreed to do certain things for one another, but this is never really enough to afford us the deep sense of fulfillment that we seek. What usually happens at this point is that one or both of us feels that the other isn't doing his or her part.

By this time, we've traveled a long, weary distance from the days when the other person's *mere presence* was all we needed, haven't we? Where once there were no expectations, there now seem to be a lot. And with an increase in the expectations there came a parallel increase in the frequency of events that caused us to feel disrespected, uncared for, irrelevant, or possibly even used.

We may then have turned to friends, or toward one

## SHAME

particular other who more fully seemed to appreciate us—who didn't cause us to feel less than, deficient, defective, sinful, or worse. Some of us became engrossed in our work; some of us became absorbed in our kids; some of us became obsessed with our careers; some of us became preoccupied with our homes; some of us became fixated on serial relationships; some of us became lost in mood-altering substances.

The process of trying to satisfy the primary interpersonal need appears to me to be a lot like peeling an onion. The outer layer is simply a visual identification for a like kind, or one that we believe is the right kind; the satisfaction of this need nearly always begins with sight. And though the process begins with sight, the more we proceed, the more we then seem to incorporate the heart, the emotions. These deeper moves toward relational union are initiated and facilitated through eye contact. Then, our heart seems to detect something in the eyes of this other being that will somehow complete us. And herein lies our greatest illusion, the source of all shame generation: we are only *images, reflections*.

> Then God said, "Let Us make man in Our image, according to Our likeness . . ." (Genesis 1:26, NKJV).

And,

> So God created man in His own image; in the image of God He created him; male and female He created them (Genesis 1:27, NKJV).

# When Shame Destroys a Human Being

### Going to the Dogs

I don't believe that the identification need is a part of our biology. In other words, animals don't seek a like kind with which to commune; they survive. Animals certainly look for a like kind with which to mate and continue the species, but animals in general—dogs, for example—don't visually identify as a prelude to a sense of belonging and then a deeper relational union.

Say, for example, you announce in your local newspaper that you are doing a study and need some volunteers. The event will take place on Saturday, July 17 at 9:00 a.m. in the gym of McKinley High School. "Free donuts and coffee will be served, along with $10.00 for an hour of your time."

The bleachers in the gym have been pulled back so nobody can sit down. Those who show up will simply have to drink their coffee, eat their donuts, stand, and mingle. Before the lock-out time of nine o'clock, 132 people have showed up.

At around 9:45 you go into the gym to have a look around. What do you think you'll see? I'll bet you can make a fairly good guess: You'll see a lot of groupings based on visual identifications. You'll see people grouped according to age, race, economic status, ethnicity, religion, and possibly even politics. In just forty-five minutes the people have done amazingly well at finding the others with whom they feel *comfortable*—people who are not going to cause them to feel less than, different, defective, sinful, or worse.

The following week you make a similar announcement in the local newspaper. Same deal, only this time you ask everyone to bring their dogs. You've erected a thirty-foot-square pen in the grass next to the parking lot. Seventy-one dogs show up before 9:00 a.m., along with their owners. The instructions are for owners to place their dogs in the pen, then do the same thing as the previous week: wait around together for an hour.

At 9:45 you walk over to the pen to have a look around. What do you think you'll see *this* time? Exactly! There are no groupings in the dogs based on age, breed, wealth, religion, or accomplishment. The poodle with a diamond collar seems to be having a fine time with a couple of mutts from the flats. And the hound from Tennessee is obviously not in the corner all alone. The Jacks aren't grouped up, and neither are the Dobermans. Why? Simply because the dogs don't give a *doggone* to belong! The Scottie and Great Dane seem to have hit it off despite their size and age differences. There is clearly something going on with us that isn't going on with the dogs. And it has nothing to do with feeling safe and secure. Simply, the dogs don't possess the primary interpersonal need. Clearly, we are driven to satisfy this need by something other than simple biology.

### *Why We Need to Identify*

The process of moving from a visual identification toward something deeper involves risk and trust. We risk feeling that we don't belong in order to find a place where we feel we do belong. Risk and trust alternate as we move deeper into identification. Some of us may have even been startled by the power that seems to pull us towards another. Some of us may even become frightened by our lack of power to resist this pull.

Have you ever wondered why individuals seem to have such a difficult time identifying themselves in the broadest way possible: as simply human beings? Why do we always seem to work toward a smaller identification instead of the larger? Why not simply be an *earthling*, a *human*, a *person*, instead of an American, a Philadelphian, a white man, a doctor, a Baptist, a surgeon, an orthopedic surgeon, a foot specialist, and so on? While many such labelings may be considered integral to the organization of culture, I suspect there's a lot more going on here than just a simple conceptualization needed for physical survival.

Within the identification need there is a tendency of movement from the general toward the particular. We identify with the many as a prerequisite toward a relational union with a single one, as shown in the progression above, from nationality to professional specialty. The identification need itself pushes us toward ever-smaller group identifications where we more strongly feel we belong and where we then seek a single other with whom to identify even more deeply: from the larger, to the smaller, to the smallest, and then onto a single one. Where we then feel that we most belong will then be a place where we are least subjected to shame and feeling we don't belong. It is actually the unsatisfied primary interpersonal need that has driven us toward smaller group identifications and fractured mankind . . . since the *beginning*.

**Sin vs. Shame**

For those of you who have some conceptualization of sin, how are you now figuring sin is related to shame? Is shame sin? Or, is shame the result of sin? In light of the previous discussion—if you buy into the idea that shame, guilt, humiliation, and embarrassment are, at their core, one and the same emotion—then obviously shame cannot be thought of as strictly a consequence of sin. For example, if you are shamed and quickly determine that the shame is without cause—mockery, scorn, contempt, prejudice, humiliation—the self has consequently determined that the wrongness is not with the self but a wrongness with the other. Since their condemnation is without cause it is they with whom the wrongness resides.

Another problem with trying to connect sin to shame is that shame isn't universally manifested across the board or equally in all situations for everyone. What causes shame in one man or in one culture might not cause shame in another. In some past cultures the eating of human flesh produced no shame. In some past cultures human sacrifice produced no shame. Shame is relative to the self, or to the culture. And what causes one man shame today might not cause him shame tomorrow, and the same could be said of cultures.

But for most of us, physical or emotional abuse of another is widely considered sinful, and often does cause shame in the abuser when it is done without cause. (But we can also abuse someone without feeling shame when we believe they deserve it!)

Is it sinful to use work as a defense against shame? What about an addiction, say, to work. Is that sinful? Is it sinful to develop any defenses against shame? Are some shame defenses sinful while others are not? Is it sinful for the self to defend itself from the shame that results from being physically abused? Is it sinful for the self to pursue respect, acclaim, honor, recognition, fame, wealth, or power as the means to lessening shame's impact? And what about the secondary responses of fear, distress, and rage—are they sinful? Or is only their expression sinful? Since shame is occasioned in our search to satisfy the primary interpersonal need, is the identification need sinful?

If you are like me, the conceptualizations of sin may seem particularly vague. It seems that each person has an individual list of things considered sinful. But what I now hope is that the concept of shame is becoming clear. I also hope that by the end of this discussion you'll have a much more defined picture of what sin really is, and what it isn't—indeed, you may begin to wonder if *sin* can really be considered to exist at all.

However, both shame and the most common perceptions of sin will each manifest whenever there is a violation of a behavioral expectation that we believe will lead us to a sense of belonging and interpersonal wholeness in the world—or more biblically, will lead us to favor from God. Whenever I *do* a *don't,* or *don't do* a *do* that I believe leads me to favor—to the diminishment of unfavorable attention—I will both have sinned *and* experienced shame.

## Shame, Humans, and God

In the next section of the book, we will take a closer look at the mechanisms of shame as they have played out in one of the world's most influential religions, the Judeo-Christian tradition. By reviewing the unfolding of shame as it is presented in the biblical record, we will discern some fascinating congruencies between ancient tradition, biblical doctrine, and the modern psychological theory of shame as presented by Dr. Kaufman.

As I stated at the outset of this book, the insights I am about to share with you came as an amazing revelation to me at a point in my life when I had slammed up against the harsh realization that I was running out of ways to find that ultimate sense of belonging and deep intimacy in my life. In many ways, I felt as if I was being given a revelation, a mission.

In fact, I have often felt as if I've been taken on an intergalactic tour by some celestial being. My journey has now come to an end, and I'm on the way back to Earth in a spacecraft that can travel the span of most galaxies in what I am told is just

# SHAME

a couple of terrestrial days, while traveling the distance between galaxies in what seemed but a few seconds. I've seen such magnificent and incredible things. The meaning of so much has been explained; I feel blessed to have been abducted.

But I am now tortured by the prospect of returning home, for how can I possibly expect anybody to believe a single word I say about my incredible journey? My celestial friend has foreseen my problem and understands my anxiety. He tells me he has a gift for me. He is going to provide me with the designs for an advanced energy technology. He tells me that it will be able to totally eliminate mankind's need for fossil fuels. The machine will even be adaptable for personal transportation. My problem is that I must write it all down in my own words! All that I've been given is a pen and paper, though I have been allowed access to the ship's computer system. I am actually quite surprised at how much I seem to understand. I feel fairly confident that with the taking of extensively copious notes that those more learned than I will later be able to figure out the rest.

Now my friend has told me that we will reach earth in just a couple of hours; I will be dropped off naked, with only my notebook—how embarrassing! I begin frantically wondering if my ranting will carry but the same validity as some *run-of-the-mill* alien abductee. If the machine doesn't work, then nothing else I say will be believed either. And though the machine is important, it pales in comparison to the rest of what I've seen. My friend only smiles when I ask him if he thinks my notes are good enough. I sense from his smile that everything is going to be just fine. Come with me now as I describe to you what I have seen on my tour of time, the universe, and the history of humanity's interaction with the Divine.

# PART 2

*Shame, God, and the Bible*

# CHAPTER 6

## How Did Shame Get Mixed up with Religion?

Before we begin our lightning tour of the Bible—thought by some scholars to contain some of the world's most ancient religious writings, by the way—it might be useful to pause and look at some basic aspects of human nature that yield interesting insights on our attitudes toward and our history with our ancient adversary, shame. If shame is, as it seems, a universal problem for humanity, and if it arises from the interactions that each of us must have in the course of "doing life," maybe we ought to look at a few foundational understandings about where our struggles against shame fit into the big picture of existence.

As we've already implied, shame is a function of the higher brain capabilities unique to humans. That is, dogs don't feel shame (from what we can tell). Nor do bacteria, amphibians, or even dolphins, the whiz kids of the non-human animal kingdom. So, where does shame fit into the picture?

**The Hierarchy of Needs**
Most of us have at least heard of the hierarchy of needs, first

## How Did Shame Get Mixed up with Religion?

posited by psychologist Abraham Maslow in 1943. Maslow proposed that human beings have a set of needs that they will try to satisfy, proceeding from the basic necessities of life—food and water—up through more complex desires or aspirations, such as a sense of personal fulfillment or achievement. Maslow's hierarchy of needs is often shown as a pyramid:

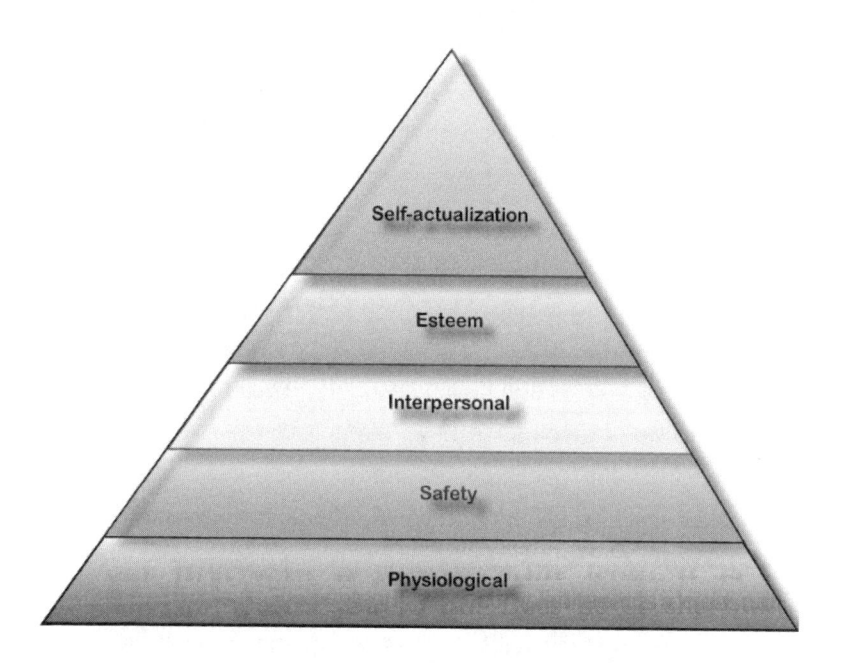

- Self-actualization
- Esteem
- Interpersonal
- Safety
- Physiological

The basic premise behind Maslow's theory is that we seek satisfaction of our needs in a sequential manner: until we have met our most basic needs for food, water, and sleep, we will not pay attention to the higher needs. That makes sense, of course. When someone is hungry, there is little else he will think about until he gets something to eat. But once the basic needs of the body and safety/security needs are fairly well assured, a person will then begin to address her higher, more interpersonally based needs: identification, belonging, and relationship.

As we have already seen, it is during our efforts to satisfy these intermediate relationship needs that we begin encountering shame: the slights, inattentions, inconsiderations, disrespects, embarrassments, and humiliations that inevitably come about when we are in contact with other humans. The having of self-esteem then becomes an issue.

In other words, if you really want to humiliate someone who is terribly hungry, it is probably best that you do it after you first feed her a meal. Similarly, a starving man is not likely to feel guilty or shamed for stealing food in order to survive. He will not be at all concerned with a sense of belonging until he has at least secured enough food to prevent starvation. At that point, when he has the luxury of assured survival, he will then be more susceptible to shame's onslaught; he will probably adopt some of the strategies we have already discussed to defend himself from the bad feelings shame produces. Self-esteem then becomes an issue of contention based on how well he or she maneuvers through shame's attack.

The attainment of self-actualization—the topmost part of Maslow's pyramid—first comes to depend on how well we can maneuver in order to prevent the occurrence of shame, and second, on how we deal with it once it occurs: the depth and integrity of our self-esteem. Is it any wonder that we often perceive that it is the wise, the powerful, the successful, the wealthy, and the famous who have high self-esteem? After all, they surely don't encounter as many occasions of disrespect as the rest of us, do they? Well, as a matter of fact, they deal with shame as much as anybody. Why? Because, as we'll see time and time again as we review humanity's failed attempts to deliver itself

## *How Did Shame Get Mixed up with Religion?*

from shame, interpersonal expectations can never be completely fulfilled through effort and action—no matter how much wisdom, position, power, or wealth we have. In fact, people in high places often experience a dramatic rise in shame's intensity when disrespect does occur. The higher their expectation that shame should not occur—because of their effort, wealth, power, fame, good looks, or whatever other criteria they may have—the worse shame feels when it comes along.

And indeed, shame always comes along. That is guaranteed, as our search for satisfaction of the interpersonal needs forces us toward interaction with others. Inevitably, the interpersonal expectations resulting from our unsatisfied primary interpersonal need collide with the same of others. No matter how much respect, fame, wealth, and power we've managed to accumulate—along with the feel and appearance of self-esteem—we must still go home at night and interact with the spouse and kids. No matter who we are to the rest of the world, we are still "just" Mom or Dad to our kids, "just" the spouse of our spouse, or "just" the partner of our partner.

So, we are all still under the affects of an unsatisfied interpersonal need which prevents us from being able to completely accept not only those with whom we are closest, but anybody else as well. And then when someone comes along and treats us differently than we expect, we feel *some kind of way* about it; and we end up either faulting them or ourselves.

**Maslow in Eden**

If we assume that all humans have certain needs that proceed more or less from the basic needs of survival up through the higher needs for personal significance as implied by interpersonal relationships, what are the implications for religion? Consider the following diagram, adapted from Maslow's hierarchy:

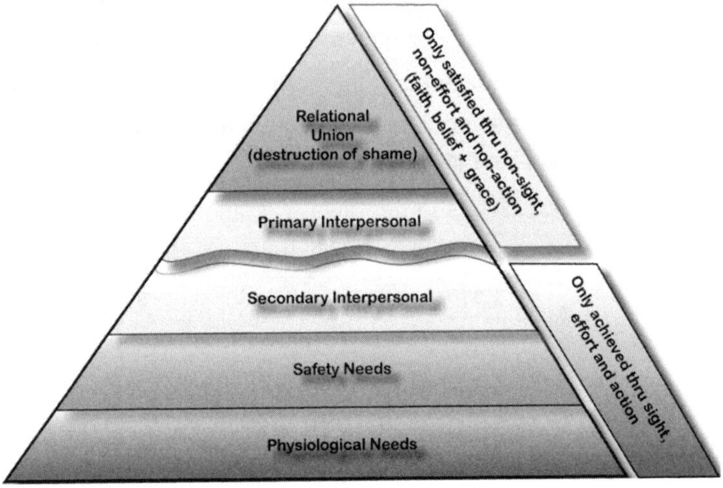
Relational
Union
(destruction of shame)
Primary Interpersonal
Secondary Interpersonal
Safety Needs
Physiological Needs
Only satisfied thru non-sight, non-effort and non-action (faith, belief + grace)
Only achieved thru sight, effort and action

If we analyze the story of the Garden of Eden from the Bible, we can see that the bottom part of the triangle—the basic needs and even some of the relational needs—were completely provided for Adam and Eve by God. Everything that they needed for their basic survival was placed within easy reach. Hungry? Have some fruit! Tired? Lie down on the soft grass and take a nap. They didn't have to worry about personal safety in paradise; according to Genesis, there was no such thing as danger there. Feeling the need for some physical affection? No problem: Adam and Eve were—quite literally—made for each other. Anything they needed for the most basic needs of life was there for the taking; all they had to do was reach out and get it.

But now we come to the second part of the pyramid. At this level, what had been working so easily and well was no

## How Did Shame Get Mixed up with Religion?

longer appropriate. Thus, when Adam and Eve used sight, effort, and action—seeing, taking, and eating—toward the external satisfaction of the primary interpersonal need—through the acquisition of great wisdom—they encountered shame.

As I mentioned early in the book, they were set up so that they would be forced to attempt to satisfy the primary interpersonal need by the methods they were accustomed to using. Even God's physical/external presence and companionship couldn't provide Adam and Eve with a sense of interpersonal completion. Remember, the Bible even uses physical imagery to discuss God's presence in the garden; Genesis 3:8 says that Adam and Eve heard God "walking in the garden in the cool of the day." But Adam and Eve—like all other humans who have ever lived—needed something that an externally perceived person could not provide . . . even if the name they gave that person was "God"!

So, the plan in the Garden of Eden was precisely arranged and perfectly executed. The primary purpose of the garden was for the inducement of a shaming experience. God's hope for Adam and Eve—once he placed them out of the garden—was for them to understand what really motivated the production of shame and then find their way to the kind of relationship with him that would be destructive to shame. Without the dear serpent and the "temptation" he provided, this would never have been even a possibility. After all, God couldn't very well tell Adam and Eve to not eat and later tell them that they could eat and still induce shame in them. Once again, the primary purpose of the garden was for the inducement of the shame experience as his mechanism of redirection unto himself, but not the externally perceived him.

Remember, too, that according to the biblical account,

# SHAME

the shame that Adam and Eve felt was accompanied by a clear example of feeling exposed and wanting to hide:

> They realized they were naked; so they sewed fig leaves together and made coverings for themselves. Then the man and his wife heard the sound of the Lord God as he was walking in the garden in the cool of the day, and they hid from the Lord God among the trees of the garden. But the Lord God called to the man, "Where are you?" He answered, "I heard you in the garden, and I was afraid because I was naked; so I hid" (Genesis 3:7–10, NIV).

We also get an example of hierarchically arranged shame transfer using blame:

> [God said to Adam:] "Have you eaten from the tree that I commanded you not to eat from?" The man said, "The woman you put here with me—she gave me some fruit from the tree, and I ate it." Then the Lord God said to the woman, "What is this you have done?" The woman said, "The serpent deceived me, and I ate" (Genesis 3:11–13, NIV).

As anyone knows who has ever been in the military, you-know-what always flows downhill! And shame works the same way; if I'm feeling shamed, one of the quickest ways to get rid of the feeling is by shifting it onto someone below me in the hierarchy.

## *How Did Shame Get Mixed up with Religion?*

The new thing that I'd like to now add to this garden analysis is this: *the serpent didn't lie!* And, of course, neither did God. Let me explain.

Another way to look at shame creation is to see it as manifesting itself when I seek to satisfy the Identification Need in the same general manner as I seek to satisfy the hunger need. When I use sight and action—seeing, taking, and eating—to satisfy my hunger need, I survive. But when I use sight and action to try to achieve an ultimate sense of external belonging, I encounter shame. And since actions I take toward the satisfaction of this primary interpersonal need increase my level of expectation, the intensity of shame upon failure will increase proportionally. Here's how it plays out in the garden:

> So when the woman saw that the tree was good for food, that it was pleasant to the eyes, and a tree desirable to make one wise, she took of its fruit and ate (Genesis 3:6, NKJV).

As Eve was soon to learn, efforts toward wisdom, just like efforts toward respect, reverence, acclaim, position, power, wealth, and fame, are all pathways toward what appears to lead to a sense of belonging and interpersonal completion in the world. These qualities give this appearance because they reduce the frequency of slights, inattentions, and disrespects. Thus, they are pursued in and of themselves so that the seeker will be treated differently—more favorably—by others. In other words, all these pursuits are shame-minimizing strategies that give us the feeling of being on the road toward interpersonal wholeness. But they will never take us to a sense of interpersonal completion, and they won't ever give us permanent relief from

# SHAME

those occasions where we feel separate and alone. Thus, when Eve took action by eating the fruit in order to become wise, an interpersonal expectation was violated.

As soon as Adam and Eve took the action of seeking wisdom and violated a request from an important *externally perceived* person, they experienced shame. (Think of similar experiences with your own parents, when you did something they asked you not to do and got caught.) Could the sense of exposure that accompanies shame—and the behavior of wanting to hide—be dramatized any better than this?

Previously, we spent a lot of time describing the devastation shame can wreak upon the self. We've spent a lot of time in describing the phenomenon Sylvan Tomkins refers to as a "sickness of the soul." I don't think it's too much of a stretch to say that shame can result in a kind of death to the self, a kind of living death—a spiritual death. When God told Adam he would die if he ate of the tree in the middle of the garden, he wasn't referring to a physical death; he was speaking in reference to the spiritual death that can occur due to the internalization of shame (though once shame becomes internalized physical life does become much more precarious).

Indeed, anybody who has ever been deeply hurt or greatly humiliated by someone knows there is no kind of pain like shame. It can almost feel like you're dying. And though shame can't kill by itself, it can be so disturbing to the self that you'll want to die.

However, when God told Adam that he would die if he ate of the fruit, Adam thought God meant that he would *physically* die. God was speaking to Adam from a spiritual-self perspective, while the serpent, taking advantage of Adam's misperception, was speaking from a physical-self perspective.

## *How Did Shame Get Mixed up with Religion?*

So, the serpent wasn't lying when it told them that it knew that God knew they wouldn't die—*physically*—if they ate of the fruit.

> "You won't die!" the serpent replied to the woman. "God knows that your eyes will be opened as soon as you eat it, and you will be like God, knowing both good and evil" (Genesis 3:4–5, NLT).

Absolutely true! For to understand the true nature and cause of shame is to indeed know what God knows about good and evil. But the serpent didn't lie! Shrewd? Yes! Cunning? Yes! Crafty? Yes! The serpent knew exactly how to entice them into taking action—eating—toward something that they believed would lead to a relative lack of shame and a sense of belonging in the world. The serpent convinced them to eat without having to blatantly deceive. In fact, there are *no* Bible translations that describe the serpent as dishonest, confounding, tricky, shady, misleading, fallacious, underhanded, incorrect, shifty, false, specious, sneaky, devious, sly, inaccurate, bewildering, wrong, puzzling, crooked, or perplexing.

The point is that the use of action toward the satisfaction of the primary interpersonal need will *always* heighten the created expectations and intensify the shame that occurs whenever these interpersonal expectations are ultimately violated. So, if this was the real teaching pertaining to the garden, how did we ever get all the others: original sin, the Fall, the consequences of Adam and Eve's "disobedience," and all the rest of it?

A lot of the answer can be found in the true nature of

shame itself. The great illusion is that shame has an *action* cause: in this case, a disobedience to God's *don't*. It only *appears* that if the actions perceived to be causing shame are discontinued then shame should be able to be eliminated from experience. This conversely means that everybody would have to be completely obedient to everybody else's interpersonal expectations in order for shame to then be eliminated and everybody to *always* feel they belong.

But the destruction of shame through action is a myth. Shame can only be eliminated through a *non-action* avenue of approach. Further, there is an important distinction between not doing something and the complete foregoing of action; simply not doing something is not the same as non-action. As long as one still believes in achieving some desired outcome by the not-doing decision, there is still a motive—driven by a need—fueling the not-doing. By contrast, with non-action one has recognized the futility of *all* action toward the satisfaction of the same goal. On one hand, there is still the belief in one's ability and power, while on the other there is the recognition of one's inability and powerlessness toward a certain outcome. For example, we know that no matter how hard we flap our arms we will never be able to fly like a bird. And it sure doesn't cause us to feel less than, defective, sinful, or evil because we can't flap our arms and fly. The New Testament uses the word "grace" to describe this non-actionable pathway toward both the satisfaction of the primary interpersonal need and the destruction of shame. We'll discuss this more fully in a later chapter.

Meanwhile, back in the garden . . . The idea that God said "Don't," Adam and Eve did, and sin entered and forever estranged us from God is a nightmare of logic and reason. Here is the purported first man and woman and—*wham*!!! This is

## *How Did Shame Get Mixed up with Religion?*

comparable to accidentally shutting down the company's entire computer network on your first day on the job—heck, in your first five minutes of your first day on the job! Or, it is like going on your first, long-sought dinner date with some hottie, getting sick, and puking on him or her. Come on! And why would God put such a tree right there in the middle of the garden anyway? Isn't this kind of like wanting to test the obedience of your children by putting a clear glass jar of poisonous cookies in the middle of the kitchen table?

When I first read the story about Adam and Eve—at the age of forty-seven—it *seemed* that the one I had previously heard about and the one I was now reading were two entirely different stories. For example, the Bible isn't explicit about Adam and Eve being the only two people on the planet. If they were, then who was the wife of their son Cain? I've heard all sorts of crazy explanations regarding this: I've heard some people say that Eve bore her son's children. Others have told me that it was one of Cain's sisters who bore his children. Much of this absurdity has arisen from the steadfast determination of those who feel compelled to maintain the idea of original sin: if Adam and Eve weren't the only people on the planet, then there might still be descendants of these others who didn't sin like Adam and Eve and were therefore sinless. *And we just couldn't have any sinless people walking around, not in need of the church, mosque, or synagogue!* Besides, if Cain had taken his mother or sister in order to have children, then the scriptures would have told us! Another contributing factor to this insistence on original sin—and probably more important for our discussion—is the perception of a sin-shame tie. Simply put, the occurrence of shame wrongfully became tied to a sinful action against God; future generations would discover an indestructible shame—

an indestructibility of sin—and would attribute its persistence to Adam and Eve. This perception of a sin-shame tie took us down a rabbit hole of illusory action causes for sin from which we in the West have still not escaped.

Another issue of contention is with the serpent being the mouthpiece of Satan. (Or was it the mouthpiece of Lucifer? Or was it the devil?) The thing about this rationale is that I never read anything in the preceding verses pertaining to God creating any of these guys. I thought that I had just finished reading that everything God created was *good*:

> Then God looked over all he had made, and he saw that it was very good! (Genesis 1:31, NLT).

One final comment on the garden involves action consequences. With most needs there are consequences for lack of fulfillment: If I don't catch the rabbit, I'll die of starvation; if I don't get out of the cold, I'll freeze to death; if I don't have sex, I won't have any children. However, remember that these same need mechanics and consequences are not applicable to the realm of shame. But because of the sin-shame tie wrongfully attributed to the garden, the occurrence of shame was perceived to mean that one had been disobedient and was therefore now deserving of punishment. All perceived punishments were hence attributed to some sinful disobedience. Besides, the perceived punishments by God in response to disobedience were not about what God would do to the transgressor, but what *we* would do in response to being shamed by someone without cause, essentially disobeyed. (Whenever someone important undeservedly does something to us that we don't expect,

## How Did Shame Get Mixed up with Religion?

causes us shame, and later something bad happens to them, we often say to ourselves, "They got what they deserved.")

> Then the Lord God said to the serpent, "Because you have done this, you are cursed more than all animals, domestic and wild. You will crawl on your belly, groveling in the dust as long as you live" (Genesis 3:14, NLT).

These "Because you did this, then . . ." causal action statements introduced by God in the garden are another basic facet of the shame experience. *Exactly like attributing the great flood to a pissed off God.* The search for some cause—now a sinful cause—is a most natural response for the wounded self, who wants to know why this has happened to it and will begin developing defenses to keep it from happening again. The self will also begin to implement consequences—ever more severe consequences—to *insure* that it never happens again. The gender scripts for women, for example, are largely the result of maneuverings by men to keep shame from occurring to *them*. (A great example of this in the Bible is found in Paul's first letter to Timothy, chapter 2, verse 14, where Paul says, "Adam was not the one deceived; it was the woman who was deceived and became a sinner.")

As we move through the Old Testament we'll notice an increase in the occurrence of these causal action/consequence statements. As shame becomes internalized, the self becomes ever more frantic and desperate in its efforts to find and eliminate the causes of shame, the causes of the now-perceived sin. Eventually the self will begin implementing punishments against those it decides are the sources of shame, the sources of sin.

# SHAME

And because of the shame/sin tie wrongly discerned from the garden, the self will now perceive itself as being in a God-approved war against the perceived action causes of sin.

As went the search for the sinful causes of shame, so went the search for the perceived consequences from God for the sin, or those that need to be implemented by man in the name of God. And if there were any perceived consequences from God—disease, famine, death, whatever—there then had to be a sinful cause that required elimination.

Futility and madness! And all because of the wrong shame-sin-consequence interpretation of the garden.

# CHAPTER 7

## *Shame and the Chosen People*

*T*he apostle Paul was one of the founding pillars of Christian thought and doctrine. A highly educated man, he was not only familiar with most of the Greek thought of his day, but as a proud Jew was the recipient of a heritage of religious teaching stretching back thousands of years. In his letters Paul grapples with the problem of shame—which he primarily recognizes as the problem of sin—he does a remarkable job of summarizing the human dilemma with shame as it has been handed down to him in the form of the doctrines and laws of the Jewish people—much of which has come to us in the document known as the Old Testament. Let's listen in as Paul tries to reason his way through the problem of the sin/shame paradigm in one of his most philosophically and theologically complex works, the letter to the Christians in Rome.

> Well then, am I suggesting that the law of God is sinful? Of course not! In fact, it was the law that showed me my sin. I would never have known that coveting is wrong if the law had not said, "You must not covet." But sin used this

command to arouse all kinds of covet desires within me! If there were no law, sin would not have that power (Romans 7:7–8, NLT).

So I find this law at work: When I want to do good, evil is right there with me. For in my inner being I delight in God's law; but I see another law at work in the members of my body, waging war against the law of my mind and making me a prisoner of the law of sin at work within my members. Who will rescue me from this body of death? (Romans 7:21–24, NIV). *We will address Paul's distorted conceptualizations of the law in much greater depth later on.*

Reading Paul's words, I can almost imagine his internal anguish: On the one hand, he is predisposed by years of study and by a lifetime of reverence to believe that the commandments of God are the means to life and righteousness—the opposite of shame. And yet, on the other hand, he sees the practical result of his ceaseless efforts to avoid *doing* one of God's *don'ts*. At the end of the day, despite his best and most committed efforts, Paul feels his incompleteness, his failure . . . his shame. Despite his misperceptions regarding the law, Paul receives some amazing insight regarding the subjectivity of shame/sin generation:

But if you have doubts about whether or not you should eat something, you are sinning if you go ahead and do it (Romans 14:23, NLT).

As Paul rightly states, what is shameful for one man might not be shameful for another. Conversely, what is sinful for one man might not be sinful for another. However, none of us can escape sin, shame, and guilt as long as we are looking for favor in the seen, or, more biblically, for belonging in the world by gaining favor with God.

> You may believe there's nothing wrong with what you are doing, but keep it between yourself and God. Blessed are those who don't feel guilty for doing something they have decided is right (Romans 14:22, NLT).

To paraphrase Paul elsewhere, he tells us that everything is permissible, but not everything is constructive or beneficial. Basically, all that Paul is really trying to convey here is that favor from God isn't earnable. By saying that everything is permissible, Paul is trying to eliminate the perception that belonging (favor) can be achieved (granted by God for obedience) through the observance of a set of *do's* and *don'ts*. The Jews thought that if they were *good,* God would reward them with a relatively shame-free position of power, wealth, respect, honor, recognition, or reverence, essentially belonging. Paul, however, surmised that it was the *do–don't* plan, the law, that was actually producing the shame; that the shame was sent by God to make him realize the depth of his sinfulness. Paul was right in his thinking that without the law—in other words, if everything was made permissible—the production of shame would greatly lessen, but it wouldn't be destroyed.

How did Paul—and presumably, many other intelligent, educated, and devout Jewish people of his day—arrive at these conclusions? How did they reach the point of seeing God's *do–don't* plan not as the means of deliverance from shame, but also,

# SHAME

at least in some sense, as a source of shaming? To discover the answer, we need to go back several thousand years, to a point in the ancient past when God was forming a special people to become a living enactment of the shame dilemma on a national scale. We need to return to the days of the Exodus from Egypt: the birth of the Hebrew nation.

### The Cleansing

By the time we finish the Old Testament book of Genesis and begin reading the book of Exodus, the descendants of Jacob's sons—the twelve tribes of Israel—have now grown to millions; they have also become slaves in Egypt. The time has now come for God to reveal himself in an extremely dramatic way. When Yahweh delivered the Israelites out of Egypt, not only did it appear to establish his presence and power, but it also indicated that Jacob's descendants were chosen for some special reason. As we're going to see, the people of Israel were indeed chosen . . . for what ended up being and excruciatingly painful lesson on the finer points of shame dynamics. God would now try a different approach for the education of his mechanism of interpersonal redirection. Things just weren't working so well since the garden. God's introduction of his Mechanism of Interpersonal Redirection to a people who were already indwelled with internalized shame was having disastrous effects. Since shame became wrongfully attributed to sin and evil, everything and anything—including murder—which gave the feeling of a shame cleansing, release, or transfer, was being seen as having the approval of God.

One of the most amazing pieces of this entire revelation concerning shame and the Bible is the one concerning blood, more specifically, blood splatter, more specifically still, the human blood splatter experienced by men on a field of battle. It was not uncommon to survive such warfare literally covered in the blood of your hated enemy. But because of the misinterpretation of the Garden of Eden linking the experience of shame to a sinful action cause, the shame transfer which took place from killing a hated enemy actually became attributed to the incurred blood splatter. The killing of your hated enemy was therefore perceived as having the blessings of God. The obvious problem with this perception was that it resulted in men killing men and both sides believing that they were in a God approved war against evil. This was the prevailing perception for everyone in the region who had heard of the story of The Garden. This of course was why when God brought the Israelites out of Egypt he commanded "Thou shall not kill" as well as instituting a strict procedure using animal blood as a substitution for the deeply ingrained perception of the shame cleansing effects of human blood on the battlefield.

God was going to try a different and highly controlled approach for guiding us to the type of relationship with himself that is destructive to the generation of shame. This approach is not unlike the kinds of experiments we see being performed within the psychology field today. Except today, such an experiment using people would be viewed as highly unethical, possibly even criminal.

Throughout the book of Genesis, shame—prior to the exodus and wilderness experience of the Israelites—was perceived as a direct communication from God indicating sin. Whenever someone experienced something which caused them shame it was an indicator that the action that generated the shame was a sin. But it was only from the perspective of those who were perceived as having found favor with God—those with

# SHAME

wealth, power, or position—that were given authority to speak for God for what was sinful. This was why homosexual acts were considered so sinful in the eyes of God—determined by men in general—while human slavery was never so much as hinted at as being even slightly sinful. But God was about to do a study and teaching on the phenomenon of shame that even from a modern-day psychological perspective is truely astounding.

Cultures that have rigid class structures and those that adopt slavery typically have strikingly similar arrangements for the disposal of shame. As we now know, shame is nearly always transferred from those with more power to those who have less—as in the garden, from Adam to Eve to the serpent; as at the office, from the boss to his or her underlings; from parents to children; from husbands to wives; and from slave owners to their slaves. While there is no doubt that there is a labor and economic motivation for the adoption of slavery—at least on a conscious level—it is equally significant that the adoption of slavery constitutes—though predominantly unconscious—a mechanism for the transference of shame. Thus, slavery amounts to a societal shame-defending strategy. Simply put, whenever a culture contains a slave component, its free citizens are provided with a ready receptacle to which their shame may be transferred.

However, this tactic cuts both ways: slavery provides the culture at large with more leisure time, resulting in an increased production of shame within its own people. Remember: Maslow's hierarchy suggests that shame generation proliferates once the self has sufficiently attended to its more basic needs. Thus, what the masters in a slave culture had at first believed to be beneficial—both on a conscious and unconscious level—has actually created an environment where shame generation now increases significantly. In the end, slavery actually turns shame upon the slave owners themselves. Cosmic justice?

Perhaps. But all the while the slaves do take the worst of it; the rising shame is in turn passed directly on to them, along with the hardest, least desirable work and the socioeconomic repression that inevitably accompanies slavery. The oppression of another human being—involving as it does the belittlement, disparagement, condemnation, and humiliation of another—is always, on some level, about shame transfer.

We could probably spend hours discussing the history of slavery, trying to determine just how much of slavery's creation, maintenance, and justification was about labor and how much was motivated by having a safe place to which to transfer shame. We could have the same discussion about cultures with rigid class structures. But regardless of the proportions—which probably shift over time—the fact remains that slaves are victims of incredible shame inducement; they nearly always have deeply internalized shame. Remember, too, that the Israelites were not only the objects for shame transfer from the Egyptians, but they were also victims of their own shame creation arising from their own unsatisfied primary interpersonal need.

### *Internalized Shame and a National Inferiority Complex*

So, in delivering them from this condition and the beginning of this grandest of psychological experimental undertakings, God announced both his presence and power and removed the Israelites from this environment of crippling shame inducement. Remember, however, that once shame becomes internalized it becomes autonomous, self-generative, and impervious to change. Low self-esteem and lack of faith and lack of trust in

# SHAME

others is characteristic of internalized shame. Throughout the book of Numbers—one of the books that records the customs and laws that were intended to govern the nation of Israel as it established itself in the Promised Land—we are provided several examples that show the depth of shame amongst the people of Israel after leaving Egypt. A particularly good example is seen when the twelve spies return from Canaan. Despite the affirming, faith-filled report of Joshua and Caleb, two spies who believed that with God's help Israel could conquer and rule the land, a diminished sense of self—a lack of self-esteem—pervades the report of the other ten spies.

> But the men who had gone up with [Joshua and Caleb] said, "We are not able to go up against the people, for they *are stronger than we.*"
> And they gave the children of Israel a bad report of the land which they had spied out, saying, "The land through which we have gone as spies is a land that devours its inhabitants, and all the people whom we saw in it are men of great stature.
> "There we saw the giants (the descendants of Anak came from the giants); and we were like grasshoppers in our own sight, and so we were in their sight" (Numbers 13:31–33, NKJV).

Despite having a fighting force that numbered around 600,000 men, these ten—clearly the majority—still lacked the belief that the land could be taken. I have no doubt that God already knew they weren't ready to take the land. (He never intended to let them settle.) But whether or not Moses knew what was *really* going on was another matter; Moses was just being obedient to God's direction. I believe that God simply wanted to show them the land before he took them into the wilderness. As events proved, the majority of the people who heard that day's report would never see the Promised Land again; they would die during the forty-year period of desert wandering that followed.

Indeed, I believe that God planned to take the nation into the wilderness even before he brought them out of Egypt. God's plan all along was to cleanse the Israelites of deep shame *before* he settled them in Canaan. There would be no better way to remove the internalized shame from within the Israelites than to have it die off naturally while keeping new shame generation to a minimum.

### Manna from Heaven—or Shame?

I've read estimates that there may have been as many as three million people brought out of Egypt by Moses. With that many people on the move in a less-than-abundant landscape, finding sufficient food would have been a problem. We have the story about God providing the manna and quail, of course, as found in Exodus chapter 16. There seems to be some debate about whether or not the Israelites were fed manna every day for forty years.

This is an important consideration in terms of God's desire to cleanse the Israelites of shame, because, as you may recall, when God provided for all the basic needs in the garden, shame was then generated. The wilderness experience of Israel was all about shame cleansing and its minimization. Thus, they needed to be in the position of having to take some care for

# SHAME

their own survival in order to avoid rising to the level of need hierarchy, where shame is most readily generated.

So, did the manna only come when survival was in jeopardy? Or did the manna come as a backup to whatever else they could provide for themselves? One thing not open to debate is that shortly after turning around and heading south, Moses gave the Israelites some supplementary instructions pertaining to plant and animal offerings. Obviously, Moses wouldn't have given such instructions if they were only eating manna. I doubt that Moses knew it would be a number of decades before they saw the Jordan again. And he sure wouldn't have given these instructions if he knew it would be another forty years before they gained the capacity to offer plant and animal offerings. I believe that these instructions were given because the Israelites either already had the capacity to make such offerings or would *soon* have that capacity.

> And the Lord spoke to Moses, saying, "Speak to the children of Israel, and say to them: 'When you come into the land you are to inhabit, which I am giving you, and you make an offering by fire to the LORD . . .'" (Numbers 15:1–3, NKJV).

God didn't take the Israelites into the wilderness—*the land you are to inhabit*—to keep feeding them manna. He wanted them to take care of their own basic needs as much as possible. God not only wanted to remove the old shame—the internalized shame from Egypt—but he also wanted to keep them below the need threshold for the proliferation of new shame. He couldn't very well provide for all their basic needs while at the same time keeping new shame generation minimized.

**Keeping a Lid on Shame?**
For any shame that did occur, God instituted a strict mechanism for the safe transfer of that shame out of the self and away from people.

> And if a person sins unintentionally, then he shall bring a female goat in its first year as a sin offering. So the priest shall make atonement for the person who sins unintentionally, when he sins unintentionally before the LORD, to make atonement for him; and it shall be forgiven him (Numbers 15:27–28, NKJV).

The implementation of guilt offerings would help keep the shame from being passed on within and amongst the children of Israel. Finally, after forty years of this incredible regimen,

> Then the Lord said to Joshua, "Today I have rolled away the shame of your slavery in Egypt" (Joshua 5:9, NLT).

The misinterpretation that linked the occurrence of shame to the commitment of a sin was begun in the Garden of Eden. This perceived linkage largely continued for the children of Israel. But since they had been cleansed of all residual, internalized, and self-generative shame, the only shame they ever felt was when they accidently violated a rule and were sent shame from God via the priests. Consequently, the occurrence of shame meant they had done something to displease God. Conversely, the relative absence of shame—gaining places of power, honor, favor, and respect—meant that they were blameless and had found favor with God. With this in mind, added to what we now know about the interpersonal generation of shame, particularly once the self's more basic needs becomes satisfied, it becomes fairly apparent where these perceptions would eventually lead the nation of Israel, as well as much of the rest of the world.

For example, as we saw in our review of Tomkins' research, the experience of powerlessness is very often accompanied by shame. It should come as no surprise, then, that in the nation of Israel, being in a position of powerlessness was therefore tied to the commitment of some sin. And since, in a society so dependent upon the physical ability of individuals to procure sustenance, being handicapped or diseased was so heavily imbued with shame, these too would also eventually become seen as the consequences of sin: of disfavor with God. This is illustrated clearly in the response of some of Jesus' disciples to seeing a man who was born blind:

> As [Jesus] went along, he saw a man blind from birth. His disciples asked him, "Rabbi, who sinned, this man or his parents, that he was born blind?" (John 9:1–2, NIV).

As we'll see later, Jesus' response to his followers' question is very instructive. However, for now, I simply want to illustrate how embedded in Jewish thought was the notion that if you were in a powerless or extremely disadvantaged position,

## Shame and the Chosen People

it was assumed that you had offended God in some way—you were the recipient of divine shaming.

### The New and Improved Shame/Sin Link

Most simply, Israel would later begin perceiving that any experience of shame meant that you had somehow sinned. We'll soon begin to see how the shame-sin tie evolves as we proceed through the Old Testament.

In fact, to this very day we see shame and guilt employed as a guide toward good behavior and a deterrent for bad; we still see it as a kind of internal moral compass. Despite these continuing perceptions, of course, the true basis for all generation of shame is actually in our looking to the seen—more specifically, externally—in an attempt to satisfy the primary interpersonal need . . . but let's not get ahead of ourselves.

Once the Israelites got settled they would increasingly come to see the generation of shame as arising from unknown sin. Say, for example, I whacked my thumb with a mallet as I was pounding in a tent stake, and a few people laughed and mocked me. Say also that these people were of more position and status than I. The shame I felt would have been perceived as being sent for some sin I had committed, knowingly or otherwise. Essentially, a sin would be looked for whenever shame was experienced—sort of a "where-there's-smoke-there's-fire" attitude.

So, at this point, shame in response to sin was either seen as sent directly from God or seen as sent through others who are perceived as being in favor with God. When shame was sent through others it seemed especially bad, for it announced to everyone present that the shamed person was a sinner. If no sin could be found in one's own life to explain a shame experience, then one could always look to one's parents, as shown in the example with Jesus' disciples, above. Failing that, one could look to one's family, tribe, or nation. And if all else failed and no cause for shame could be found, one could always blame it on Adam and Eve, or better yet, the serpent.

Also, since all sin had to be punished, one would look for an occasion of punishment as well. All perceived punishments therefore had to have a sinful cause and ultimately be tied to shame. And if no punishments could be found immediately, one would always come along eventually; the next calamity, illness, or misfortune would be interpreted as the consequence of some sin or shortcoming. This mindset, of course, evokes all the later evolving statements in the Old Testament involving the formula, "Because you have done X, then Y has happened."

Unfortunately, all these lines of thought and reasoning were dead-end branches down the rabbit hole that prevented the Israelites' escape from the shame cycle—and ours as well. All of us got lost in a labyrinth of causes and consequences, when all along, neither shame, nor, by extension, sin could ever be defeated by *doings* or *not-doings*. This predicament led to the development of a multitude of rather creative explanations for why shame—and sin—continued to occur, despite our best efforts.

**The Cleansing . . . Failed**
As we will see, shame would eventually become generated at exponential levels under Mosaic law. Because of the increasing human expectations concerning the law's ability to deliver from shame, the generation of shame for the settled Israelites would continue rising to new levels. In fact, without all the written-in protections for the cleansing and safe transfer of shame

through sacrifice, shame would have became internalized and institutionalized even more quickly than it did.

Then, when the threat of eternal damnation was eventually added to the list of tactics to combat shame, extremely fertile ground existed for some of the worst shame-based syndromes ever seen in humankind. Of course, as Paul would note a couple of thousand years later, it wasn't the law in and of itself that did this, but the Israelite's expectations—their belief that obedience to the law could destroy shame—that caused shame to continually increase over time.

So, by the time the wandering Israelites finally entered the Promised Land and began its conquest, the shame/sin linkage was firmly established in the national consciousness. And, as we'll see, their history over the next generations would do nothing to weaken this tie. In fact, it became more entrenched than ever.

# CHAPTER 8

## *When Shame Defines a Nation*

By now, we've seen how God planned to extract Israel not only from slavery, but also from the shame that was heaped upon them by occupying the bottom rung of Egypt's socioeconomic ladder. He has led them into the desert and arranged events so that they would spend enough time wandering there to eliminate, via the death of an entire generation, much of the residual shame that still lingered in his chosen nation. It was critically important for God to expunge as much shame as possible from amongst the Israelites before he settled them into Canaan. God's hopes for the children of Israel were very similar to his hopes for Adam and Eve. He hoped they would recognize shame as a mechanism of interpersonal redirection unto himself—more specifically, to the HIM that is within us. But as we'll see, the illusion that shame has an action cause is stubbornly pervasive. All that God has ever wanted is an all-consuming personal relationship, the kind of relationship that would hopefully then lead them to the place where that relationship with HIM is completely destructive to shame.

Toward these ends, God surely wasn't going to subject them to the heavily shamed Canaanites whose homes and lands he was about to give to the children of Israel. God took extra severe steps to insure that his chosen people would not become objects for shame transfer from the peoples that were heavily shamed by killing them and taking their lands: he instructed the Israelites to completely exterminate the peoples whose land they were taking.

Notice this example, taken from the conquest of Ai, one of the first Canaanite cities overrun by the Israelites:

> When the Israelite army finished chasing and killing all the men of Ai in the open fields, they went back and finished off everyone inside. So the entire population of Ai, including men and women, was wiped out that day—12,000 in all . . . Joshua impaled the king of Ai on a sharpened pole and left him there until evening (Joshua 8:24–25, 29, NLT).

How could such barbarism be justified or rationalized? How could such cruelty be attributed to an order from God? Nevertheless, the Old Testament book of Joshua, which describes the military conquest of the Promised Land, is filled with many such examples of what appears to be wanton butchery. I've heard it said that the Israelites weren't really any worse than anybody else; I disagree—they were much more brutal, because they wiped out entire tribes of people. However, there were some very specific reasons for this cruelty towards others. After all, complete exterminations were not commonplace; if they were, why would God have needed to intervene and give such explicit orders?

I pondered this for a long time before I finally came to

an understanding: These actions were foundational to the great teaching about shame that God intended to perform, using the entire nation of Israel as a visual aid. Simply put, the conquered Canaanite people were sacrificed as part of that teaching.

There were basically two reasons for all this mercilessness. First, God wanted to eliminate any exposure to these other people's shame; second, he wanted the Israelites to earn these people's deep hatred. God not only wanted to keep the Israelites as isolated as possible from the surrounding nations, but he also wanted them to be despised as much as possible by their geographic neighbors. By having neighbors who hated them also kept the Israelites below the need level where shame generation would begin to escalate—when we are always concerned with our physical safety we don't give as much attention to attending to our higher interpersonal needs. By doing it this way, God also made it virtually impossible for them to blame anybody but themselves for what he knew *would* one day possibly happen—he would have the tree of life if it was needed. But for this current effort God wanted a sterile Petri dish for the growing of this spiritual mechanism of interpersonal redirection. We'll return to some additional implications of such ethnic cleansing a bit later.

**The Law and Shame Mitigation**
After Moses was dead and buried, Joshua, the new leader of the nation, received these instructions from God:

> Be strong and very courageous. Be careful to obey all the instructions Moses gave you. Do not deviate from them, turning

either to the right or to the left. Then you will be successful in everything you do. Study this Book of Instruction continually. Meditate on it day and night so you will be sure to obey everything written on it. Only then will you prosper and succeed in all you do (Joshua 1:7–8, NLT).

The law and instructions would serve the Israelites well in gaining material prosperity, but it wouldn't satisfy their primary interpersonal need. And the perception of a localized God—in the pillar of fire, in the cloud, above the Ark of the Covenant, in the tabernacle—would actually inhibit the Israelites from finding the kind of relationship with God that was completely destructive to shame.

The law was many-faceted, providing guidance and regulation for a multitude of personal and public health issues. It provided for personal protections and administered civil and criminal justice. It also provided for the dissipation of shame.

We know that anger can be really damaging when it is allowed to build within the self. Many of us are probably familiar with the concept of role-playing in the field of counseling and therapy. The therapist, a counselor, or a therapy group member will play the role of the parent, spouse, boss, friend, or whomever the counselee is feeling anger toward. When inability to express anger is the issue at hand, this *stand-in* is used as a safe replacement for the object of the anger. The counselor or other stand-in doesn't actually accept the anger in such a situation, but it is only the *expression* of anger towards another person that matters in terms of dissipating the harmful inner effects of anger buildup.

# SHAME

The expression (sending) of anger is very similar to the expression (sending) of shame. However, if the Israelites carefully observed the law, any and all shame that was generated could be safely purged from amongst them. In other words, to paraphrase scripture, "I promise that if you are obedient to all my law, shame will not build up and become internalized" (Deuteronomy 28:18, paraphrase).

## *To Be Forgiven*

We learn in Exodus 28:38 that God had decreed during the wilderness wandering that Aaron (Moses' brother and chief priest of the nation) would be the one through whom the people's shame would be transferred. Ultimately, it was the animal sacrificed by the priest that was perceived to receive the shame. A careful reading of Exodus 28 and 29 seems to indicate that the shame was transferred through Aaron's priestly garments. Exodus 28:36 tells us that it was the gold medallion that Aaron wore on his turban that allowed him to take on the shame of the people. Verse 43 of chapter 28 tells us that Aaron and his sons were to wear these special linen garments in order to protect them from taking the shame on themselves. In other words, Aaron and the other priests were a combination of spiritual sanitation workers and psychological bomb-disposal squad. They mediated and performed the ceremonies and practices that provided the all-important perception of God's forgiveness, vital to the prevention of the buildup of shame in the nation of Israel.

Let's say that I say or do something that hurts a friend. I have damaged the interpersonal bridge between my friend and myself, resulting in shame and guilt. If I truly care about the relationship, I will apologize; my apology will be an attempt to be cleansed from the guilt I feel. If my friend accepts my apology, my shame will appear to have left me. It can almost appear that my friend has accepted my shame. However, if my friend doesn't accept my apology, my shame appears to remain. In other words, my shame appears to transfer when there is an understanding or perception of forgiveness, and to remain when forgiveness is absent. If forgiveness is perceived to have occurred, there will also result a feeling of being cleansed of shame. *(This lingering of shame is what gave Cain the perception that his offering wasn't accepted by God—this lingering of shame despite the offering was undoubtedly due to the fact that shame had already become internalized in Cain.)*

In a similar way, the nation of Israel needed a way to apologize to God for transgressions and be perceived forgiven. Shame was seen as arising from the violation of one of God's do's or don'ts. If shame remained, it appeared that there was no restoration in their relationship with God. They could confess their wrongs and give an offering, but unless their shame dissipated—unless their apology and offering were understood as accepted—there was no appearance of a restoration with their relationship with God. Thus, the sacrifices and offerings to God performed by the priests on behalf of the people were actions demonstrating that the apology was divinely accepted. Shame was dissipated through the sacrificial process. This release from shame gave the feeling that forgiveness was granted. Because of this relief, it also appeared that God was no longer angry. In other words, the sacrifices appeared to restore one's good standing with God; they dissipated the shame of the broken relationship.

# SHAME

**The Endless Treadmill of Shame**

But there was a problem: shame continued to build within the Israelites, resulting in the perception of an increasing estrangement from God. This must have been maddening for the Israelites to witness: the slow build up of shame within their culture. This also resulted in a lot of paranoia—to use a modern psychological term—motivating a hyper-vigilant search for the hidden causes of sin.

The fact is, God knew what he was up against regarding the generation of shame. God knew the Israelites were seeing him as an external being; he knew they would come to perceive him as angry. He knew they might eventually come to see their relationship broken. He knew they might come to feel estranged. All of this stage-setting by God was in preparation for a possible future unfolding drama. We are given a glimpse of these possibilities as early as Deuteronomy 30:

> In the future, when you experience all these blessings and curses I have listed for you, and when you are living among the nations to which the Lord your God has exiled you, take to heart all these instructions (Deuteronomy 30:1, NLT).

This verse contains a clear prediction of the possible deterioration of the Israelites. Some will say these curses were prophetic. But given what we now know about shame generation and the perception of a sin-shame-action tie, I believe that we too could make similar predictions. It's not very difficult to now see how these misperceptions developed and where they might eventually lead the nation of Israel.

First, we could obviously have predicted the possible continuing occurrence and rise of shame among the people of Israel. Because of the sin-shame tie, it would also have been fairly easy to predict the perception of a continuing rise in the perception of sin. Once the Israelites were settled in Canaan, shame generation would accelerate as their greater prosperity allowed them to tend to the higher-level interpersonal need. As the internal generation of shame began to increase they would in turn begin to develop defenses to combat the rising occurrence of shame. This developing internal war with shame would preoccupy the Israelites and cause them to become increasingly vulnerable to the surrounding enemies who hated them. However (and paradoxically), and as just mentioned, their enemies would initially serve the purpose of slowing their descent into shame: when one is concerned with safety and security needs, the internal generation of shame is minimized (remember Maslow).

With the development of defenses to deal with the rising occurrence of shame, we would also expect a development—and enforcement—of the behavioral pathways to decrease shame's effects. These behavioral paths would be generally developed most specifically for men and women—the male and female gender scripts—but scripts would also develop for the culture at large; the pursuit of wealth, position, wisdom, and accomplishment would increasingly be utilized in an effort to minimize the rising sense of shame. *These addendums to combat shame were of course not of God.* Success in these efforts would in turn be wrongly perceived as favor granted by God for blamelessness. However, since these scripts would be enforced using shame itself, they would actually up the ante, so to speak.

# SHAME

In response to shame's rise there would be a corresponding increase in desperation to find shame's cause—or should I say, the sinful cause of shame. This would ultimately result in the interpretation of the events in the garden as *the Fall*. The idea of *original sin* would also develop. This would also eventually pave the way for the adoption of belief in an underworld—complete with its king and his minions—as an explanation for the invincibility of shame, or should I say, the invincibility of sin.

So, would the words of Deuteronomy 30:1 have required the gift of prophecy or just a clear understanding of the workings of shame? The Old Testament is full of accounts of disobedience by the people of Israel. They were always looking for some sinful action to explain the continuing occurrence of shame, and instances were always ready at hand. They did not know that shame could not be defeated using effort and action, and each time they looked to the seen to try and satisfy the primary interpersonal need—and failed—it always appeared that shame resulted from some action cause—seen or unseen, intentional or unintentional.

We could have also predicted that some would eventually perceive the law as the creator of shame. As Paul would point out many centuries later, the law would wrongfully be seen to have the effect of forcing someone's hands onto a hot stove and then admonishing them for screaming "Ouch!"

The tediousness of shame's continuing occurrence and the tediousness for its continuous cleansing could also have been predicted. The process of *sinning* and *restoration* sure could get old year after year after year after year. Likewise, the institution of nearly immediate and rather severe consequences to even the slightest wavering from the law also could have been predicted. Consider the statements in the following verses from Deuteronomy 28 (NLT):

> 1. If you fully obey the Lord your God and carefully keep all his commands that I am giving you today, the Lord your God will set you high above all the nations of the world.

(But what God didn't say was that the careful keeping of commands couldn't completely stem the tide of proliferating shame—particularly when they reached a place of power and wealth. In a twisted sort of way, God could almost be seen as setting them up for destruction by shame.)

> 11. The Lord will give you prosperity in the land he swore to your ancestors to give you, blessing you with many children, numerous livestock, and abundant crops.

(Do/don't plans are great at providing for physical prosperity, but they are ineffective in completely destroying the production of shame.)

> 15. But if you refuse to listen . . . and do not obey all the commands and decrees . . . all these curses will come and overwhelm you . . .

(Obedience to the law was great at supplying the basic needs, and though it could keep shame from becoming internalized, it could not prevent its occurrence.)

# SHAME

> 20. The Lord himself will send on you curses, confusion, and frustration in everything you do, until at last you are completely destroyed for doing evil and abandoning me.

(Indeed, God would be perceived to use the enemies who hated Israel to destroy them when they turned from the law.)

> 21. The Lord will afflict you with diseases until none of you are left in the land you are about to enter and occupy.

(Significantly, portions of the law dealt directly with the control of disease, fever, inflammation, blight, and mildew.)

> 25–26. The Lord will cause you to be defeated by your enemies . . . You will be an object of horror to all the kingdoms of the earth. Your corpses will be food for all the scavenging birds and wild animals . . .
>
> 28–29. The Lord will strike you with madness, blindness and panic. You will grope around in broad daylight like a blind person groping in the darkness, but you will not find your way.

(Could the internalization of shame and the development of its syndromes be dramatized any better than this? Could the fear, distress, and rage responses that accompany the occurrence of shame be illustrated more forcefully?)

## When Shame Defines a Nation

The revelations in the Old Testament that derive from our new understandings about shame are almost unending. However, with each new revelation there remains one consistent theme: sight, effort, and action—even when motivated by obedience to divine law—are incapable of totally resolving the problem of shame. This is similar to saying that the Israelites were incapable of ultimately resolving the problem of their guilt under law. It is also now perfectly understandable how the law eventually caused them to believe that they were just hopeless sinners. This of course resulted in the perception which linked shame, and consequently sin, to an action cause.

The reason for the law was to teach the nation of Israel that sight, effort, and action were useless towards the total eradication of shame. The law was meant to:

1. provide for an abundant physical life;
2. teach about shame;
3. prevent the internalization of shame;
4. teach that human sight, effort, and action are useless towards a sense of relational wholeness; and
5. keep the children of Israel free of internalized shame until they hopefully found their way out of shame through the establishment of a particular kind of relationship with God.

The law was *not* meant to

1. make us into defective sinners;
2. create an evil underworld as an explanation for continuing shame;
3. create shameless pathways—hierarchically designed

# SHAME

and enforced—in an attempt to defeat shame;
4. cause shame to be internalized; or
5. have addenda added.

    I have a childhood memory that may be helpful in understanding the law and its effects upon the Hebrew nation. I believe it was on the *Ed Sullivan Show* that I saw a performer do an act with spinning ceramic plates. He would spin these plates on the ends of very tall wooden dowels and then step back from the standing stick with the spinning plate on top of it. One by one he would quickly add more spinning plates to his standing, rotating collection.

    After a couple of minutes, a few of the first plates would begin to slow down and wobble. With a quick hand motion to the middle of the stick, he would restore the velocity of the wobbling plate. Soon, in addition to adding more spinning plates, he also had to maintain the ones already spinning. There were times when a number of the plates would start wobbling at the same time. I instinctively knew that if one plate fell, it would cause a chain reaction of breaking plates and falling sticks.

    Perhaps the law—the precepts, instructions, and commands outlined by Moses—worked a lot like these spinning plates. The law required one's absolute attention to sight, effort, and action. Also like the plates, it was impossible to tell which rule or commandment one could safely ignore. The commandments, like the spinning plates, were all dynamically connected to one another. And in both cases, there was no rest from the spinning plates. The spinning plates were maintainable—just barely—but eventually, *there could be no more plates added*. In the same way, the law was perceived as stringent in its demands, but manageable. The law was life and the consequences of walking away were dramatic.

By the end of the book of Joshua, the land of Canaan had been significantly subdued and divided amongst the twelve tribes of Israel. Joshua has gotten old and was approaching death, but the land had not been completely cleared of its previous inhabitants. This was a problem.

> Joshua, who was now very old, called together all the elders, leaders, judges, and officers of Israel. He said to them, "I am now a very old man . . .
>
> "So be careful to follow everything Moses wrote in the Book of Instruction. Do not deviate from it, turning either to the right or to the left. Make sure you do not associate with the other people still remaining in the land" (Joshua 23:2, 6–7, NLT).

By failing to destroy or drive out all the previous peoples, the Israelites risked being subjected to the shame of those they had conquered. When someone's families, friends, and relatives are brutally killed, essentially murdered, the shame suffered by the self is unfathomable. It would have been impossible to have any close association with such people and not be affected by their shame and their hate, particularly if they were taken into one's household. The Bible gives idol worship as the reason for Joshua's instruction, but this was only part of the story. God did not only not want the Israelite men worshipping Baal, but he also equally didn't want any of the foreign women transferring their shame to the Israelite men.

Joshua goes on to tell them what will happen if they

marry any of the remaining women:

> They will be a snare and a trap to you, a whip for your backs and thorny brambles in your eyes, and you will vanish from this good land the Lord your God has given you (Joshua 23:13, NLT).

Could the warning of exposure to the deep shame in these women be made any clearer than this? Most of these girls had had their entire family slaughtered. They surely held deep-seated resentments and hatred. To take one of these women as a wife would surely subject the man to her shame. After all, nobody is more able to make a man feel less than or inadequate than the woman with whom he shares his bed. But in some cases, these warnings of Joshua's were not heeded, and men were permitted to intermarry with women from the conquered lands.

Some of the allure for not carrying out these orders may have arisen from the fact that these girls were not a physical threat. And though Joshua himself had carried out these "clearance" orders with particular thoroughness, it appears that these very same orders had once been previously overlooked by Moses in a very big way. Moses gave the following instruction after an earlier military campaign where the Israelites had destroyed the Midianites and taken a large number of captives.

> So kill all the boys and all the women who have had intercourse with a man. Only the young girls who are virgins may live; you may keep them for yourselves (Numbers 31:17–18, NLT).

## When Shame Defines a Nation

It is deeply puzzling that Moses would allow the sons of Israel to take these deeply shamed young girls into their homes—some, no doubt, as wives. And even if they were not made wives, these girls would at least be taken into Israelite homes as servants.

Consider: the Israelites had just finished wandering in the wilderness for forty years in order to be cleansed of the shame of Egypt. Their lives had purposely been made difficult in order to keep new shame minimized. They had been making sacrificial offerings to expunge the shame that did generate.

These Midianite girls had just witnessed the slaughter of everything and everyone they cared about and loved. Simple hatred probably doesn't even come close to describing the way these girls felt toward the Israelite men. The only conclusion I could come up with was that Moses wasn't privy to the real reason God was asking him to do what he did; perhaps Moses was simply following orders.

For whatever reason it was done, by allowing these girls to live, the Israelites were subjected to a great shame transfer. Is it possible that the integration of the Midianite girls—and the other women who were similarly joined to Israel—was intentional? There would have been no more powerful way for God to plant a seed of shame within the nation of Israel than to have thirty thousand emotionally traumatized—and vengeful—young girls dispersed throughout this relatively shameless people. And what a huge crop of shame was seeded in Israel! To get a perspective of this, male readers might think of the most tumultuous and difficult romantic relationship they've ever been in and worsen it by a factor of ten! That is what these young girls undoubtedly did to these Israelite men!

The purposefulness of this act by Moses dramatically

changes the underlying motivation of God's entire educational study with the Israelites! If God did this intentionally it means that God had planned to send the tree of life all along and that he wanted the Israelites to succumb great shame growth—to come to view themselves as hopeless sinners in need of a savior. I don't believe this. I believe the taking of these thirty thousand virgins was a mistake by Moses. This mistake isn't solely responsible for what would one day probably happen anyway within the kingdom, but it surely didn't help. God would probably have to use the tree of life regardless; he knew all along the inherent difficulties for eliminating the perception that linked shame and, conversely, sin, to an action cause. But I believe God's foremost hope was for the Israelites to find their way out of shame without having to resort to the tree of life. I believe God wanted to keep shame from becoming internalized as long as possible—thus giving the Israelites better chances of finding their way out of shame.

Not only would Israel now be subjected to the shame of these girls, but with the conclusion of the conquest of Canaan, they would now begin to increasingly generate shame within themselves. Remember: they were no longer living in tents. They began to acquire homes and farms and businesses. They would even begin making their own wine with their own grapes. Essentially, there was now an assuredness in their daily lives that hadn't been there in over forty years. They could now relax and enjoy life in a way that they hadn't been able to do before. And since they now had their own homeland, their interpersonal expectations would soar. The Israelites would now be able to devote much more attention to all their interpersonal needs.

Thus, shame would begin to build quickly without devoted compliance to sacrificial law. In response to a rise in shame they would slowly begin developing shame defenses, and they would also wrongfully start attributing the rising sense of shame to sin in the people.

With the deaths of Joshua and the head priest Eleazar, the people of Israel were without any binding military or spiritual leadership. The twelve tribes became like twelve siblings whose parents had just died. Each sibling would now return home to his own land and family, and each would soon have to learn how to deal with the rising occurrence of shame.

The years following the death of Joshua are accounted in the Old Testament book of Judges. This period of three centuries is described by some as the dark ages of Israel's history. Paradoxically, though they may have been dark by some standards, these were actually years of relatively little shame buildup. This would be a period characterized by a cyclic rise and fall of shame, the external oppression of hateful enemies—inducing shame—and a return to law—for the cleansing of shame. This of course would be understood and perceived as a repetitive cycle of sin, oppression, and repentance. What wasn't realized by anyone was that their enemies were actually keeping shame generation minimized by keeping them beneath the threshold where shame would then begin proliferating greatly from within. In terms of shame control, Israel's enemies were actually doing the nation a favor!

Many hundreds of years later Nehemiah would say this about this seemingly endless cycle of sin, oppression, and repentance: "But as soon as they were at peace, your people again committed evil in your sight, and once more you let their enemies conquer them" (Nehemiah 9:28, NLT). Of course! Once the people felt safe and secure, once they had leisure to attend to all interpersonal needs, the occurrence of shame—stoked by failure to satisfy the primary interpersonal need—skyrocketed and quickly accumulated, particularly without anything or anyone external to absorb the blame. Meanwhile, the rise in shame would always be attributed to some sinful cause.

These first few centuries of the Israelite nation would also be an era of evolving perceptions of God. Where once God was often seen as largely localized—in the pillar of fire or cloud, in the commotion atop Mount Sinai, or hovering above the Ark of the Covenant—he would increasingly be perceived as remaining "above" and sending his spirit. These early "sendings" were job- and mission-specific. God's spirit would thus be perceived as sent to do a job, but then be perceived to leave when the task was finished.

During this period we also begin seeing an expanding misperception of God's more intimate involvement with everything connected to shame: sin, punishment, fear, distress, and rage. Since shame was now rigidly tied to sinful infraction, anything severely shameful was now being seen as a punishment. God was seen as being personally involved in *everything* dealing with shame.

We can assume that when the children of Israel first settled into Canaan they were incredibly shame free. We would be amazed to see what such a society looked like. I don't believe we would have seen any expressed contempt, belittlement, or disrespect amongst the people who came out of the wilderness. When punishments were carried out, they were done without shame transfer. This must have been an incredible sight to see—to witness violence without the attached rage. And since there was so little shame, the only condemnation one might ever feel from a brother was when a rule was violated, and this too would have been done without the accompaniment of anger: in cold blood, so to speak. Shame was only perceived as sent for rule violations. However, these perceptions would begin to drastically change as shame began to build within the people of Israel.

Indeed, as we have already discussed, once they were no longer nomadic wanderers in a hostile environment, but settlers in a rich land of their own, shame would inevitably begin building in the nation of Israel. In fact, God would now begin using politics to bring about the next phase in his great object lesson for the human race.

# CHAPTER 9

## Shame on the King

*P*erhaps at this point it's appropriate to pause and take stock of where we've come so far in our journey with the Hebrew nation. They have come from slavery and its internalized shame. They have wandered in the wilderness for a generation, facing the daily struggles of existence that have kept their lives at a level where the development of new shame is minimized. They have ceremonial and religious procedures in place to deal somewhat with shame as it accrues in the course of everyday life.

Now, they have entered the land to which God has been guiding them—albeit with the seeds of great shame sown among them, either accidently or on purpose—in the persons of the thirty thousand virgins who have most likely intermarried with their men. However, they have the law and its protections against the internalization of shame.

**The Law and Shame**
But let's again consider what the law could and couldn't do with regard to shame. First, we need to remember that it is not

shame that *prevents* us from doing the wrong things; it is shame which actually *causes* us to do the wrong things. Thus, the moral code in Israel—and everywhere else, most likely—was largely developed in response to the occurrence of great shame. Basically, the moral code was and still is a shame-defending strategy: one designed, implemented, and enforced by those who hold the relative power, largely, the religious power.

So, the Jewish law was not really what you would call a moral code. Instead, the law's primary purpose—at least initially—was to provide for the flourishing of physical life and the orderly conduct of daily affairs. However, Israel made the law into something—and continued expanding it into something—it was never intended to be and develop into. Because of the pervasive human perception of an action cause for shame, the Israelites thought that the problem of shame was tied to obedience. Thus, they came to think that a more perfect law-keeping could eliminate the occurrence of all consequential shame. The moral code, then, developed in an effort to stem and destroy the continuing rise in shame and its accompanying responses, defenses, and syndromes.

Indeed, there are many people in our culture today who feel that a return to a strict moral code would cure all our ills. This is exactly what the children of Israel thought—three thousand years ago! But, as we have seen and as I will continue to emphasize, obedience or any other type of "doing or not doing" as a way to favor—human, societal, or divine—doesn't destroy shame.

**Personal Shame**
The children of Israel have now inhabited the Promised Land for

# SHAME

nearly three hundred years. They have begun to murmur that they want a king just like everyone else in the region. The story of the rise of the Israelite kings begins in the Old Testament book of First Samuel with a woman named Hannah: a woman who is deeply shamed.

Hannah is barren. Since barrenness for a woman was so shameful—notice that in the Bible the barrenness of a woman is never attributed to the deficiency of a man!—it was believed that God had done this to her as a consequence to some sin. Barrenness was perceived as a consequence of having fallen out of favor with God.

Hannah thus initially perceives her barrenness as justified. And though she finds it difficult to endure, she believes the taunting—the shaming—she is receiving from her husband's fertile other wife, Peninnah, is deserved. However, once Hannah does become pregnant—in response, she believes, to a promise made to God, which we will discuss in a moment—there is a dramatic change in the way she views the shaming she received at the hands of Peninnah. She now believes the shaming was either never deserved, or at the least, only temporarily warranted. Either way, she now perceives that she has regained favor with God. She now no longer believes that Peninnah has a right to make her feel less than, inferior, deficient, defective, and worse. If Peninnah continues to cause her to feel this way, Hannah would view her as an enemy because of the unwarranted shame she is sending Hannah's way. Notice how in Israel by this time, people, presumably because of their own deepening sin and its concealment, are now beginning to be seen as carriers and spreaders of shame themselves.

But let's return to Hannah's perceived deliverance from shame. In 1 Samuel 1:11, we read of the promise she makes to

God: "If you will look upon my sorrow and answer my prayer and give me a son, then I will give him back to you" (NLT). In other words, Hannah was trying to please God—to bargain with him—in order to gain favor, or freedom from shame. While "giving to get" in our human relationships works extremely well toward survival, it doesn't work so well toward the satisfaction of our primary interpersonal need. Similarly, "giving to get" something from God—trying to please him so he'll help us toward survival or interpersonal wholeness—doesn't work so well either. When we try to apply "giving to get" toward satisfaction of the primary interpersonal need—whether from people or by obedience to God—it increases expectation and further amplifies the intensity of shame when it does occur.

But Hannah doesn't know all this. Since she was willing to give the boy away, it was not so much the having of the child itself that motivated her bargaining, but the shame of barrenness that caused her to make this sort of deal with God. Simply, Hannah believed that having a son would make her interpersonally complete—as well as free from shame's onslaught.

Hannah tells her husband Elkanah that once the boy is weaned she will make good on her promise to God and take the child to the tabernacle in Shiloh. Eli was the priest there at this time. Sure enough, Hannah presents her son to Eli and he begins to live with the priest and his sons, assisting with the duties of the tabernacle—the elaborate tent and surrounding complex that was the center of religious activity in Israel at that time.

First Samuel 2:26 tells us, "And the child Samuel grew in stature, and in favor both with the Lord and men" (NKJV). This makes perfect sense, for the perception was that if one had

# SHAME

the favor of society, then one also had it with God. Essentially, the experience of visible favor was perceived as having been awarded by God for sinlessness. Samuel obviously wasn't causing any shame to be felt by any of those who perceived themselves in favored positions with God; thus, he too was favored, both by humans and, presumably, by God.

Samuel continues to grow in favor, and the time eventually comes when Eli and his sons fall out of favor—with the people and, presumably, with God—because of the sons' practice of accepting bribes and engaging in other shady practices that cause them to be regarded as deeply sinning in the eyes of the LORD, "for they treated the Lord's offerings with contempt" (1 Samuel 2:17, NLT). Samuel becomes the most respected man in Israel, and continues for many years as a "judge," or a leader to whom the people look for guidance and decisions. First Samuel 7:15 says that "Samuel continued as Israel's judge for the rest of his life" (NLT).

**Long Live the King!**
Because of his position of respect and favor, then, it was only natural that the elders of Israel went to Samuel and asked him to give them a king. Samuel went to God with their request and returned with this warning:

> The king will draft your sons and assign them to his chariots . . . making them run before his chariots . . . some will be forced to plow in his fields and harvest his crops, and some will make his weapons . . . The king will take your daughters from you and force them to cook and

## Shame on the King

bake and make perfumes for him. He will take away the best of your fields and vineyards and olive groves and give them to his own officials. He will take a tenth of your grain and grape harvest and distribute it among his officers and attendants. He will take your male and female slaves and demand the finest of your cattle . . . you will be his slaves . . . you will beg for relief from this king you are demanding, but then the Lord will not help you (1 Samuel 8:11–18, NLT).

Somewhat predictably, "the people refused to listen to Samuel's warning. 'Even so, we still want a king,' they said" (1 Samuel 8:19, NLT). But why would the people of Israel ignore such dire warnings? What was it about having a king that they thought would provide them with that missing something that Samuel's leadership, the law, and their current perceptions of God were incapable of providing? Maybe the reasons were actually pretty basic; maybe they were just sick and tired of being tormented by the surrounding nations who hated them; they hoped that a king might completely destroy their neighboring enemies. Indeed, they tell Samuel, "Our king may judge us and go out before us and fight our battles" (1 Samuel 8:20, NKJV). In other words, if the surrounding peoples—who had kings—were giving them so much trouble, maybe what they needed was a king of their own, to protect their lands and possessions. But as we'll also see, having a king to destroy their neighboring threats would have consequences which nobody foresaw.

So, Samuel returns to God with the people's response. God tells him to go ahead and give the people a king, but that he will tell Samuel whom to select.

# SHAME

Perhaps it had always been God's plan for the Israelites to have a king, but he needed for them to first ask for one. It may be, in fact, that much of God's instruction pertaining to shame demanded a national leader who would unite the people; a king may also have been important to provide a more detailed look at the way shame plays out in an individual's life over time. And, since the king occupies the most elevated position on the societal and cultural ladder, the establishment of a monarchy in Israel provides an especially unique view of shame dynamics. But as we'll also soon see, the destruction of the enemies who hated them would create a national environment where shame generation would rise dramatically. In a similar vein as allowing thirty thousand traumatized virgins to be integrated into the Israelite culture, a king would end up creating ideal conditions for the explosion of shame within the kingdom. God would try to accommodate this escalation in shame generation as best he could, but this too would ultimately prove futile.

Whatever all the underlying reasons may have been, Samuel, in response to God's direction, anoints Saul, from the territory of Benjamin, as king.

### "To Fall from Grace"

What is it about fame, favor, honor, respect, recognition, position, power, and acclaim that make them so difficult to give up once one acquires them? It is almost always an excruciating transition to go from being a *somebody* in the world to being a *nobody*. We have plenty of current examples of athletes, politicians, and entertainers who have failed miserably at transitioning into relative *nobody-ness*. It can be particularly devastating to be subjected to an *unexpected* move from a place of immense

## Shame on the King

favor to one where we are mocked or ridiculed. Indeed, some will choose death over such *falls from grace*—and by the way, isn't that an interesting phrase to describe a demotion from a position of power and favor? However, experience teaches us that some will kill—themselves or others—in an effort to prevent such a change in their place in the world. The point is, to echo the words of Gershen Kaufman, some of us will do anything to prevent the exposure to shame. And so it was with Saul.

Saul was a warrior king—just what the nation ordered—who apparently loved the adoration of his people. He was willing to do nearly anything to prevent feeling disliked by his troops. Modern psychology would probably indicate that Saul had issues involving self-esteem.

In what would prove the pivotal event of his reign, Saul was instructed by God, through Samuel, to make war against the Amalekites and to completely annihilate them, down to the last man, woman, and child. In fact, he was not even to leave their animals alive!

However, after destroying the Amalekites, Saul allowed his men to keep the best of the sheep, goats, and cattle for themselves. This indicated that Saul was more concerned with the favor of his troops then he was with being obedient to God. When Samuel confronts Saul about this he tries to justify his disobedience. Saul tells him that they took the best livestock so that they could sacrifice them to God. Samuel explains to Saul that if there has been no disobedience there wouldn't be any guilt that would then need to be cleansed. Saul was subsequently *made guilty*—shamed by Samuel before the people.

And Samuel told him, "Although you
may think little of yourself, are you not the

## SHAME

leader of the tribes of Israel? The Lord has anointed you king of Israel. And the Lord has sent you on a mission and told you, 'Go and completely destroy the sinners, the Amalekites, until they are all dead.' Why haven't you obeyed the Lord? Why did you rush for the plunder and do what was evil in the Lord's sight?" (1 Samuel 15:17–19, NLT).

Though Saul continues for a number of additional years as Israel's king, this act of disobedience is seen as resulting in the withdrawal of God's favor from his reign. First Samuel 15:35 states, "And the Lord was sorry he had ever made Saul king of Israel" (NLT). As a result, God has Samuel anoint a future king in private: a boy named David. And once David is anointed by Samuel, "the Spirit of the Lord came powerfully upon David from that day on" (1 Samuel 16:13, NLT).

However, "the Spirit of the Lord had left Saul, and the Lord sent a tormenting spirit that filled him with depression and fear" (1 Samuel 16:14, NLT). Indeed, Saul had probably been suffering from internalized shame for quite some time. His paranoia and bouts of depression were more likely shame-based. These symptoms became much more pronounced after the well-known events of David killing Goliath. Saul simply couldn't handle all the positive attention that was now being diverted from himself and bestowed upon David. The tipping point was finally reached a number of years later when Saul hears the women singing in the streets: "This was their song: 'Saul has killed his thousands, and David his ten thousands!' This made Saul very angry" (1 Samuel 18:7–8, NLT).

No doubt it did! Whenever we look to the seen for

## Shame on the King

a sense of belonging and something we do causes us to momentarily question our worthiness of belonging, we are more than likely to respond with fear and distress. However, when it is someone else's actions that cause us shame—in the form of a disrespect, embarrassment, or humiliation—and we then determine it to be a shaming without cause, we are likely to become angry or enraged. These anger and rage responses seem justified when it appears that it was the actions of others that have caused us shame and pain without cause. Also, by expressing our anger toward those who have caused us to question our worthiness, we attempt to transfer the shame to them.

However, we are not so inclined to do this if there is a high likelihood of physical retribution for the expression of our rage. For example, we are far less likely to angrily confront a guy for butting in our line when he is 6'6" and 280 pounds than we are to confront a guy who is 5'4" and 140. We instinctively know that it is not wise to embarrass or humiliate the big guys. It is for these very same reasons that shame is rarely transferred from weaker to stronger. This explains much of the advantage humans perceive in physical strength—especially true three thousand years ago.

However, when the other person causes us to feel shame through actions that are not specifically directed at us—such as David's military successes, which were, after all, beneficial to Saul's land and people—it doesn't work so well for us to try and use anger to try and return the shame. For example, it doesn't work so well to get angry at a spouse when we got caught having an affair. We feel shame, but we can't transfer it to the other when the other is not at fault.

So, as we consider Saul's response to his fall from favor

# SHAME

and David's rise, we may realize that his envy and jealousy were a manifestation of inexpressible anger in response to a person that, for some reason or another, was causing him to feel less than, defective, or worse. Because David hadn't done anything that would validate an expression of rage in response to shame, Saul secretly seethed within. Indeed, in our own lives, jealousy and envy arise as the result of a comparison with someone else in which we find ourselves deficient. We feel shamed because of the actions or qualities of someone else, though neither has been directly used by the other person to shame us. Thus, we respond with envy and jealousy, since we can't justifiably use rage as a mechanism to return the shame.

We can really only guess at the specific causes which made Saul so envious and jealous of David. We do know, however, that Saul's pent-up rage in response to shame would still occasionally burst forth, despite the invalidity of such a response as a means of shame transfer.

> The very next day a tormenting spirit from God overwhelmed Saul, and he began to rave in his house like a madman. David was playing the harp, as he did each day. But Saul had a spear in his hand, and he suddenly hurled it at David, intending to pin him to the wall. But David escaped him twice (1 Samuel 18:10–12, NLT).

For Saul, the next few years would bring a continuing descent into shame, even as David's star continued to rise—so to speak. David, though he is married to one of Saul's daughters, must eventually flee the court and live as an outlaw in order to escape Saul's uncontrollable rage. In the Bible, this period of Hebrew history is seen as an example of how God protects David—because he is favored—while continuing to allow Saul to reap the consequences of his disfavor. Finally, Saul and his sons fall to Israel's archenemies, the Philistines, and the way is paved for David to take up the throne for which he was anointed as a young boy.

It would be tempting to believe that David's reign would be characterized by God's favor, and thus that the experience of shame would be virtually unknown during his kingship. But that belief would be false. In fact, David will display many vivid details that illustrate the futility of obedience in avoiding shame. Indeed, through the psalms that he wrote, we receive an eloquent expression of what shame looks and feels like when it is experienced by an articulate, artistic, and passionate individual.

# CHAPTER 10

## *David, the "Man after God's Own Heart"*

From the people to whom he had given his law, God wanted both complete devotion to himself and complete obedience to his commands, precepts, and requirements. While he never expected them to be *faultless*—and therefore perceive themselves as immune to the effects of shame—he expected them to be obedient as best they could.

David was a nearly perfect example of what God wanted from those under his law; he was also an individual of stark contrasts. He was a man's man, a warrior's warrior: ruthless and fearless on the battlefield. But David was also an exceptionally expressive individual—a classical extrovert—who wore his emotions on his sleeve. Many of his psalms express his deep feelings for God and his law.

> The law of the Lord *is perfect, converting the soul;*
> The testimony of the Lord *is sure, making wise the simple;*
> The statutes of the Lord *are right, rejoicing the heart;*
> The commandment of the Lord *is pure, enlightening the eyes;*
> The fear of the Lord *is clean, enduring forever;*
> The judgments of the Lord *are true and righteous altogether.*
> (Psalm 19:7–9, NKJV).

## David, the "Man after God's Own Heart"

The psalms of David are also exceedingly rich in their expressions of shame: disgrace, dishonor, scorn, contempt, hate, distress, rage, and humiliation. Simply, they are full of shame's many faces. Shame is clearly David's greatest enemy, though because of the perceived sin-shame tie, he believes the true enemy is sin. Throughout the Psalms we see the record of his personal war on sin.

Do not let me be put to shame, nor let my enemies triumph over me . . . No one whose hope is in you will ever be put to shame, but they will be put to shame who are treacherous without excuse . . . Remember not the sins of my youth and my rebellious ways . . . Look upon my affliction and my distress and take away all my sins. See how my enemies have increased and how fiercely they hate me! Guard my life and rescue me; let me not be put to shame, for I take refuge in you (Psalm 25:2–3, 7, 18–20, NIV).

David is obviously distressed about the shame he is being sent. He wonders if it is the sins of his youth that are the cause of his now being sent shame. But we now know that it is the violation of expectations resulting from the unsatisfied primary interpersonal need that is the real cause of David's emotional turmoil. Despite his distorted perceptions concerning the origin and workings of shame, David still sensed that the solution to shame rested in God. But there was no amount of obedience or hope in God that could in and of itself prevent him from experiencing shame.

David sees those who send him shame without cause as his personal enemies. But what has actually begun to happen is a significant rise in shame amongst the people of Israel. The destruction of Israel's enemies had begun under Saul and was now coming to complete fruition under David. Israel's safety and security needs were becoming completely satisfied under King David. There was also no longer a hated enemy whose blood would keep David and his military cleansed of shame.

I did a lot of things for them but they didn't do anything for me. They hurt me. I took care of them when they were in need. I am now being disrespected by people I don't even know. They play me and slander me. They use me when I am vulnerable. They snarl at me. Please don't let my enemies laugh at me in my troubles. May those who rejoice in my difficulties be humiliated and disgraced. Humiliate and disrespect tomorrow all those who do me that way today (Psalm 35, paraphrase).

Much like Saul, David was terribly concerned with the favorable attention of others and was greatly tormented by the disrespect, mockery, scorn, contempt, indifference, and hate of others. David lived in a culture that was by now awash in people trying to dissipate their own internally generated shame (much like what we have in our culture today). But unlike Saul, David would not take action against those who were causing him shame unless he could be absolutely sure that the shame was without cause—that he was sinless and undeserving of the condemnation from others.

David's torment by others is often attributed to his sins involving Bathsheba, as recorded in 2 Samuel 11 and 12. We may interpret this, however, as a *sinful cause* that was *found* in order to explain the shame sendings. Punishments would later be attributed to those sins and shame sendings. But David had been forgiven by God for those sins, so from his perspective, this should have discontinued any sent shame.

Then I acknowledged my sin to you and did not cover up my iniquity. I said, "I will confess my transgressions to the Lord"—and you forgave the guilt of my sin (Psalm 32:5, NIV).

## *David, the "Man after God's Own Heart"*

Thus, the continuance of condemnation now caused David to highly suspect others as spreaders of indwelled shame due to their own sins.

But some of the reasons why people shamed David were the same reasons why Saul experienced shame with David: comparison-making resulting in self-generative shame. David was not only a particularly good inducer of self shaming in some people—manifesting itself as envy and jealousy—but he was also a particularly easy target for their shame transfers. We would say today that David was *thin-skinned,* but definitely not in the sense that he was physically fearful of others; the only person David feared was God. But because of his reverence for God, David realized that reacting to the mockery, contempt, disrespect, hate, and scorn of others was possibly to act against God. And David was simply not going to take that chance.

Lord, please don't just sit there while they tell lies and slander me. Though I care for them they spew hate towards me for no reason. They accuse me of all sorts of things even as I pray for them (Psalm 109, paraphrase).

In you, O Lord, I have taken refuge; let me never be put to shame; deliver me in your righteousness . . . Because of all my enemies, I am the utter contempt of my neighbors; I am a dread to my friends—those who see me on the street flee from me . . . I am forgotten by them as though I were dead; I have become like broken pottery . . . Let me not be put to shame, O Lord, for I have cried out to you; but let the wicked be put to shame and lie silent in the grave (Psalm 31: 1, 11–12, 17, NIV).

Yes, David wants the wicked, who he perceives dead in shame—because of their own deep sin—to simply shut up and stop spewing their shame toward him and others.

Oh Lord, shouldn't I hate those who hate you? Shouldn't

# SHAME

I despise those who oppose you? (Psalm 139:21, NLT).

David is wondering if it is okay for him to feel enraged toward those who he perceives as sending him shame without cause. He is also wondering if it is okay for him to take action and return the unwarranted shame. It can seem like a justified response to want to hurt those who hurt us, particularly when we perceive that we were hurt without cause. If we can somehow claim that they did evil, then our own shame-defending strategy can be rationalized as good, valid, and warranted.

David seems to do amazingly well in keeping his retaliatory urges under control with respect to his own people. But when it came to punishing God's more obvious enemies, it was another story. David's violence on the battlefield—perceived as God-approved because of the feel of being cleansed of shame—was largely to do with shame transfer. It wasn't animal blood that kept David free of shame buildup, but the violent spilling of human blood—*the killing of God's enemies*—that David perceived as *blessed* because of the way it made him feel afterwards.

But no matter how hard David tried to live a blameless life, he continued suffering from the increasing feeling of condemnation. He believed that God not only controlled shame but also that God could help him avoid any known or unknown sins that would cause the warranted shame to be sent.

I will be careful to live a blameless life—when will you come to help me? (Psalm 101:2, NLT).

David recognized that not only could he not keep himself blameless and therefore free of deserved shame, but that he also couldn't protect himself from the undeserved sent shame by shame-filled, sinful others. This of course was *more or less* what God wanted David to realize—to teach him of his

## David, the "Man after God's Own Heart"

inability to combat and defeat shame without God's help.

Save me, O God, for the floodwaters are up to my neck. Deeper and deeper I sink into the mire; I can't find a foothold. I am in deep water, and the floods overwhelm me (Psalm 69: 1–2, NLT).

I love the metaphors that David uses to describe the feel of monumental shame: like *rising floodwaters*, like *sinking into the mire*. Beautiful! Who among us hasn't felt similarly whenever we were betrayed, mocked, scorned, insulted, humiliated, hated, or disrespected by others?

David figures that since God is so personally involved with the sending of shame to sinners that he should also be able to do something about the shame that is being sent to him without cause. He writes, "I am exhausted from crying for help; my throat is parched. My eyes are swollen with weeping, waiting for my God to help me. Those who hate me without cause outnumber the hairs on my head" (Psalm 69:3–4, NLT).

The favor David seeks from God is an elimination of all forms of shame, for to be in favor with God was to see it reflected in the favor of humanity.

Rescue me from the mud; don't let me sink any deeper! Don't let the floods overwhelm me, or the deep waters swallow me, or the pit of death to devour me . . . Don't hide from your servant; answer me quickly, for I am in deep trouble! Come and redeem me; free me from my enemies. You know of my shame, scorn, and disgrace. You see all that my enemies are doing. Their insults have broken my heart and I am in despair. If only one person would show me pity; if only one would turn and comfort me (Psalm 69:14–15, 17–20, NLT).

David is lost in this whirlwind of trying to determine whether the shame is justified—that he is deserving of the shame

# SHAME

because of sin—or whether it is unjustified. He doesn't know if he should just continue to ask God for forgiveness or start killing the sinners who are sending him shame without cause.

About the only real difference between David's experiences of shame and ours is the acuteness of his perception of God's intimate involvement and sending of shame due to sin. But like David, we still perceive the shame experience as an indicator of a wrongfulness of the self. *Only now*, however, do we realize that shame results because of the self's looking externally in an attempt to satisfy the primary interpersonal need. David, for all his piety, had no idea that a complete elimination of all shame could only be truly satisfied through the development of a personal relationship, and ultimately, in a relational union with God the person.

Keep in mind that internal shame generation had been incrementally rising within the kingdom ever since Saul won his first battle. For well over fifty years now the enemies of Israel have been gradually meeting their end. The people of Israel were now beginning to enjoy a freedom from external threat that they hadn't known since they first settled the land. Simply, they now felt safe enough to give their full attention to the complete satisfaction of all their interpersonal needs. And, like their sensitive and articulate king, they were all feeling more and more shame despite their increasingly invigorated efforts to be extra obedient to law.

And since David and his people perceived a sin/shame tie, and since there weren't any laws obviously being broken, the rising shame was attributed to sin—largely secret sin:

They visit me as if they were my friends, but all the while they gather gossip, and when they leave, they spread it everywhere... Even my best friend, the one I trusted completely, the one who shared my food, has turned against me (Psalm 41: 6, 9, NLT).

Of course! It is never the stranger, the enemy, or even the casual acquaintance that hurts us the deepest; it is those whom we believe are most essential to our interpersonal wholeness that possess the greatest potential for causing us the most pain.

It is not an enemy who taunts me—I could bear that. It is not my foes who so arrogantly insult me—I could have hidden from them. Instead, it is you—my equal, my companion and close friend (Psalm 55:12–13, NLT).

And, since shame continued to increase regardless of how obedient one was to the law, David and his people began to conclude that they were just born sinners, and any perceived found punishments were simply the acts of a god who was justifiably angry because of the inherent sin.

Surely I was sinful at birth, sinful from the time my mother conceived me (Psalm 51:5, NIV).

David actually believes that it is God's desire to break him using shame. In a way this is kind of true. Shame's purpose is to interpersonally *redirect us*. Shame was not meant to become internalized and make us into hopeless sinners, but to teach us the futility of sight, effort, and action toward the satisfaction of the primary interpersonal need, to simply redirect us from looking to each other and instead look to THE PERSON within.

Purify me from my sins, and I will be clean; wash me, and I will be whiter than snow. Oh, give me back my joy again; you have broken me—now let me rejoice (Psalm 51: 7–8, NLT).

God doesn't desire for us to be *broken*, but he does desire that we learn the vanity of our efforts at ridding ourselves of the occurrence of shame.

# SHAME

David knew that the ultimate solution for the continuing occurrence of shame somehow rested with God, not with himself or with others.

The Lord is my rock, my fortress, and my savior; my God is my rock, in whom I find protection. He is my shield, the power that saves me, and my place of safety (Psalm 18:2, NLT).

But David still sought belonging and interpersonal completion in the *seen* and he still looked externally for satisfaction of the primary interpersonal need. He believed that gaining favor with God would translate and reflect into gaining favor—into a complete freedom from the feel of condemnation—from people. He believed that God would reward him for his obedience by protecting him from shame.

The Lord rewarded me for doing right; he restored me because of my innocence. For I kept the ways of the Lord; I have not turned from my God to follow evil. I have followed all his regulations; I have never abandoned his decrees. I am blameless before God; I have kept myself from sin. The Lord rewarded me for doing right. He has seen my innocence (Psalm 18: 20–24, NLT).

But despite the confident tone of David's words in this psalm, the best that obedience could provide was to inhibit the internalization of shame within the self; it couldn't protect David or his people from the condemnation of *shame-filled, sinful others*. Thus, while Psalm 109:31 (paraphrase) states, "God stands ready to save us from those who shame us," God would never be able to protect them from those who illicitly caused them to feel deficient, defective, sinful, or worse. The protection David sought would not come in a way David expected. The protection David sought would not be implemented on the outside, but on the inside. It would be the feel of shame that would be destroyed, not the attributable shame-causing act. David was so close to finding his way out of shame, but also still so far away. Though his heart was perfectly ready, his mind could still not yet grasp. It would be another thousand years before God would implement his most dramatic, effective, and logistically difficult plan for the education of a more clearly delineated way unto the satisfaction of the primary interpersonal need and the complete destruction of shame.

David foresaw that the solution to shame sent without cause would one day be found with God. He also knew that the complete resolution of shame would involve more than just obedience to the law. In other words, I believe David had begun to figure out much of what had still not been formally revealed. He began to experience something in his devotion to the Lord that was completely destructive to shame, whether that shame manifested itself for cause or not. He sensed that shame—and conversely sin—would one day be destroyed by means of some kind of relationship with God, the likes of which he could not yet comprehend.

Those who look to him for help will be radiant with joy; no shadow of shame will darken their faces . . . No one who takes refuge in him will be condemned (Psalm 34:5, 22, NLT).

David knew that shame would one day be destroyed by having a heart for God and taking refuge in him. But how were he and his people to look to God and take refuge in him when they really didn't know how to relate to him? The destruction of sin would require a lot more—actually, a lot less—than strict obedience. It would require a *real relationship*. It would require an individualized personal relationship. And they couldn't very well find their way unto an intimate *personal relationship* with a God whom they increasingly viewed as pissed.

# SHAME

**The Rebellion of Absalom**

A series of related events that happened while David was king provide a lot of insight into the way sin and shame were viewed at the time.

In 2 Samuel 15, we learn that David's son has organized a rebellion against his father. Absalom wants the kingdom for himself. In response to the rising tide of rebellion, David gathers his family and flees Jerusalem with his bodyguards and six hundred men from Gath. A few days later, as they approach a village called Bahurim, a man comes out toward them.

His name was Shimei son of Gera, and he cursed as he came out. He pelted David and all the king's officials with stones, though all the troops and the special guard were on David's right and left. As he cursed, Shimei said, "Get out, get out, you man of blood, you scoundrel! The Lord has paid you for all the blood you shed in the household of Saul, in whose place you have reigned. The Lord has handed the kingdom over to your son Absalom. You have come to ruin because you are a man of blood!" (2 Samuel 16:5–8, NIV). Shimei is essentially making David feel guilty by shaming him. But the prevailing question in David's mind is whether the condemnation is for cause or without cause. In other words, was the shame being unjustly spread by a shame-filled sinner, or was it being deservedly sent for some sin of his own?

One of David's officers has this to say about the shame sending:

"Why should this dead dog curse my lord the king?" Abishai son of Zeruiah demanded. "Let me go over and cut off his head!" (2 Samuel 16:9, NLT).

Abishai is indirectly asking David if there is a cause for the shaming. As far as he is concerned, there isn't one. David

## David, the "Man after God's Own Heart"

is his lord the king. Abishai views the condemnation of his lord by Shimei in much the same way as sending shame to God. David's response, however, is very interesting:

"No!" the king said. "Who asked your opinion, you sons of Zeruiah! If the Lord told him to curse me, who are you to stop him?" (2 Samuel 16:10, NLT).

Though David isn't sure whether the condemnation from Shimei is for cause or not for cause, he still wants to play it safe. David perceives that if he approves the killing of Shimei and is wrong—in other words, if he commits a sin by killing God's shaming conduit—he could bring even more shame and punishments onto himself.

Then David said to Abishai and to all his servants, "My own son is trying to kill me. Doesn't this relative of Saul have even more reason to do so? Leave him alone and let him curse, for the Lord told him to do it" (2 Samuel 16:11, NLT).

Fascinating! David is resting in what he believes is the safest position: that the shaming by Shimei is warranted. Besides, what real harm is there with a few thrown stones and words? I don't doubt that David is still holding to the hope that *none* of what is happening is a deserved punishment for some sin. More evidence would be needed before a contrary decision could be made, as David points out:

And perhaps the Lord will see that I am being wronged and will bless me because of these curses today (2 Samuel 16:12, NLT).

A few days later, twenty thousand men die in a battle between David and Absalom's forces.

During the battle, Absalom happened to come upon some of David's men. He tried to escape on his mule, but as he rode beneath the thick branches of a great tree, his hair got

# SHAME

caught in the tree. His mule kept going and left him dangling in the air (2 Samuel 18:9, NLT).

Joab, one of David's commanders, sinks three daggers into Absalom's heart while he dangles from the tree.

With the death of his son, David realizes that none of the shame or punishments from Shimei or his son were justified. It was all evil. Neither his son's nor Shimei's actions were for sinful cause. David was not only blameless in regard to the deservedness of losing the kingship to his son, and other humiliations committed by Absalom as well, but he was also blameless with regard to the deservedness of the condemnation by Shimei.

David and his people begin their return toward Jerusalem and soon arrive at the Jordan River.

As the king was about to cross the river, Shimei fell down before him. "My lord the king, please forgive me," he pleaded. "Forget the terrible thing your servant did when you left Jerusalem. May the king put it out of his mind. I know how much I sinned. That is why I have come here today, the very first person in all Israel to greet my lord the king" (2 Samuel 19:18–20, NLT).

It is almost comical how the death of Absalom could create such a monumental shift in everyone's perceptions. But shame was an extremely serious matter, particularly when it involved one of God's perceived *favored*. Where the shaming was previously looked at as *possibly having cause*, it is now looked at as *positively never having cause*. Both Shimei's and Absalom's actions are now seen as utterly evil.

Accordingly, Abishai says to David, "Shimei should die, for he cursed the Lord's anointed king!" (2 Samuel 19:21, NLT). Notice how Abishai uses the designation "the Lord's anointed

## David, the "Man after God's Own Heart"

King." Previously (2 Samuel 16:9), Abishai wasn't so sure who was really God's anointed king, but now he is. He is also surer that Shimei should die for sending shame to David without cause. Shimei's actions are not only seen as wicked, but they are also now definitely seen as sins against God himself. David has this to say to his loyal servant Abishai:

"Who asked your opinion, you sons of Zeruiah!" David exclaimed. "Why have you become my adversary today? This is not a day for execution but for celebration! Today I am once again the king of Israel!" Then, turning to Shimei, David vowed, "Your life will be spared" (2 Samuel 19:22–23, NLT).

So, it's a happy ending, especially for Shimei, right? Wrong! But before we get to the rest of the story, let's consider a few questions that might give us some clues and insights as to how this shaming scenario plays out.

Have you ever had someone shame you in front of a large group of people when there was no cause, reason, or justification for shaming? If you have ever been humiliated like David was by Shimei, there is a pretty good chance you may still be harboring a resentment. Despite the fact that it may have happened decades ago, you may still be angry about the way this person *wrongfully* treated you. We can develop resentments from these kinds of experiences—particularly when we have determined that they are done *without cause*—that can last a lifetime. *When these events are severe enough and recurring enough, shame can become internalized and we can begin shaming ourselves.*

Furthermore, imagine David's perception of the sin-shame tie. David perceived this resentment of lingering shame as a kind of lingering evil which had been sent to him by Shimei.

Years later, we find David approaching death and giving

# SHAME

final instructions to his son and heir, Solomon. When I first read the following passage I was stunned by the content, but then came the *realization* . . .

"I am going where everyone on earth must someday go. Take courage and be a man. Observe the requirements of the Lord your God, and follow all his ways. Keep the decrees, commands, regulations, and laws written in the Law of Moses so that you will be successful in all you do and wherever you go . . . And remember Shimei son of Gera . . . He cursed me with a terrible curse as I was fleeing to Mahanaim . . . I swore by the Lord that I would not kill him. But that oath does not make him innocent. You are a wise man, and you will know how to arrange a bloody death for him (1 Kings 2: 2–3, 8–9, NLT).

David is still feeling the shame that Shimei sent him that day long ago! Modern psychology would say that David is still holding a deep resentment toward Shimei. But resentment is really internalized shame from a shaming that is perceived to have no deserving cause, and it continues to propagate without any new shame-generating events.

It's tempting to view David's words as the final, vengeful act of a resentful old man. However, we need to remember how everyone perceived shame during these times—that all shame had sinful action origin. And all that David knows is that he has not yet been cleansed from being made guilty without cause. He also possesses a basic understanding of the way residual shame can be passed on to successive generations: the idea that the son could be punished for the sins of his father. It was thus important to David that his shame be cleansed and not passed on to his son Solomon.

Remember, too, that David was so well acquainted with the sense of shame cleansing that came from spilling and being splattered by the blood of God's hated enemies on the battlefield. And when it became apparent that Absalom's revolt would fail, Shimei was seen to have made himself God's enemy by cursing God's anointed king. Thus, Shimei's bloody death would be perceived to cleanse the illegally sent shame—the sin—and thereby keep its evil from being passed on to his son.

Under King David, Israel has finally achieved utter peace and completely secure borders. The Tabernacle, though very elaborate and rich in design, is still a tent, and is no longer seen as a fit place for the center of the nation's religious observance. Accordingly, a temple is planned to house the Ark of the Covenant. It is to be a time of peace and building.

But along with great peace and prosperity comes great shame. The law is now nearly useless in preventing the exploding generation of shame within the people. The temple would help provide for the newly needed en masse cleansing of exploding shame amongst the children of Israel. And though observance of the law could keep one relatively guiltless and free from the buildup of shame, it contained no real mechanism to protect one from the sloughed-off shame of others, the shame sent without cause.

There had been no other man in Israel's past who had enjoyed as much favor amongst the people as David—in some ways, he was the first rock star! But it was from his peers and equals that he suffered most from shame. David became an easy target for their shame transfers because he was so fearful of returning it without cause.

Now, it was Solomon's turn. And, as we will see, under Solomon, the kingdom of Israel would become both the envy of much of the ancient world, but it would also be a kingdom ill-equipped to stem the rising tide of shame.

# CHAPTER 11

## *Solomon and the Golden Age of Israel*

*I*n many ways, Solomon was the opposite of his father. Where David was the spontaneous, emotionally expressive, extroverted, song-writing warrior king who wore his emotions on his sleeve, Solomon was a thoughtful, reserved, introverted, goal- and accomplishment-oriented type-A personality: more philosopher and administrator than poet or warrior. Where David kept himself largely cleansed of shame by the spilling of men's blood, Solomon cleansed himself by the ceremonial splattering of animal blood; he was obedient to the law. Solomon was also the lover of many, many women. Solomon was not as much of a people person as his father; this helped decrease his exposure to shame-indwelled others, making him a less accessible target for shame transfer. Solomon also didn't commit any of the heinous sins—like the murder and adultery perpetrated by his father—that could be used to legitimize such shame transfers from others.

**Settling an Old Score**
Remember Shimei, whom we met when he cursed David as

he fled Absalom's rebellion, then recanted following Absalom's defeat? True to David's deathbed request, after the death of his father Solomon devises a plan to cleanse the evil that had been sent to his father by Shimei and was now believed to indwell David's children.

> The king [Solomon] then sent for Shimei and told him, "Build a house here in Jerusalem and live there. But don't step outside the city or go anywhere else. On the day you so much as cross the Kidron Valley, you will surely die; and your blood will be on your own head" (1 Kings 2:36–37, NLT).

Because blood was perceived as so essential for the cleansing of shame (to receive atonement, forgiveness, and redemption) it was also therefore believed that blood was needed for the cleansing of illicitly sent shame. Though Shimei admitted his sin and pleaded for David's forgiveness, this didn't make him innocent of the shame-sending. David was still feeling the shame he had been sent by Shimei those many years earlier. The bloody death of Shimei would therefore be perceived as necessary to prevent the evil of the illicitly sent shame from passing on to David's future descendents.

Obviously, then, Solomon wanted Shimei nearby so he could keep an eye on him. He *knew* that Shimei would one day violate their agreement and leave the walled city for some reason. When that happened, he could then splatter Shimei's blood, according to the terms of his royal warning.

Sure enough, one day three years later, Shimei finally left the city to look for a runaway slave. He was immediately brought before Solomon, who told him,

> You certainly remember all the wicked things you did to my father, David. May the Lord now bring that evil on your own head. But may I, King Solomon, receive the Lord's blessings,

# SHAME

and may one of David's descendents always sit on this throne in the presence of the Lord (1 Kings 2:44–45, NLT).

Solomon apparently believes that Shimei's wickedness—his sent shame—could have prevented David's bloodline from staying on the throne. Solomon also greatly feared shame because of the way it was *perceived* to be tied to sin, and because of the way sin was always perceived to be tied to a punishment. Thus, ridding himself of the taint of Shimei's sent shame was not only the fulfillment of a promise to his father, but also a step toward the perception of making his throne and his dynasty more secure, as shown by the next words in the scripture passage:

Then, at the king's command, Benaiah, son of Jehoiada took Shimei outside and killed him. So the kingdom was now firmly in Solomon's grip (1 Kings 2:46, NLT).

Thus, now that shame had been cleared from David's bloodline, the kingdom was believed to be firmly in hand.

Unfortunately for Solomon and everyone else, however, shame was exploding in the land. After all, the people now slept in utter peace; their interpersonal expectations were incredibly high. Where once sinful, evil (shame-filled) people were primarily seen as "others," now shame-indwelled people are increasingly perceived as indwelling the Israelite people.

Remember that up until this time, things had been pretty simple for the Israelites: be obedient (to the law) or else; it's us (the chosen, righteous Israelites) versus them (the surrounding, shame-indwelled, sinful nations). But all this clear delineation was now becoming distorted; shame was now proliferating within and amongst Israel's own people. Also, because of David and Solomon's military and political successes, there was no longer a hated enemy whose blood could be spilled to help keep the nation cleansed from the buildup of shame. While it was true that the temple was now massively institutionalized, along with its ceremonial animal sacrifices to help compensate for the lack of spilt human blood, the internal generation of shame was far outstripping any mechanism for its removal. After all, sacrifices were generally only effective for the guilt that arose because of one's own actions—for the removal of deserved shame. There was no effective means whereby one could be cleansed of the shame when it was determined to occur—sent—without cause. There was also no perceived effective means to prevent shame from being sent without cause except through the punishment, or the threat of punishment, of shame-indwelled, *sinful* others.

### The Proverbs of Solomon: Shame Inoculation?

The Old Testament book of Proverbs, usually attributed to Solomon, may be seen as the king's attempt to teach the people how to cope with and combat the perceived rising wickedness amongst them. Consequently, Solomon devotes a lot of time to attempting to teach others how they should deal with the shame sendings of "mockers": people who use contempt as a method of combating shame by transferring it onto others. Due to internalized shame, mockers have essentially become shame-slingers. But "those who are wise" are able to endure the mockers' shame sendings and defuse the fire ignited by their contempt (a lot easier said than done when you yourself have become the target of their derision):

> Mockers can get a whole town agitated, but the wise will calm the anger (Proverbs 29:8, NLT).

We learned earlier that contempt (mockery) is an affect blend of anger and dissmell. We also learned that contempt

## SHAME

is a *learned* strategy for defending against shame; one learns to be a mocker by watching others mock. This spreading characteristic of mockery had Solomon especially concerned. He saw mockery being transferred from one person to another, much like a disease. Mockery appeared to Solomon to be the manifestation of a particularly virulent form of evil, so he believed mockers should be made examples of, such as when he says, "Flog a mocker, and the simple will learn prudence" (Proverbs 19:25, NIV).

In this way, Solomon actually starts his people down the very slippery slope of humiliating and shaming someone and causing them to feel even more defective—sinful—than they felt previously. He begins using shame to combat shame.

Penalties are prepared for mockers, and beatings for the backs of fools (Proverbs 19:29, NIV).

So don't bother correcting mockers; they will only hate you (Proverbs 9:8, NLT).

Of course they will! For whenever we criticize or rebuke someone—usually because his behavior offends (shames) us—we do nothing more than add fuel to the fire. When we send shame to someone already shame-indwelled by criticizing, insulting, or condemning him, he will often return the shame using rage, particularly if he is more extroverted. Besides, when we openly *correct* someone we are often using that person as a target for our own shame transfers.

Drive out the mocker, and out goes the strife; quarrels and insults are ended (Proverbs 22:10, NIV).

Mockers hate to be corrected, so they stay away from the wise (Proverbs 15:12, NLT).

Absolutely! Shame-filled people are not going to hang around anybody who condemns them and makes them feel even worse about themselves than they already do.

Because of their intended preventative qualities regarding shame, Solomon's proverbs can, in a sense, be looked at as an addendum to God's law. Solomon's proverbs are still looked at as a mechanism to control and combat sin!

## Taming the Tongue

You may have noticed by now how the tongue can be an especially effective device for both the inducement and transfer of shame. While physical violence can be extremely effective in inducing shame, violence itself is usually punished—heavily shamed—particularly when it is committed without cause.

The verbal transfer of shame, on the other hand, can be both extremely subtle and relatively risk-free. Indeed, verbal abuse can actually be a worse torment than physical abuse; we can sometimes heal much faster from a physical trauma than we can from an emotional one, which can be transmitted solely by the use of speech.

Humans have learned some incredibly clever and creative ways to verbally transfer shame. Consequently, the book of Proverbs is filled with passages that address this *evil* capacity of the tongue.

For example, according to Solomon, it is now considered sinful to condemn one's neighbor without cause: "It is a sin to belittle one's neighbor . . ." (Proverbs 14:21, NLT). Further, Solomon teaches that those who shame their friends are godless: "With their words, the godless destroy their friends . . ." (Proverbs 11:9, NLT). They obviously must have become shame filled, evil, because of sin . . . they must have turned from God's law. In fact, according to Solomon, "The words of

## SHAME

the wicked are like a murderous ambush . . ." (Proverbs 12:6, NLT). And indeed, an unexpected humiliation, disrespect, condemnation, belittlement, or embarrassment can surely feel like being ambushed.

Solomon also admonishes his people to speak the truth when he says, "The godly hate lies; the wicked cause shame and disgrace" (Proverbs 13:5, NLT), and, "Telling lies about others is as harmful as hitting them with an ax, wounding them with a sword, or shooting them with a sharp arrow" (Proverbs 25:18, NLT). Indeed, when we tell lies about someone we usually do it with the intention of shaming the person and causing him or her to feel less than, defective, or worse; we seldom tell lies about someone in order to make them appear better than us.

Solomon also wants to keep his people from inciting shame by quarreling. He unequivocally states, "He who loves a quarrel loves sin . . ." (Proverbs 17:19, NIV). And, after all, quarrels are nearly always about the defense and transfer of shame. The shame in a quarrel gets batted back and forth until someone finally relents and accepts it. People who love to quarrel are often using it to slough off their own deep shame in an attempt to feel better than others. He also warns, "An offended friend is harder to win back than a fortified city. Arguments separate friends like a gate locked with bars" (Proverbs 18:19, NLT). When we shame a friend we knock down the interpersonal bridge that was established between us. It will then be beyond our own power to re-erect the bridge unless our friend forgives us. Arguments, like quarrels, are nearly always about the defense of shame.

## Solomon and the Golden Age of Israel

### *Steps to a Shame-Free Life?*

Solomon believes that human effort and restraint can effectively combat shame, and therefore, effectively combat sin. Many of his proverbs illustrate the belief that shame could be totally destroyed if everyone became completely obedient to God's law and lived a life of humility and wisdom.

The fool is quick-tempered, but the wise person stays calm when insulted (Proverbs 12:16, NLT).

Better to be patient than powerful; better to have self-control than to conquer a city (Proverbs 16:32, NLT).

Doing wrong leads to disgrace, a scandalous behavior brings contempt (Proverbs 18:3, NLT).

To discipline a child produces wisdom, but a mother is disgraced by an undisciplined child (Proverbs 29:15, NLT).

Pride ends in humiliation, while humility brings honor (Proverbs 29:23, NLT).

Godly people find life; evil people find death (Proverbs 11:19, NLT).

Though these proverbs may appear to be effective in combating shame, they really do nothing more than push it somewhere else; they do nothing to indicate and address shame's true root cause. In fact, whenever we use effort toward shame's destruction we actually heighten expectation and thereby increase shame's intensity. *All* escalating do/don't effort action plans toward the control and/or destruction of shame will actually fan the flames of shame generation and can, and did, give the appearance of an escalating evil.

The Israelites were now enjoying peace and unprecedented prosperity. No doubt, they believed they should also have been finding satisfaction for all of their interpersonal needs. Besides, weren't their peace and prosperity indicators that they had finally achieved God's favor?

But why did something still seem to be amiss? Wasn't the law supposed to be able to take care of all their needs? It seems likely that Solomon himself wondered why, in a time of such material bliss, there still seemed something so significantly wrong and getting worse.

We are told in the Bible that this wrongness was due to sin—dutifully found, of course, in Solomon's taking of foreign wives and their gods, among other causes. But the law couldn't eliminate shame nor provide the ultimate interpersonal satisfaction that everyone now sought and expected. The law provided little in the way of suggestions to help them cope with the shame-filled, *sinful* others who were now seen increasingly as being among them, part of the "chosen nation." Israel was now undergoing a nuclear shame meltdown that no amount of wisdom, obedience, patience, restraint, or threat of punishment could prevent.

Significantly, Solomon himself defines the predicament inevitably found by those—like himself and his nation—who seek to be rid of shame by means of personal effort when he states, "There is a path before each person that seems right, but it ends in death" (Proverbs 14:12, NLT). Indeed, this proverb is even truer and more profound than Solomon himself realized! Looking externally for someone or something to satisfy our primary interpersonal need indeed seems right; but in fact, such attempts inevitably lead to failure and spiritual death.

**Solomon's Despair**
That shame was seemingly so virulent and undefeatable would soon result in the perception that it was a facet, or symptom, of

something that was against man and opposed to God. Shame was no longer being seen as something solely sent by God in consequence to the commitment of some sin. Evil began to be increasingly seen as something in and of itself that was separate and apart from God. Some would adopt Adam and Eve's sin in the Garden of Eden as the cause for the pervasiveness of shame, while others would adopt Satan as its cause.

How frustrating it must have seemed to Solomon that each time he attempted to construct a response to a "sinful" behavior that was obedient to the law, and conducive to the life of restraint and wisdom, his sense of shame only seemed to increase! Despite his pithy and frequent warnings in the Proverbs about the futility of anger, the benefits of patience, the advisability of punishment for wrongdoing—including that of children—and all the rest of the behaviors he was trying so hard to institute among his people, all he succeeded in doing was to create new occasions for shame to be experienced. For example, by tying anger to sin, Solomon creates an affect-shame bind, so that now even the feelings of anger within the self will become shame inducing. His famous dictum, "Spare the rod and spoil the child," has been used to justify many an instance of corporal punishment! Not only were the anger and rage responses—to a shaming without cause—starting to be shamed, but so were the shame responses of fear, jealousy, distress, and pride. Everything and anything connected to shame—the secondary responses, the defenses, the methods of shame transfer, the syndromes resulting from internalization—were all beginning to be shamed in an effort to combat sin. But instead of reducing shame it only escalated at a faster rate.

As suggested previously, Solomon's Proverbs were perhaps man's first systematic attempt to control what he

# SHAME

perceived as evil using effort, restraint, and punishment. This was not what God had hoped for. This in turn would bind humanity ever more deeply to the search for an actionable solution to the problem of shame, taking us ever deeper down into the rabbit hole . . . and to the point where we were no longer even allowed to express *any* fear, distress, or anxiety. To express these emotional responses to shame—or to even express these same *emotional responses to physical life*—became indicative that we were now being controlled by sin. Need-shame binds, affect-shame binds, drive-shame binds, and gender scripts are all results of man's waged war against shame. The final step in the progression of this proliferating and all-consuming war against shame was the adoption of physical violence in an effort to destroy evil.

By this time, many people have begun to believe that humans were simply born into sin; there seemed no other explanation in light of the continuing occurrence of shame. "Hidden sin" was the "found cause" that was blamed for the continuance of shame. So while it may have *appeared* that we were born into sin, it also appeared that physical punishment was having the effect of eliminating the behaviors that caused the shame.

Keep in mind that the behaviors that induced shame—evil behaviors—were predominantly determined by those who held the more relative power. The king would combat evil by punishing the subjects who caused *him* shame. Parents would combat wickedness by punishing their children when *they* were disrespected or mocked. Husbands would combat the devil by punishing their wives for behaviors that caused *them* shame. The *shameless* female behaviors, largely decided by male consensus, would determine the proscriptions of female gender scripts. And on and on it went.

## Solomon and the Golden Age of Israel

### "Vanity, Vanity . . . All Is Vanity . . ."

Much like his father, Solomon's greatest fear and enemy was shame. And also like his father, Solomon perceived shame as a consequence to sin. Shame was either sent directly from God (guilt) or through someone else higher on the ladder (condemnation) for disobedience. When someone lower on the ladder caused someone higher on the ladder shame, it was called evil.

God was no longer being seen as the originator and sender of shame; shame flourished despite the Israelites' best efforts to be obedient.

When we read Proverbs and Song of Songs we can hardly help but get caught up in Solomon's hope. For a long time he honestly believed that human effort and restraint could solve the inadequacies of the law in combating shame. We still believe it. And it seems that we will forever continue to believe that some repackaged, action-oriented "do this/don't do that" plan will ultimately fix us at last.

However, as Solomon finally concluded,

Everything is wearisome beyond description. No matter how much we see, we are never satisfied. No matter how much we hear, we are not content (Ecclesiastes 1:8, NLT).

Indeed, when we then read Ecclesiastes we can't help but to get caught up in Solomon's despair. At the end of his efforts, his relentless striving for righteousness and wisdom—for an ultimate sense of interpersonal completion—he must finally admit, I devoted myself to search for understanding and to explore by wisdom everything being done under heaven. I soon discovered that God has dealt a tragic existence to the human race. I observed everything going on under the sun, and really, it is all meaningless—like chasing the wind (Ecclesiastes 1:13, NLT).

# SHAME

There are no effort or sight cures for our achievement of a sense of interpersonal completion. Both wisdom and the law were powerless toward the destruction of shame and the attainment of this foremost interpersonal need . . . it is all meaningless—like chasing the wind. In other words, nothing we *do* accomplishes anything toward the satisfaction of the primary interpersonal need.

At a certain point in my own life, I began to feel a lot like Solomon:

The greater my wisdom, the greater my grief. To increase knowledge only increases sorrow (Ecclesiastes 1:18, NLT).

In other words, the more I learned, the more I realized that my education wasn't taking me to a place of ultimate interpersonal satisfaction. The more deeply I sought respect, the more severely I encountered disrespect. The more I sought to belong, the more I felt out of place. The more deeply I believed I had finally found that special someone to complete me, the more deeply I felt deficient, defective, and alone. I increasingly turned from my interpersonal search towards interests, excitements, enjoyments, and pleasures as the means of distraction. But nothing distracted me for long, and even the world of amphetamines—and my position in it—eventually stopped working. I discovered a place of incredible loneliness and despair where I walked and talked amongst the dead.

There is an Eastern saying which I've often heard misquoted as a blessing when it is actually a curse: "May you live during interesting times." When the person telling you this is also smiling, you may even thank him! But, what the person is actually wishing for is for you and yours to become *lost* in interesting times: to develop what essentially amounts to an addiction to your interests. The "well wisher" could have equally wished for you and yours to live in *exciting* times. The same could similarly be said for enjoyments and pleasures. The net result is the same: that you and yours become lost in the attention-grabbing diversions used to cope with shame's onslaught.

Like Solomon, we will ultimately arrive at a place where nothing we do can give us relief. We too are essentially *out of looking places*.

There is no other book of the Old Testament that touched me quite as deeply as Ecclesiastes. I totally identified with both the intensity of Solomon's search and his ultimate level of frustration, despair, and resignation at the failure of that search. I too have sought interpersonal satisfaction through the pursuit of knowledge and wisdom. I too have sought favor and belonging through the pursuit of achievement. I too have not withheld anything that I believed might gratify me—nothing! I've tried pleasure, pleasure, and more pleasure. I was not only out of looking places, but I was also out of causes to blame it on.

Shame has a way of greatly distorting reality. It always seems that there is some action cause for its occurrence: that either I *did or didn't do something*, or someone else *did or didn't do something*, all of which has caused me to feel deficient, defective, *sinful*, or worse. But I can never arrange others' behavior or behave my own way into an elimination of shame. I can never arrange or behave my way unto a state of absolute favor and belonging. I believe that Solomon was able to grasp some of these dynamics concerning shame, but surely not able to make the more essential determinations made by his Jewish brothers—Maslow, Tomkins, and Kaufman—these many millennia later.

Though Solomon initially believed in human restraint and thought, he later realized the vanity of all such efforts

# SHAME

toward a place of interpersonal wholeness. He also realized how extremely difficult it was to remain objective while undergoing the shame experience. He first thought that it was wise to have a predetermined set of responses for whenever we are made to feel guilty without cause: mocked, cursed, humiliated, disrespected. Because being shamed without cause could rapidly escalate into violence, he espoused discipline in dealing with the shame-filled *wickedness* of others. But all these insights and efforts were for naught because Solomon never found his way to interpersonal completion. The more clearly shown way to interpersonal completion, and to the complete eradication of shame, would not be revealed for centuries.

So few people truly realize that a clearly defined solution to shame had not yet been revealed to Solomon. Most—especially religious folk—attribute Solomon's predicament to this or that sin, but "this, too, is vanity"—simply more *looking for causes*. And though the Israelites were slowly coming to the end of places to look, they were really only beginning to look for unseen causes and unseen things to blame.

# CHAPTER 12

## *A Kingdom (Self) Divided, a Prophet's Voice*

Despite Solomon's best efforts, both he and his nation became ever more plagued by shame. No amount of obedience to the law, no amount of sober, patient, and wise living has been able to mitigate the tidal wave of shame now being experienced by the people of Israel. And despite the peace and prosperity of the land, everyone still feels the nagging inner sense that something—something vital—is both missing and increasingly going wrong.

What is missing, of course, is the satisfaction of the primary interpersonal need. God's ever refined lesson for humanity continues to take shape as the people he has called out of slavery in Egypt, whom he has shaped by forty years of wilderness wandering, and to whom he has delivered both a code for an orderly society and a homeland in which to build that society, continue to suffer from looking in all the wrong places for an escape from an increasingly burdensome feeling of shame. In fact, as we have just seen, they are running out of looking places.

As shame begins growing within the self, the self becomes ever more frantic in its search for causes. The Old

# SHAME

Testament reflects this increasing desperation of the self with its increased use of "because . . . then" and "since . . . then" causal action statements. The two types of statements are essentially no different in their ultimate message, though "if . . . then" statements are forward looking—with the purpose of hopefully heading off any future occurrences of consequential shame—and "since . . . then" statements occur after the fact, explaining the reasons or perceived causes of shame that have been or are being experienced.

**"Because You Have Done This . . ."**
As shame deepened in the land of Israel, the use of these statements proliferated. Most often, "if . . . then" and "since . . . then" statements are not so much a direct response to shame as an intellectual effort to find the casual relationships and consequences to the actions believed to have caused the shame.

> "Because of the violence you did to your close relatives in Israel, you will be filled with shame and destroyed forever" (Obadiah 1:10, NLT).

Unfortunately, when shame is used in an attempt to control or eliminate shame, the intensity of shame rises dramatically and becomes more readily internalized. And, as shame becomes internalized, the self attempts ever more forcefully to disown and cut off that part of itself which it sees as defective, corrupt, nasty, dirty, sinful, or worse. Then, as shame increasingly comes to lie at the core of the self, the activation

## A Kingdom (Self) Divided, a Prophet's Voice

of shame becomes more and more autonomous. The self will not only continue using its defenses for the external sources of shame, but it will increasingly begin using those same defenses to deal with the evil that it now increasingly perceives to lie within. As we have seen in earlier chapters, the self eventually declares war against that part of itself it sees as sinful, dirty, defective, or whatever; that part of itself it now sees as deficient or defective or sinful is now cut off and disowned. Truly, the kingdom of the self becomes divided against itself—perpetually engaged in a war it cannot win.

Not surprisingly, this same process may be observed in Israel, as the shame internalization at work in its people is writ large in the history of the entire nation.

**"A House Divided against Itself"**
During Solomon's reign, a man named Jeroboam was noted by the king for his enterprising behavior and outstanding leadership qualities. However, Jeroboam fell out with Solomon (though the Bible attributes the cause to Solomon's sin and perhaps his jealousy over apparent favor shown toward Jeroboam by God) and fled for his life to Egypt. After Solomon's death, Jeroboam returned to Israel. Meanwhile, Solomon's son Rehoboam became king in Jerusalem. "Rehoboam went to Shechem, where all Israel had gathered to make him king" (2 Chronicles 10:1, NLT), and Jeroboam and many of the leaders from the Hebrew clans in the northern part of the kingdom went to Rehoboam with a request:

> "Your father was a hard master," they said. "Lighten the harsh labor demands

# SHAME

and heavy taxes that your father imposed on us. Then we will be your loyal subjects" (2 Chronicles 10:4, NLT).

Rehoboam asks for three days to consider his answer, then confers first with his father's trusted advisers, followed by the young men his own age. While the seasoned officials counsel him to follow the peoples' advice and ease their burdens, the young Turks—presumably his boyhood companions among them—advise Rehoboam against clemency, and even encourage him to turn up the heat. Sadly for himself and the kingdom of Israel, Rehoboam decides to follow the advice of his contemporaries. He tells the waiting representatives of the northern tribes:

> My father laid heavy burdens on you, but I'm going to make them even heavier! My father beat you with whips, but I will beat you with scorpions! (2 Chronicles 10:14, NLT).

Thus, the stage is set for a civil war in Israel, with Rehoboam and the southern tribe of Judah on one side, opposed by Jeroboam and the northern tribes.

Was it a mere coincidence that the kingdom was about to be split apart by two men with such similar sounding names? Rehoboam—whose name, ironically, translates as "he who frees the people"—and Jeroboam—"he who opposes the people"—are in their opposition highly symbolic of the shame-induced splitting of the self, which now views itself as inherently sinful.

Not surprisingly, "Rehoboam and Jeroboam were continually at war with each other" (2 Chronicles 12:15, NLT).

## A Kingdom (Self) Divided, a Prophet's Voice

From this point forward, the Israelite kingdom's direction—like the self's direction with internalized shame—is starkly downward. Though there will be a few bright spots in subsequent generations, the now-divided kingdom of David and Solomon will gradually dissolve in a combination of fratricidal strife and the depredations of powerful outsiders.

Beginning immediately with Rehoboam's kingship, matters in Judah (the southern kingdom) began to deteriorate. Rehoboam reigned in Jerusalem for seventeen years, then passed the crown to his son Abijah, who reigned for three. In an effort to slow the kingdom's descent, Abijah's son Asa implemented some extremely harsh measures to combat the exponential rise of shame within Judah:

> They agreed that anyone who refused to seek the Lord, the God of Israel, would be put to death—whether young or old, man or woman (2 Chronicles 15:13, NLT).

However, even threats of death are ineffective at stemming the generation of shame within the self, which has by this time become autonomous in the people of Judah and Israel (the northern kingdom). As Kaufman describes it,

> The internal shame process has become painful, punishing, and enduring beyond what the simple feeling of shame might produce. The internalization of shame has produced an identity, a way of relating to oneself, which absorbs, maintains, and spreads shame even further (p. 115–116).

# SHAME

Indeed, as we know, once shame becomes internalized there is now no action, no "do-don't" plan possible to even minimally combat shame's increasing onslaught. It would now be just a matter of time before the people started being taken captive by shame-based syndromes such as addiction. And in fact, when we read the words of the prophets, who try to counteract the moral and ethical slide they observe among their people, we read clear evidence of this: "When the rulers of Israel finish their drinking, off they go to find some prostitutes. They love shame more than honor" (Hosea 4:18, NLT).

Hosea doesn't have it quite right. Though what they were doing may have made it appear that they loved shame, they were actually trying to escape the torment of shame that had now become internalized. A self with internalized shame also becomes ever more watchful for anything or anybody that might cause it to activate its own deep shame. This includes distancing itself from anything or anybody which now might remind it of its deficiency, defectiveness, sinfulness, or evil—especially the voices of those pesky preachers, the prophets:

> What have I done to you, man of God, that you come here and condemn me and cause me to feel deserving of punishment? (1 Kings 17:17–18, paraphrase).

> You are obviously a sinful nation, since you are so incredibly burdened by shame. I can find plenty of sinful causes. You've bumped your head; your body is in tatters, shattered from head to toe. You are covered with wounds that no amount of care and medicine can heal (Isaiah 1:4–6, paraphrase).

## A Kingdom (Self) Divided, a Prophet's Voice

But the shame-filled self has now become frantic in its search for anything that will keep it distracted from itself: pleasures, enjoyments, interests, excitements. The prophet Isaiah comes remarkably close to the real cause of shame: "Stop looking to humanity for favor and belonging" (Isaiah 2:22, paraphrase).

### Elisha and the Taunting Boys: A Case Study in Shame-Sending

As with King David, the prophets of God were themselves far from immune to the effects of shame-sendings. Consider the following story about Elisha, one of the most important prophets from the early period of the divided kingdom:

> Elisha left Jericho and went up to Bethel. As he was walking along the road, a group of boys from town began mocking him and making fun of him. "Go away, baldy!" they chanted. "Go away, baldy!" (2 Kings 2:23, NLT).

As with the shaming of David by Shimei, here is another shame sending that is perceived to be without cause (though Elisha perceives the sending as *wicked* much more quickly than David). Where we previously had an "anointed" king we now have an "anointed" prophet. As far as Elisha is concerned, there is absolutely *no cause* for the condemnation by the boys. Consequently, they are immediately perceived by Elisha to be evil: shame-filled because of sin, possibly the sin of their

# SHAME

parents. So, "Elisha turned around and looked at them, and he cursed them in the name of the Lord" (2 Kings 2:24, (NLT).

What we really have here is a retaliatory verbal shaming: insult for insult, cursing for cursing, and humiliation for humiliation. Simply, Elisha's *feelings were hurt* when the boys called him names. But of course Elisha saw it very differently. He had just done a good deed in Jericho by purifying the city's water supply. I expect that he was feeling pretty good about himself as he strolled out of town; he was definitely not feeling of deserving of being sent any shame. Besides, he was God's *anointed prophet*! But here he is suddenly being humiliated by a bunch of young boys. And since what they did was seen as sinful—because they were shame-filled and had obviously sent it without cause—there must now be found a consequence or punishment to complete the "because . . . then" model—some might even call it the "karmic model."

Here's what happened: "Then two bears came out of the woods and mauled forty-two of them" (2 Kings 2:24, NLT).

Notice the placement of the word, "then." Are we to assume that forty-two boys were justifiably mauled because they verbally disrespected some prophet? "That's ridiculous!" we might say. However, that was exactly the people's perceived understanding of these events. But at least *now* we know the truth. Whether the mauling occurred in an hour, a day, a week, or even a year later, the important thing was that a "then"—a consequence for the undeserved shaming—was found. Sin always had to be shamed and have a consequence, and perceived punishments had to always have some found sinful cause.

We have all had at least one experience with someone that left us enraged. We may have later told someone else how "so-and-so really pissed me off!" What has usually occurred

## A Kingdom (Self) Divided, a Prophet's Voice

was that the person said or did something which caused us to feel betrayed, disrespected, discounted, or less-than: we felt shame. We probably then saw this person as an enemy of sorts for what was done, particularly when there was no perceived cause for the shaming. For whenever there is no perceived cause for someone causing us shame, we usually respond with anger or rage—either expressed or held inside—and it happens so quickly we hardly see that we've first been hurt. The rage is often seen as being "caused by them" ("they made me angry"). In other words, rage is often seen as a valid response to a shaming perceived without cause.

Since a shame-sending without cause was viewed as sinful, the rage response to that shaming was seen as of God. Elisha actually believed that his angry cursing of the boys was *of the Lord*. Rage was thus seen as an appropriate response of God himself toward sinners.

> In my anger I have trampled my enemies as if they were grapes. In my fury I have trampled my foes. Their blood has stained my clothes (Isaiah 63:3, NLT).
>
> Don't be angry with us, Lord. Please don't remember our sins forever (Isaiah 64:9a, NLT).

In fact, rage will become so tied to God as a consequence to sin that an enraged enemy will often be seen as sent by God when one believed there was cause. To now feel guilty or shameful—particularly now that shame had become internalized—was to feel deserving of God's rage! And deeper we went down into the rabbit hole. Madness, madness, madness!

# SHAME

**The Shame-Induced Laundry List**

As shame increased in the leaders and people of Israel, so did the defenses and the relentless search for causes. Behavioral scripts became ever more developed and harshly enforced. In the war against sin, the list of do's and don'ts got longer and longer. The actions of others that caused those of higher relative authority to feel shame were continually added to the list, and once on the list, these actions were now deemed sinful, complete with attached punishments for their violation.

The people of Israel and Judah believed that obedience to "God's" ever-expanding list of do's and don'ts would be awarded with favor—and a consequent elimination of shame—and result—at last!—in a sense of interpersonal completion. Indeed, the urge to make more rules is a most natural response to rising shame, and *it has occurred within every culture on the planet*. But it is an effort that is inevitably doomed to failure.

> The Lord says: "These people come near to me with their mouth and honor me with their lips, but their hearts are far from me. Their worship of me is made up only of rules taught by men" (Isaiah 29:13, NIV).
>
> So then, the word of the Lord to them will become: Do and do, do and do, rule on rule, rule on rule; a little here, a little there—so that they will go and fall backward, be injured and snared and captured (Isaiah 28:13, NIV).

As we now know, when we look externally for deliverance, the occurrence of shame always seems to have an event cause. It appears quite reasonable to believe that we

## A Kingdom (Self) Divided, a Prophet's Voice

should be able to destroy sin by eliminating the behaviors that "caused" the shame. But shame is such that whenever we push down on it in one spot, it comes out in another, and usually only worse—like a Whack-a-Mole game from hell! "Do-don't" plans believed to result in favor only increase shame's intensity. We then develop defenses against the shame and often end up turning those same defenses against ourselves. We perform what essentially amounts to psycho-emotional self-surgery; we cut off or cover over the deficient, defective, or sinful part of ourselves, even if doing so emotionally cripples us.

This war within the self can cause such internal havoc that an addiction may actually "save" us from emotional destruction. And, by this time, shame was becoming so burdensome and toxic to the people of Israel and Judah that some were willing to do and try anything in order to try and gain relief from the emotional anguish due to internalized shame.

> He [King Manasseh] sacrificed his sons in the fire in the Valley of Ben Hinnom . . .
> (2 Chronicles 33:6, NIV).

(This is a good example of where it may have been better for King Manasseh to take up drinking to cope with shame rather than killing his sons.)

When a person (in this case, an entire nation) becomes dependent on any substance or activity as a means of coping with emotional distress, daily life is altered; the ability to take care of oneself is jeopardized. Addictions can become particularly devastating for a nation surrounded by enemies who hate them.

# SHAME

Then tell them, 'This is what the Lord says: I am going to fill with drunkenness all who live in this land, including the kings who sit on David's throne, the priests, the prophets and all those living in Jerusalem'" (Jeremiah 13:13, NIV).

Then tell them, 'This is what the Lord Almighty, the God of Israel says: Drink, get drunk and vomit, and fall to rise no more because of the sword I will send among you'" (Jeremiah 25:27, NIV).

Indeed, wine betrays him; he is arrogant and never at rest. Because he is greedy as the grave and like death is never satisfied . . . (Habakkuk 2: 5, NIV).

Woe to him who gives drink to his neighbors, pouring it from the wineskin till they are drunk, so that he can gaze on their naked bodies. You will be filled with shame instead of glory. Now it is your turn! Drink and be exposed! (Habakkuk 2:15, NIV).

They couldn't stand the thought of food, and they were knocking on death's door (Psalm 107:18, NLT).

They will be appalled at the sight of each other. . . (Ezekiel 4:17, NIV).

In fact, it was appearing that there were no benefits to obeying God's law. Strict obedience to God's law could—at one time long ago—only help keep shame from becoming internalized; it couldn't grant favor and belonging in the

## A Kingdom (Self) Divided, a Prophet's Voice

world. And obedience to God's law couldn't keep shame from occurring. But now no amount of obedience—or anything else for that matter—was having even the slightest effect on the shame that was now being generated solely from within.

> You have said, "It is futile to serve God. What did we gain by carrying out his requirements and going about like mourners before the Lord Almighty?" (Malachi 3:14, NIV).

However, despite the fact that all the discipline in the world wasn't having much of an effect on shame, God still wanted their attention, as the prophets would attest:

> When a man turns from the things that caused him to be sent shame, and becomes obedient to all my decrees, he will at least live (Ezekiel 18:21, paraphrase).

> Your wickedness will bring its own punishment. Your turning from me will shame you (Jeremiah 2:19, NLT).

> They turned their backs to me and not their faces; though I taught them again and again, they would not listen or respond to discipline (Jeremiah 32:33, NIV).

Though God's hopes for the Israelites finding their way out of shame were pretty much dashed now that shame had become internalized, he had yet to reveal his *just in case back-up plan* to more clearly show the way out of shame; the solution to shame would ultimately lie *in* him. But God still wanted both their obedience and their hearts. Even those who relied on God

# SHAME

and didn't turn their hearts to evil still had a need to cope with the many faces of shame. First and foremost, there was the inherited shame *because of the sins of their ancestors*:

> Oh my God, I am too ashamed and disgraced to lift up my face to you, my God, because our sins are higher than our heads and our guilt has reached to the heavens. From the days of our forefathers until now, our guilt has been great. Because of our sins, we and our kings and our priests have been subjected to the sword and captivity, to pillage and humiliation at the hand of foreign kings, as it is today (Ezra 9: 6–7, NIV).

Then, of course, there was always an abundance of autonomous, internally generated shame, not to mention the shame that was sent without cause.

> You have made us the butt of their jokes; they shake their heads at us in scorn. We can't escape the constant humiliation; shame is written across our faces. All we hear are the taunts of our mockers. All we see are our vengeful enemies (Psalm 44:14–16, NLT).

Indeed, Jeremiah, one of the greatest prophets of the Old Testament, suffered both personal shame and the collective shame of his people. Indeed, he goes so far as to express a sense of betrayal by God for the shame he is being sent for no reason.

## A Kingdom (Self) Divided, a Prophet's Voice

> Why did I ever come out of the womb to see trouble and sorrow and to end my days in shame? (Jeremiah 20:18, NIV).
>
> O Lord, you deceived me, and I was deceived; you overpowered me and prevailed. I am ridiculed all day long; everyone mocks me (Jeremiah 20:7, NIV).
>
> So these messages from the Lord have made me a household joke (Jeremiah 20:8, NLT).

### Shame Rehab

Both Israel and Judah would eventually be conquered by powerful nations: Israel by Assyria in 722 BC, and Judah by Babylon in 597 BC. Though attributed to the ongoing sin of the people by the Old Testament, these conquests and subsequent periods of foreign captivity would actually function as a sort of temporary "rehab" for the chosen people.

> Now we are being punished because of our wickedness and our great guilt. But we have actually been punished far less than we deserve, for you, our God, have allowed some of us to survive as a remnant (Ezra 9:13, NLT).

God further explains:

> Your injury is incurable—a terrible wound. There is no one to help you or to bind up your injury. No medicine can heal you. All

# SHAME

your lovers—your allies—have left you and do not care about you anymore (Jeremiah 30:12–14, NLT).

Why do you object so strongly to these consequences for a sickness that has no cure? I have to do this because of the depth of your shame. If I don't send you to rehab you will surely die (Jeremiah 30:15, paraphrase).

But God, even in these dark days for the people of Israel, was pointing them to a future time when a more clearly defined way of deliverance would be revealed:

Then my anger will cease and my wrath against them will subside, and I will be avenged. And when I have spent my wrath upon them, they will know that I the Lord have spoken in my zeal (Ezekiel 5:13, NIV).

"My wayward children," says the Lord, "come back to me, and I will heal your wayward hearts" (Jeremiah 3:22, NLT).

Do not be afraid; you will not suffer shame. Do not fear disgrace; you will not be humiliated. You will forget the shame of your youth and remember no more the reproach of your widowhood (Isaiah 54:4, NIV).

Search will be made for Israel's guilt, but there will be none, and for the sins of Judah, but none will be found, for I will forgive the remnant I spare (Jeremiah 50:20, NIV).

They will forget their shame and all the

## A Kingdom (Self) Divided, a Prophet's Voice

unfaithfulness they showed toward me when they lived in safety in their land with no one to make them afraid (Ezekiel 39:26, NIV).

I will lead blind Israel down a new path, guiding them along an unfamiliar way. I will brighten the darkness before them and smooth out the road ahead of them (Isaiah 42:16, NLT).

For I am about to do something new (Isaiah 43:19, NLT).

It will not be like the covenant I made with their forefathers when I took them by the hand to lead them out of Egypt . . . (Jeremiah 31:32, NIV).

Instead of their shame my people will receive a double portion, and instead of disgrace they will rejoice . . . (Isaiah 61:7, NIV).

You will never be put to shame or disgraced, to ages everlasting (Isaiah 45:17, NIV).

The generations of Israel will no longer suffer shame when in the Lord (Isaiah 45:25, paraphrase).

You will seek me and find me when you seek me with all your heart. I will be found by you . . . (Jeremiah 29:13–14, NIV).

And I will put my Spirit in you . . . (Ezekiel 36:27, NIV).

No longer will I make you hear the taunts of the nations, and no longer will you suffer the scorn of the peoples . . . (Ezekiel 36:15, NIV).

# SHAME

> I will put my instructions deep within them, and I will write them on their hearts (Jeremiah 31:33, NLT).
>
> They will no longer obsessively or compulsively desire some experience or attach themselves to some object; I will cure them completely from the ill effects of shame (Ezekiel 37:23, paraphrase).
>
> But those who still reject me are like a restless sea, which is never still but continually churns up mud and dirt (Isaiah 57:20, NLT).

**School Is Out**

There are estimates that as many as three million Israelites, a people who had been incredibly cleansed of residual shame, had settled in Canaan eight centuries earlier. More than three centuries have passed since the kingdom split apart. Over a hundred years have passed since the split off part of the kingdom was taken captive by the Assyrians. Shame definitely had its way in the land of milk and honey for the remaining portion of the kingdom was later taken captive as well. King Nebuchadnezar had found less than ten thousand Israelites that were worth taking as prisoners.

The fact that the kingdom of Israel had survived as long as it had is a testament to the power of the law; eight hundred years was actually a pretty good run for a nation of peoples in those times. But with extreme prosperity and safety, there always comes a proliferation in the generation of shame. "Do-don't" plans believed to yield favor—God's or otherwise—only increase shame's intensity.

## A Kingdom (Self) Divided, a Prophet's Voice

We have seen much in these eight hundred years that has highlighted the tenacity and indestructibility of shame. The psychological and emotional mechanics of shame are also such that the harder one tries to subdue it, the worse it becomes. And though the real cause of shame—and the real cause of sin—has effectively eluded us for ages, it is now truly astounding to view the garden retrospectively and realize the deeper truths it has contained all along:

- The sight-action components to shame generation (seeing and eating);
- The existence of an interpersonal need that wasn't satisfied by one another or by their perceptions of an external God;
- The elimination of the most basic needs as factors of consideration in the generation of shame (e.g., food, water, safety, sex);
- A hierarchically organized shame transfer;
- The use of blame as the most common form of shame transfer;
- The use of "because . . . then" consequential deductions.

When we examine the most basic elements of shame generation—for example, that it initially occurs interpersonally—then any possibility for the elimination of shame must also somehow involve a person (sure, we could eliminate it by eliminating all human interaction, but usually at the cost of suffering extreme loneliness). Of course, when we do find a person who we really believe is the one for whom we have been looking all our lives, the more devastating the shaming potential! But there is an alternative—a solution, actually—which resolves both dilemmas.

We are now supposed to learn from the garden that neither a wife nor husband, nor any other human or group of people, is capable of satisfying this primary interpersonal need. We are now supposed to learn that shame is the mechanism of interpersonal redirection. And, there is and has always been another person, or more properly, a PERSON, who is uniquely willing and capable of satisfying this foremost interpersonal need. And, as will become clearer in the next few chapters, this is not a relationship which takes place with a person who is external—though for all intents and purposes, it more often than not begins that way. But before humanity could accept this truth, we had to have tried every other conceivable alternative for ourselves and learned that none of them filled the bill. We also had to learn about shame and what it really is. In other words, we had to be out of looking places—and that is where we find ourselves now.

By the middle of the sixth century BC, sixty years had passed since the Babylonian captivity of Judah began. The Jews were allowed to live somewhat normal lives under both Nebuchadnezzar as well as the Persians who had later conquered Babylon. The Persian ruler Cyrus then issued a proclamation allowing the Jews to return to Jerusalem and rebuild their city and its temple.

After lying destroyed for decades, the temple was completed in 515 BC, though it is only a shadow of its former glorious self. And though the temple is rebuilt there is still another concern: "What should now be done differently in order to prevent such a national disaster from happening again?" This is essentially the same as asking, "What can now be done to keep shame from rising again?" Those advocating various causes

## A Kingdom (Self) Divided, a Prophet's Voice

and solutions to shame generation organized themselves into groups called Pharisees, Sadducees, Zealots, Herodians, Essenes, and others. These groups are really nothing more than the proponents of various approaches for the explanation, control, and reduction of shame.

Nearly a hundred years have passed since the rebuilding of both the temple and the walls around Jerusalem, Malachi is God's current spokesperson. And though the people had once been energized by the fulfillment of the prophesies concerning the rebuilding of the temple and wall they are now becoming discouraged, because the prophesies concerning the destruction of God's enemies and the coming of a messiah have not yet materialized. Though the Israelites enjoyed immense freedoms under the Persian kings Cyrus and Darius, they are increasingly looking forward to the coming of the one who will establish a kingdom of utter peace and prosperity.

Look! I am sending my messenger, and he will prepare the way before me. Then the Lord you are seeking will suddenly come to his Temple (Malachi 3:1, NLT).

Despite Malachi's words, however, it appears to some that God no longer has anything to say to his people. *This is understandable, for they are no longer seeing shame as communications from God indicating sin.* To others it appears that God has abandoned them. But such is not the case. In fact, God is about to do something dramatic that will bring the world a giant step closer to knowing a more clearly delineated way unto interpersonal completion and a complete eradication of shame.

# CHAPTER 13

## *Jesus—Sent to Show Us the Way*

What is commonly referred to as the Old Testament of the Bible ends with the book of Malachi. Four hundred years would then pass during which, according to some biblical authorities, God was silent.

During these four centuries the Persian Empire would end and Alexander the Great would bring most of the known world—from the eastern end of the Mediterranean, across the Levant and Persia, and as far as India—into contact with Greek culture as part of the Macedonian Empire. Consequently, the Jews would become heavily influenced by the Greek culture. Though they would be highly resistant to adopting Greek religion, they would learn to speak the language, since it was the language of trade and culture for the entire empire. The Jews would even translate many of their religious writings into Greek. Upon Alexander's death, his empire would be divided among three of his chief generals: Seleucus, whose capital was in Syria; Ptolemy, who ruled in Alexandria, Egypt; and Antigonus, who ruled Greece.

Early in the second century BC, Judas Maccabeus led a revolt against the Seleucids and achieved the first self-rule enjoyed by Israel since the time of the Babylonian conquest. However, this independence was short-lived. The rising Roman Empire turned its sights on Jerusalem, and in 63 BC the city was overtaken by Pompey. The Jews were once again placed under foreign rule as Rome installed Antipater as governor of Jerusalem. Antipater's son, Herod, was ruling the region when Jesus was born.

**The Coming Messiah**

There were many ideas floating around amongst the Jews regarding the messiah, the anointed one who was to come. Some thought he would be like Moses or Elijah. Since the nation was at that time under Roman domination, many were hoping that this anointed one would be like David and free them from foreign oppression. Even Malachi, hundreds of years earlier, seemed to imply that the messiah would be some kind of warrior:

> But who will be able to endure it when he comes? Who will be able to stand and face him when he appears? For he will be like a blazing fire that refines metal, or like a strong soap that bleaches clothes. He will sit like a refiner of silver, burning away the dross (Malachi 3:2–3, NLT).

On the other hand, hundreds of years before Malachi, Isaiah seemed to emphasize a softer side to the one who would come. Has anyone noticed that most of the prophesies concerning such a one also began to occur once shame had

# SHAME

become internalized—when the nation, *the self*, was split apart?

> Here is my servant, whom I uphold, my chosen one in whom I delight; I will put my Spirit on him, and he will bring justice to the nations. He will not shout or cry out, or raise his voice in the streets. A bruised reed he will not break, and a smoldering wick he will not snuff out (Isaiah 42:1–3, NIV).

But one thing that all the prophets agreed on: the anointed one would be God's special envoy—he would be perceived and understood as "sent." This "sent one" would be called by many names:

Son of God (Luke 1:35)
Immanuel (Isaiah 7:14)
Son of David (Luke 20:41)
Rabbi (Matthew 26:25)
Lord (John 20:28)
The Christ (John 1:41)
Son of the Blessed One (Mark 14:61)
King of the Jews (Matthew 27:37)
Jesus of Nazareth (Matthew 26:71)
Holy One (John 6:69)
Lamb of God (John 1:29)
Messiah (Matthew 1:16)
Savior (Titus 3:6)
Teacher (Matthew 12:38)
Chosen One of God (John 1:34)

## Jesus—Sent to Show Us the Way

And, of course, there were many, many more. But Jesus identified himself most often as the "Son of Man." "Jesus" is the Latin version of the Greek "Iesous." "Christ" means "the anointed one" and equates to "Christos" in Greek and "Messiah" in Hebrew.

### The One Who Was Sent

John the Baptist believed that Jesus was sent:

> For the one God has sent speaks the words of God . . . (John 3:34, NIV).

Indeed, many in centuries past had spoken the words of God, but never before had one been *sent* to speak the words of God. To be "sent" obviously assumes a "sender." Equally obvious in this case is that the sender is assumed to be God.

But for Jesus to convince others that he was sent by God would be no easy task.

> "Unless you people see miraculous signs and wonders," Jesus told him, "you will never believe" (John 4:48, NIV).

> In fact, the Father will show him how to do even greater works than healing this man. Then you will truly be astonished (John 5:20 NLT).

Several persons queried Jesus about his "sent" status:

> Are you the person who was predicted to come or should we continue waiting for someone else? (Luke 7:19, paraphrase).

# SHAME

As we'll see, Jesus' foremost concern was convincing his hearers that he *was* the sent one. What didn't seem to matter as much were the particulars concerning his "sent-ness," but only that they might believe that he *was* sent.

> But I have a greater witness than John—my teachings and miracles. The Father gave me these works to accomplish, and they prove that he sent me (John 5:36, NLT).

However, even with the witness of his miracles, Jesus was not able to convince everyone:

> But despite all the miraculous signs Jesus had done, most of the people still did not believe in him (John 12:37, NLT).

Yes, to convince them he was sent was no easy task! Not only was Jesus continuously bent on trying to prove he was sent, but he was also forever modeling the intimate relationship that he had with God, to whom he referred on numerous occasions as "the Father" and "my Father."

> The Father who sent me is with me (John 8:16 NLT).

The Pharisees found this intimate and personal form of address blasphemous:

> For he not only broke the Sabbath, he called God his Father, thereby making himself equal with God (John 5:18, NLT).

## Jesus—Sent to Show Us the Way

But how else was Jesus to portray the primary interpersonal relationship in such a way that we would more readily understand? And how else was he to describe the conceptualization of relational union except to say:

> And the one who sent me is with me . . . (John 8:29, NLT).

And:

> For when you see me, you are seeing the one who sent me (John 12:45, NLT).

There is perhaps no relationship that is more primal, intimate, and non-sexual than that of the relationship between a father with his son.

### Who Is Jesus?

Jesus clearly indicates on numerous occasions that he isn't God. It was the PERSON with whom he was in relational union who did the miracles. Jesus himself didn't possess the ability to draw the people, only God did. Jesus never indicates that he is like, equal to, or the same as God!

> Not to do my own will but to do the will of him who sent me (John 6:38, NIV).
> So Jesus told them, "My message is not my own, it comes from God who sent me" (John 7:16, NLT).

## SHAME

Jesus also never said, "If you don't believe that I am God . . ." but this is exactly what many thought he said.

Because you are trying to find a sense of belonging in the world you will die in your shame. I don't belong to the world. Unless you believe I am what I claim to be you will never find your way out of shame (John 8:24, paraphrase).

When we read Jesus say "I am" in John 8:58, the people start to stone him. When the Pharisees come to the Garden of Gethsemane to arrest him, Jesus says "I am" not only once, but twice! Jesus knew from experience the effect these words had on many people, particularly the Pharisees. He said these words twice that night at Gethsemane to insure the Pharisee's rage and his crucifixion.

As Jesus "was," we can also "be," for his Father is also *our* Father.

But go find my brothers and tell them,
"I am ascending to my Father and your Father,
to my God and your God" (John 20:17, NLT).

The miracles that testified to his special status as the sent one, the messiah, were performed by the PERSON with whom he was in relational union. Jesus not only never indicates that he is like, equal to, or the same as God; in fact, he is at some pains to explain that he is doing what he does on behalf of, or at the bidding of, someone else:

## Jesus—Sent to Show Us the Way

> Because I carry out the will of the one who sent me, not my own will (John 5:30, NLT).
> I don't speak on my own authority. The Father who sent me has commanded me what to say and how to say it (John 12:49, NLT).

In proclaiming his sent-ness and modeling relational union, Jesus walked an extremely fine line between persuasion and provocation. His primary focus, however, was on the belief of his followers—even if that meant provoking the Pharisees and violating the rules of the complicated do/don't system they had developed in an effort to earn God's favor and minimize the occurrence of shame. As I already mentioned, Jesus' use of the "I am" statement was a deliberate provocation—a shaming—to insure his own crucifixion.

> Yes, you know me, and you know where I come from. But I'm not here on my own. The one who sent me is true, and you don't know him (John 7:28, NLT).
> You say, "He is our God," but you don't even know him. I know him. If I said otherwise, I would be as great a liar as you! (John 8:54, 55, NLT).

Though Jesus was admitting that the Pharisees might indeed know *him*—including facts about his family and the town where he was from—they didn't *know* the one who sent him.

And just when the Pharisees figured Jesus' message couldn't become more blasphemous and shame-inducing, he said things like this:

# SHAME

The Father and I are one (John 10:30, NLT).

So, not only did Jesus say he was sent with a message, but he was now further implying that the message-giver himself was with him and in him. The more common misunderstanding of this verse is to take it to mean that he was saying he himself was God. However, the much more subtle understanding of this verse—particularly in light of our study of shame—reveals that he was in a relational union, or oneness, with the Father. But of course the Pharisees saw it more *superficially*, which would eventually cause them to seek his death. After all, when Jesus asserted that they didn't know God, he had greatly shamed them. They of course then perceived this shame-sending as having no legitimate cause. And much like King David, it would then only be through the shedding of his blood that could cleanse them and transfer this illicit shame back to where it came from.

Relational union can also have a way of antagonizing—even without a word being said—those in higher positions of power and authority because of the Person in union's insusceptibility to shame transfer. Jesus made a reference to this inherent resistance to hierarchical shame transfers when he told them that those who don't belong to the world are hated by those who are seeking belonging in the world.

**"To Him Who Has Ears, Let Him Hear!"**
As I read the Gospels, I find myself in absolute awe at the determination with which Jesus resisted clarification. To be clear would have been to draw a line in the sand.

To say he was either *this* or *that*—to identify himself as

## Jesus—Sent to Show Us the Way

*this* or *that*—was the last thing Jesus wanted to do or felt the need to do. There are many instances in the New Testament where Jesus asks his disciples, "Who do the people say I am?" Jesus also remained purposely vague in order to give some room for the PERSON to work out of the moment with those who believed he was the sent one. And he surely couldn't straighten out the wonderings of the religious elite; he had to not only give them reasons for wanting him killed but reasons for having him crucified! For from the Jewish perspective—as well as everybody else in the region—there could be no transfer and cleansing of shame without the splattering, *the shedding*, of blood.

We do see Jesus get much more explicit about relational union in John 17, at a time when the Pharisees are not around. I believe this chapter, as well as the previous three (chapters 14 to 17), are particularly revealing, for they not only cover Jesus' last few hours of ministry, but they occur when he is completely alone with his friends. Though I have spent many, many hours reading all these chapters, I have a particularly deep love for John 17. The chapter is essentially a prayer to God for each of his disciples, for every future believer, and for everyone in the world at large. The prayer cuts to the core of his entire teaching. If I were to entitle this chapter, I'd call it the "Jesus Prays for Oneness" chapter, or, more specifically, the "Jesus Prays for Relational Union" chapter . . .

> I pray that they will all be one just as you and I are one . . . (John 17:21, NLT).
> Father, I want these whom you have given me to be with me where I am (John 17:24, NLT).

# SHAME

For to be with him *where he is* does not indicate a location at some other time, but speaks of enjoying a state of being with him *in this particular moment*. Being "where he is" implies being with him right now, possessing a state of being that is derived from a personal relationship—a relational union—with the PERSON *right now*.

**The Kingdom of God and Relational Union**
In Luke 17–20, Jesus tells the Pharisees that the kingdom of God is not a place or location they could point toward, but that it was already among them. Please don't make the ageless mistake of thinking that Jesus was referring to himself; if Jesus was implying that his visible person was the kingdom of God, he would have been contradicting himself, because he himself was obviously something you could point toward and say, "There it is!"

The truth is that the kingdom of God has always been among us and within us and available to us since the Garden of Eden. Jesus was *sent* to clearly show us the way to interpersonal completion—and a complete eradication of shame—*right now*, not for when we die. Chapter 17 is all about the "am-ness" or "one-ness" with the PERSON, in this eternal moment!

Some may think this notion has an Eastern feel to it, but unlike that proclaimed by Eastern religions, the oneness pronounced by Christ is the result of an interpersonal relationship involving two distinct and separate people—two beings, two minds, two shared consciousnesses. In fact, what is commonly referred to as *Eastern* is actually a slight distortion of relational truth: in the way taught by Jesus there is no real diminishment of the one in order to become united with the other. There is

## Jesus—Sent to Show Us the Way

simply a union of two into one that then becomes a composite of the two. In becoming one as Jesus taught, we will never totally lose our own sense of individuality. The one can never actually become the other. Think of it as *the SELF and a self becoming a Self*, or *the PERSON and a person becoming a Person*. Jesus was a Person. A *Person* will also never be able to totally lose the sense of space and time until his or her body dies.

Not only had Jesus been indicating he was sent with a message, but he was now further implying that the message-giver himself was with him and in him. The more common misunderstanding of this verse is to take it that he was saying that he *was* God. The much more subtle understanding of this verse reveals that he was in a kind of co-relational union, or oneness, with the Father. But of course the Pharisees saw it more superficially. And this is what Jesus intended, and which ultimately drove the Pharisees mad. Jesus wasn't really doing anything more here than modeling and describing a relational union, albeit with a glaring innuendo for the grooming of enemies. The Pharisees took the bait. They actually believed Jesus was telling them he was God. But the disciples understood the deeper concept Jesus was modeling.

>"My Lord and my God!" Thomas explained (John 20:28, NLT).

I believe that the best way to describe this phenomenon is to see it as a *developed* personal relationship that results in a relational union. A personal relationship is never developed and established by simply knowing something *about* the other person, but only by *knowing them personally*. This is why Jesus talks about his am-ness, his one-ness, and his union with the

# SHAME

Father on numerous occasions throughout the four Gospels. He mentions *knowing* the Father many, many times.

Remember, as Jesus was speaking these words, he was still very much a human. He had a mother, brothers, sisters, a father, friends, cousins, aunts, and uncles. He worked at a job for which he was paid. He sweated, belched, and urinated. He also bled when cut and bruised when traumatized. But when he said, "I and the Father are one," he was referring to the relational union that he was in with the PERSON—even while he was in the same bodily form that you and I have. It is in this place, this state of being—where *I am* with *him*—that the generation of shame is entirely halted. When Jesus prays for his followers in John 17, he is praying that they also find their way to this state of being.

Something else very special happened on that last night that greatly relieved Jesus. Through the course of his ministry, Jesus had probably referenced his "sentness" on countless occasions. In John's gospel alone, some form of "sent" is used nearly forty times! Here it is the last night that he will be with his disciples and they finally turn to Jesus and say:

> Now we can see you know all things and that you do not even need to have anyone ask you questions. This makes us believe that you came from God (John 16: 30, NIV).
>
> Jesus excitedly responds, "You believe at last!" (John 16:31, NIV).
>
> Moments later Jesus tells the Father the good news: "They knew with certainty that I came from you, and they believed that you sent me" (John 17:8, NIV).

## Jesus—Sent to Show Us the Way

Remember: the sense of interpersonal wholeness we so desperately seek can never be brought about from someone externally perceived on the outside, but only from an *inside* relationship. No church, mosque, or synagogue can give you what you're looking for. Nor could the external relationships that Adam and Eve and Moses had with God or the apostles' relationships with the visible Jesus satisfy their primary interpersonal needs. However, once we are with him, by being in him, we'll have that vital sense of belonging regardless of wherever we are physically. This sense of interpersonal completion is fully gained and maintained by the continuous and abiding conscious/unconscious relationship. It is then in this *knowing* him that we find the union—the way, the truth, and the life.

We can have the exact same type of relationship that Jesus had. Just as he was a *son*, we can also be *sons* and *daughters* through the establishment of a primary interpersonal relationship. That indeed was why it was necessary that they perceived him as being sent, for unless they believed him as sent they would never have pursued a personal relationship with *him* once they perceived he rose.

> But to all who believed him and accepted him, he gave the right to become children of God (John 1:12, NLT).

Notice here that the belief and acceptance of Jesus only gives the right to become children of God. The rest of the process requires that we get to know him personally.

# SHAME

### Where Is Jesus?

As I've said, Jesus *had* to die and disappear before an unseen personal relationship with him would be pursued and oneness could then occur. Jesus had to die and disappear and then be looked for, so that his followers would not only know the *kind* of person for whom they were searching, but also that they would then recognize him when he was found. With the phrase "so that they may be one as we are one," Jesus is telling his listeners that he has to go away before they'll be better able to find the kind relational union with the Father like the one that he has with the Father.

> I said in a little while you won't see me,
> but a little while after that you will see me again
> (John 16:19, NLT).

To restate in slightly different words, Jesus knew that spiritual oneness occurs via an interpersonal relationship between a person (a human) and the PERSON (God), not a relationship between a person and a person—even a perceived "sent" other Person. Looking to visible others as providers of interpersonal completion is what creates the potential for the shame in the first place, exactly like the external face-to-face relationship Adam and Eve had with God in the Garden of Eden. *(By the way, this was also like the external face-to-face relationship that Moses had with God).* Thus, when Jesus prayed "so that they may be one as we are one," he knew that the answer to his prayer would necessitate his leaving his followers. Indeed, he told them,

> But I tell you the truth: It is for your

good that I am going away. Unless I go away, the Counselor will not come to you; but if I go, I will send him to you (John 16:7, NIV).

So, rather than being saddened that we can't still see Jesus walking among us today, we should be grateful. This too argues for the position that his *return* will not be a physical one. Indeed, his mission as the sent one could not be completed without his leaving. He came to demonstrate and embody the life completely devoid of shame, the life of relational union—and then, just as the Father intended, he left, in order that each of his followers—each of us!—might then better find our way to a relational union with the PERSON.

**Jesus Prays for You!**
As mentioned briefly above, the prayer of Jesus in John 17 is, in a very real sense, his prayer for all those seeking the way of relational union, both present and future; he was praying for *each of us*. With this in mind, I invite you to read Jesus' prayer as shown below, stressing the italicized "to be" verbs and placing your own name in the provided spaces:

> I also pray for each of those who believe in me because of the message of my disciples, that_____may be one, as you *are* in me and I *am* in you. May_____also *be* in us, so that the world will believe you sent me.
>
> I have given_____the glory that you have given me so that <u>he/she</u> may be one as we are one, I in <u>he/she</u> and you in me. May

# SHAME

_____be brought to *complete unity*, to let the world know that you sent me, and have loved him/her even as you have loved me. Father, I want_____to be with me where I *am*, and to see my glory, the glory you have given me because you have loved me before the creation of the world.

What is even more "unearthing" is to have your spouse or a close friend read this prayer while you're sitting comfortably in a chair with your eyes closed. Have the reader use your name and appropriate pronouns. Ask them also to emphasize both "one" and the italicized verbs. It can be a truly moving and revealing spiritual experience.

It is also important to notice that Jesus' prayer for oneness also included the desire that his followers would enjoy a new type of relationship, not only with the PERSON but with each other. Indeed, the disciples of Jesus would soon be traveling to the ends of the Greco-Roman world. And though they would never again be as much together physically, they would soon discover a way of relating to one another that they had never experienced before. This "connection" they would have with each other was not with each other directly, but was facilitated through the relational union they now had with the PERSON. This "tie" to each other was of a kind that could be maintained across miles and even across time; it was the kind of tie that existed between them without the need for being in physical proximity with each other. The disciples would essentially become the first members of the kingdom—a kingdom not characterized by space and time.

The implications for us today may be somewhat obvious;

## Jesus—Sent to Show Us the Way

by entering into relational union, we, too, can experience a new type of connection—one not based on sight—with other people who are also in oneness with the PERSON. Imagine the effect on our discordant world if enough of humankind entered into relational union and discovered a new sense of connectedness with each other around the globe!

**The Mission and Message of the Sent Messiah**
Humankind had never seen an example of relational union before the coming of Jesus.

He was the first to have and display the kind of personal relationship that was actually completely destructive to the generation of shame—even the shame sent by others without cause. It had been God's hope ever since the garden that we would recognize shame as the mechanism of interpersonal redirection unto the *him* within us. What's amazing is that so few have found their way to such a union. It seems that we got lost in this millennial-long argument pertaining to Jesus' divinity. The belief that Jesus was the *Son* of God does nothing in and of itself toward shame's destruction!

So, what have we learned about Jesus?

- He was viewed as somehow sent;
- He did some incredible stuff;
- He had an unprecedented type of relationship with God, to whom he referred by the intimate epithet of "my Father";
- He indicated that not only was the Father "out there" somewhere, but that he was also with him and in him, in a kind of interpersonal fusion which Jesus described

as being one with the Father;
- He taught that if we believed in him, and got to know him, he would provide a peace and joy far beyond that of the world's;
- He taught that this peace and joy was not achieved through obedience to some action plan—thus appearing to completely throw out the law as the means to favor from God—but rather as a result of a relational oneness with the PERSON.

Those who belong to God are in a personal relationship with him. We are either seeking belonging in the world—the seen—or else we are seeking belonging in him. When we belong *in* him—and he belongs *in* us—we gladly listen to his words and he gladly listens to ours, and the generation of all forms of shame is completely destroyed.

> I tell you the truth, whoever *hears* my word and believes him who sent me has eternal life and will not be condemned (John 5:24, NIV).

Jesus clearly had to come to show us where he was, what he looked like, and how we could personally get to know him. Who could have ever conceived that God was a person in the likeness of a father with whom we each could have an intimate relationship? Who could have ever conceived that we were created for this particular kind of Relationship? Who could have ever conceived that shame's purpose was to redirect from looking toward an externally perceived PERSON and rather forcefully turn us toward the inner PERSON instead? Who could have ever conceived that we are all already indwelled—at birth—with HIS indwelling SPIRIT?

> And I will ask the Father, and he will give you another Advocate, who will never leave you (John 14:16, NLT).

Indeed, prior to the coming of Jesus, nobody could have grasped that not only had God always been available for a deeply intimate and personal relationship, but he had always been *wanting* such a relationship. The Israelites had previously perceived God as externally localized: up in heaven, at the temple, etc. He was perceived as unapproachable to everyone but the high priest. The purpose in Jesus' perceived sending was to assist us in overcoming the perceived barrier between ourselves and the God with whom we were evolved and created to be in relational union. He had to be perceived as *coming* in order to give us a personal name that we could use in order to have the vitally needed type of personal relationship—with the HIM within us—that was required for gaining relational union.

Truly, the perceived coming of Jesus changed everything. Two thousand years have passed since his earthly presence, and humanity is still grappling with his intended impact. Within just a few weeks of his leaving, his disciples began altering the world in which they lived because of the newfound power of the spiritual indwelling that Jesus made possible.

One of the chief architects and evangelists of this new life of the spirit was a devout and deeply learned Jewish rabbi from the city of Tarsus, on the southern coast of the Roman province of Asia Minor—what we know today as the country of

# SHAME

Turkey. He was so devout a Jew, in fact, that he did his best to stamp out the new sect of those who were followers of Jesus of Nazareth. That is, until he himself had a dramatic spiritual encounter on the road to the Syrian city of Damascus. His name was Paul, and it is to his influential body of writing that we will turn next.

# CHAPTER 14

## *Paul the Apostle and His Long Journey toward Understanding*

*T*here can be little doubt that the Apostle Paul, originally known as Saul of Tarsus (Acts 9:11), was one of the most influential figures in shaping the early beliefs, practices, and doctrines of the church in the first century following the death of Jesus Christ. He was well educated, both in the Jewish scriptures and in Greek thought. He was ambitious—actually, "driven" would probably be more accurate—tireless, and apparently fearless where his convictions were concerned. In many ways, he was the perfect ambassador for the new faith that was taking shape around the figure of Jesus of Nazareth.

Saul of Tarsus was a Jew's Jew. He was educated and trained in the scholarly and legal traditions of the Pharisees. For such a Jew as Saul, the law was everything: the department of health, the Pope, the civil and criminal court systems, the police department, and the mental health profession all rolled into one. To turn from the law would undoubtedly cause an abrupt and devastating end to the culture he knew and loved; Saul would have found it incomprehensible that any kind of discontinuance or dismantling of the law could possibly be approved by God. Saul certainly recognized the law's utility—he would have seen

# SHAME

it as absolutely necessary—for the cleansing of guilt. He also recognized the law's inability to defend him from the sloughed off shame of shame-filled, sinful others. In order to combat shame, he would simply be obedient and shed the blood of sinners by stoning them. Neither Paul nor his contemporaries realized that it was actually their efforts toward favor that were causing the manifestation of shame in the first place. However, despite his belief that shame and guilt were tied to a sinful action cause requiring punishment, Paul—as he later become known—came remarkably close to seeing the total picture by the end of his spiritual journey.

Saul of Tarsus became an exceptionally zealous advocate for the destruction of all who were followers of Jesus Christ, whom he and his colleagues considered a blasphemer and a lawbreaker (Acts 9:1). He believed that these followers of the man from Nazareth were not only a threat to the nation of Israel but also unrighteous (and probably shame-filled). How could the foregoing of law, which the believers in Jesus appeared to advocate, possibly earn favor from God?

But everything changed for Saul one day on the road to Damascus. A profound—even temporarily debilitating—spiritual encounter convinced Saul that not only had God been walking in union with Jesus, but that Jesus was still very much alive (Acts 9:5). Saul was so traumatized by this paradigm-shifting experience that he went away to Arabia for three years of solitary contemplation. Though Saul had never known the physical Jesus, he began the unnecessarily slow process of getting to know him. It may have also been at this time that Saul decided to start going by his Roman name: Paul.

*Paul the Apostle and His Long Journey toward Understanding*

## The Epistles of Paul

Paul became a determined missionary and a prolific correspondent. His instructional letters—often known as "epistles," from the Greek word for "letter"—sent to the followers of Jesus in various communities around the Mediterranean rim, contained the fruit of his contemplation of the implications of the new spiritual realities to be found in a new kind of relationship with God made possible by the teachings and examples of Jesus Christ.

Where Paul once believed that faith in God meant one was obedient to God's law, he now understood it somewhat differently; through faith one *became* obedient (Romans 1:5). This was actually a pretty radical shift in his perception, since it takes attention away from obedience to the law and puts it on the living, unseen PERSON. Though I don't think Paul ever realized that it was actually the relationship itself that destroyed shame (sin), he did come to realize that faith, grace (extended by God), and belief were integral to the new spiritual life he was embracing (Romans 1:16–17). But despite this potentially significant shortfall Paul still received some incredible understandings pertaining to shame dynamics and the satisfaction of the primary interpersonal need.

For example, in Romans 2:1 he tells us that whenever we partake in the evaluation (judgment) and condemnation—the shaming—of others, we cannot help but apply the same *action* standard to ourselves, thus laying the groundwork for the production of shame in ourselves:

> You, therefore, have no excuse, you who pass judgment on someone else, for at whatever point you judge another, you are

## SHAME

condemning yourself, because you who pass judgment do the same things (Romans 2:1, NIV).

Good advice! On the other hand, Paul's fuzzy picture regarding both the relationship and shame shows itself in Romans 2:5–10:

> But because of your stubbornness and your unrepentant heart, you are storing up wrath against yourself for the day of God's wrath, when his righteous judgment will be revealed . . . To those who by persistence in doing good seek glory, honor, and immortality, he will give eternal life . . . But for those who are self-seeking and who reject the truth and follow evil, there will be wrath and anger (Romans 2:5, 7–8, NIV).

In the context of our current understandings about relational union, Paul's characterization of the continuance of sin as simply a "stubbornness and refusal to turn" falls short. Release from unproductive behaviors (sin) isn't something God grants us because we believe and have faith in him; the power to lay down unproductive behaviors—such as addiction, perfectionism, comparison making, or the condemnation of others—is gained as we get to personally *know* him.

We must recognize Paul's belief that all condemnation has arisen in consequence to sin, either known or unknown:

> When the Gentiles sin, they will be destroyed, even though they never had God's

written law. And the Jews, who do have God's law, will be judged by that law when they fail to obey it (Romans 2:12, NLT).

Paul believes we can become spreaders of shame when we ourselves have become indwelled with shame from sinning. He believes in a sin/shame tie and sees the self's experience of guilt as a validation of sin.

For merely listening to the law doesn't make us right with God. It is obeying the law that makes us right in his sight (Romans 2:13, NLT).

Paul further believes there is a kind of unwritten law for the Gentiles, and that they too will suffer shame when it is violated, just as the Jews will suffer for disobeying the written law. All of these perceptions have stemmed from Paul's belief that God will grant us favor depending on what we do or don't do.

### *Paul, the Law, and Shame*

However, as we now know, the problem with the law, as well as any other do/don't plan believed to yield favor from God, is its tendency to keep us looking at it to see how well we're doing; the problem isn't so much with the law itself, but what we think such a law can provide. Whether we are looking for favor from God or looking for it directly from people, the primary motivation of both is the elimination of incidental shame and an acquisition of a sense of interpersonal wholeness. It just won't work; only the personal relationship can destroy both the shame which we determine to have cause for—when we are criticized, convicted, condemned, or judged—and the shame which we determine to not have cause for—when we are prejudiced, disrespected, belittled, mocked, or scorned.

I have no doubt that Paul had an extremely difficult time in trying to impart his new understandings to others, particularly when his audience contained both Jews and gentiles. I believe this is why Paul preferred to teach the "Good News" to gentiles; he didn't have to contend with the problems of trying to overcome the age-old Jewish perception (that right action leads to a right relationship with God) in favor of the new teaching that knowing a person leads to right action. I see this as the foremost issue that caused Paul most of the beatings, whippings, and stonings from the hands of his Jewish brothers (see, for example, Acts 14:19).

Because of his belief in the sin-shame tie and the fact that shame continued to occur for those under law regardless of how well they obeyed, Paul concluded that the reason for the law was to make people feel guilty:

> Obviously, the law applies to those to whom it was given, for its purpose is to keep people from having excuses, and to show the entire world guilty before God (Romans 3:19, NLT).

However, the law's purpose was not to induce shame; we each cause our own shame when we believe that our obedience to some action plan can satisfy our primary interpersonal need. Paul comes somewhat close to understanding this:

> For no one can ever be made right with God by doing what the law commands. The law simply shows us how sinful we are (Romans 3:20, NLT).

But Paul is only 50 percent correct here. It is true that obedience to the law cannot end shame. But even those without the law suffered shame, and even complete obedience to the law couldn't destroy shame—particularly shame determined to not have cause.

Still, to give Paul his due, he is 100 percent correct when he states,

> But now God has shown us a way to be made right with him without keeping the requirements of the law (Romans 3:21, NLT),
>
> And when he says,
>
> We come into a right relationship with God by believing in his Personhood. And regardless of who we are, we can each come to know Him if we first believe in Him (Romans 3:22, paraphrase).

Paul comes even closer to a right understanding when he says,

> Can we boast, then, that we have done anything to be accepted by God? No, because our acquittal is not based on obeying the law. It is based on faith (Romans 3:27 (NLT).

# SHAME

Paul correctly suggests that our freedom from shame is now not based on obedience, that our favor with God can no longer be gained through the law, but based on faith.

But what about the implications of faith for ethical and moral behavior? If what we do or don't do doesn't matter, then anything goes, right? Wrong! As Paul explains it,

> Well then, if we emphasize faith, does this mean we can forget about right actions? Of course not! In fact, it is only thru faith that we can truly have right actions (Romans 3:31, paraphrase).

Once again, Paul is emphasizing that right actions are not produced by obedience to the law, but rather by faith in the Person. Or, as he states it elsewhere:

> Clearly, God's promise . . . was not based on obedience, but on a right relationship with God that comes by faith (Roman 4:13, NLT),

and,

> Shall we now keep on doing things that we know are not wise even though they might not cause us the shame they once had? Of course not! Though we are no longer being shamed under law, how can return to acting in ways that clearly used to bring condemnation about? (Romans 6:1–2, paraphrase).

# Paul the Apostle and His Long Journey toward Understanding

When we no longer feel shame we will no longer need to act in the ways we once did to combat shame. Our long-held defenses to shame begin to dissolve as the satisfaction of our primary interpersonal need enables us to live our daily lives at an incredible level of interpersonal acceptance—for both ourselves and for others. The unconditional love exhibited by Jesus is a natural outgrowth of relational union.

## Paul's Understanding of Sin and Atonement

We noticed earlier how merely an *understanding of forgiveness* was all that was really needed for shame to transfer. But we also noticed that once shame became internalized it wouldn't transfer, thus giving the appearance of not being forgiven—that *God was still angry!* For those under the law, the sacrifices initially gave them a sense of being forgiven by God; they perceived the spilling of blood as absolutely essential for the forgiveness of sin.

Paul and other Jewish converts therefore saw the crucifixion as Jesus dying on their behalf as a blood sacrifice to God—and to cleanse them from sin once and for all—even those who were already dead because of internalized shame. However, we have already noted the earlier story in the Old Testament that relates how Judah's King Manasseh sacrifices his own sons to pagan gods. The verse clearly states how evil this was considered in God's sight. So, how was it now even feasible for them to believe that Jesus died for the cleansing of their sins? For God to offer his own son would seemingly be no less evil than King Manasseh's action. Furthermore, if Jesus had died as the *perfect sacrifice* for all our sins—past, present, and future—then nobody should ever still be feeling any shame!

This is obviously not the case. There is no more abhorent—and quite frankly, wrong—perception held by modern Christianity than the one that suggests that God sent his own son to die as a sin sacrifice unto himself—for *our* sins!

Still, Paul states, "He was handed over to die because of our own sins" (Romans 4:25, NLT). This of course was the *Jewish perception* of why Jesus died, arising from the mistaken perception linking shame to an action cause—that obedience to the law could earn favor and completely eliminate the feel of all shame. This belief and perception was very much a perception from down in the rabbit hole.

While I don't wish to fault Paul for his perceptions, we must remember that he was once a devout Jew and radically devoted to Jewish law. Likewise, I don't wish to now fault him for his belief that obedience to the law could earn favor and destroy shame. Still, from our new perspective on shame and relational union, his views are a lot like looking up from deep in the rabbit hole and thinking that the small, blue circle above is the full extent of the sky. Thus, when we read Paul's words in Romans 5:10 (NLT)—"For since our friendship with God was restored by the death of his Son while we were still enemies, we will certainly be saved through the life of his Son"—we first need to realize that we were never God's enemies! The belief that we were his enemies was largely derived from the perception of a shame-sin-action-law tie!

Because of considerations like these, I tend to sometimes believe that Paul didn't fully grasp the revelations he was given. I know there is a tendency to align revelations through our personal, human frames of reference. However, from the perspective of new scientific and psychological insights revealing that embarrassment, guilt, humiliation, and condemnation are simply different faces of the same phenomenon—shame—and that these faces all manifest themselves because of frustrated interpersonal expectations, we can now read Paul's epistles and other scriptures from a new, wider perspective. When we now read Paul's words, we can actually understand them in ways in which he himself may actually have had no comprehension. Essentially, we are out of that rabbit hole with a much more encompassing view of the sky—but it's the *same sky*!

**Paul and the Inner Struggle**

The concept of sin was familiar to many people other than the Jews. Shame had become tied to sin for everyone in the Tigris-Euphrates region who had been told the story of the Garden of Eden. And when the Israelites were given the law, it was the law itself that became an additional stumbling block to Jewish conversion. Consequently, Paul spends an incredible amount of time in his epistle to the Romans trying to resolve some of these sticking points for Jewish converts—as well as for himself. Indeed, when we read parts of Romans 7, it is almost as if we are listening in on an argument Paul is having with himself about what the law could do—and what it couldn't.

What got Paul in so much trouble with his Jewish brethren—and what probably troubled him, too, on some level—was how his teaching sometimes seemed to imply that it was the law that created sin. He tries to discourage this interpretation:

> What shall we say, then? Is the law sin? Certainly not! Indeed I would not have known what sin was except through the law (Romans 7:7, NIV).

# SHAME

Indeed, Paul goes on to suggest that the law "taught" him about sin precisely by saying things like "Thou shalt not covet." He observes,

> But sin used this command to arouse all kinds of covetous desires within me! (Romans 7:8, NLT).

Actually, there are few cultures on the planet that don't recognize some rights and protections of personal property. The urge to covet is largely a response to internalized shame—we see something that we *really, really* believe will make us feel better. Coveting became exceedingly shameful under law when it snowballed into the belief that it was sinful to desire anything! It wasn't "sin" that caused shame to compound itself and cause more of a desire to "sin," but rather a distorted perception of what the *not coveting* command was capable of.

Remember that the commandment doesn't say that a deep desire for *anything* is sinful; instead, what this commandment tried to inhibit was a preoccupation and envious longing for, and possibly the taking of, something of your neighbor's. A deep desire for *a* wife isn't sinful, but the deep desire for your neighbor's wife *is*. Though this commandment was initially meant as nothing more than a protection for personal property, it was extrapolated into a realm of meaning that was never intended when the condemnation continued to occur despite their best efforts to be obedient, when a deep desire—and in some cases, even a moderate desire—for *anything* was eventually considered sinful.

Paul at times appears validly conflicted about his perceptions of the law:

> Once I was alive apart from the law, but when the commandment came, sin sprang to life and I died. I found that the very commandment that was intended to bring life actually brought death (Romans 7:9–10, NIV).

But the fact is that Paul would still have experienced shame even if he had never learned the law. Shame became enhanced under law because of the rising interpersonal expectations regarding the law itself.

> But how can that be? Did the law, which is good, cause my death? Of course not! Sin used what was good to bring about my condemnation to death (Romans 7:13, NLT).

No! Sin didn't do anything. Paul's "condemnation to death" resulted from nothing more than his looking to the law while under the effects of an *unsatisfied* primary interpersonal need: his ultimate belief that obedience to law could destroy shame.

Remember that the law's foremost purpose was to keep a people healthy and functional while hopefully teaching them that sight and effort were of no help toward achieving interpersonal completion. Notwithstanding Paul's angst, the law was never intended, nor able, to bring "complete life." Still, Paul concluded, as do many today, "The trouble is with me, for I am all too human, a slave to sin. I really don't understand myself, for I want to do what is right, but I don't do it. Instead, I do what I hate" (Romans 7:14–15, NLT).

# SHAME

> But if I know that what I am doing is wrong, this shows that I agree that the law is good (Romans 7:16, NLT).

No, what this shows is that Paul is still heavily bound to effort and action. He still largely believes in some action pathway toward favor and belonging. He knows that the answer lies in Christ, but he is also still trying to combat shame. The good/bad and right/wrong duality is vitally important for survival, but with respect to the satisfaction of the primary interpersonal need, it is no longer relevant. The mere delineation of "right" and "wrong," "sinful" and "not sinful" actually increases shame's intensity because it heightens expectations of satisfaction of the primary interpersonal need.

> And I know nothing good lives in me, that is, in my sinful nature. I want to do what is right, but I can't (Romans 7:18, NLT).

But it is the goal to *be right* that fuels the motivation to *do right* that in turn brings the condemnation. Looking to the seen for favor resulted in the perception of an angry god, for the harder they tried to find favor and a sense of belonging in the seen, the worse shame deepened and caused the perception of an angry god. Besides, interpersonal wholeness isn't something he can grant or give us; he is our relational wholeness; he is our interpersonal completion.

So there is nothing "wrong" with us! We indeed are human, also meaning that our survival needs are predominantly met through sight, effort, and action. But we are also not slaves to the seen, for we have the capacity of choice. While non-sight, non-effort, and non-action—faith, belief, and grace—may be difficult adjustments for us to make because of our creaturehood, the adjustments are still possible. We are not bound to the slavery and frustration of the seen, and we are definitely not slaves to it once we get to *know* him personally.

However, the sort of shame spiraling evidenced by Paul's self-indictment, "I do what I hate," is very symptomatic of internalized shame. When we see some part of ourselves as deficient, defective, bad, wrong, nasty, sinful, or worse, we lay the groundwork for the splitting of the self. This internal war of right vs. wrong gets replicated externally and soon the world—or at least our perception of it—becomes torn in half by a war between good and evil.

> I want to do what is good, but I don't.
> I don't want to do what is wrong, but I do it anyway (Romans 7:19, NLT).

Once we have categorized all human actions as either good or bad, right or wrong, we set about a search for just the right combination of *goods* and *rights* which we believe will take us *there* at last. But hopefully—before we're dead—we come to the realization that nothing we *do* or *don't do*, and nothing anybody else *does* or *doesn't do*, will ever bring us to a place of interpersonal completion. "Blessed are those" who get to this point while they're still alive (see Mathew 5).

> But if I do what I don't want to do, I am not really the one doing wrong; it is sin living in me that does it (Romans 7:20, NLT).

# SHAME

What is "wrong" is when we blame what we do that's "wrong" on sin. What is "wrong" is our looking for a sense of favor and belonging in the world. What is "wrong" is our looking to the seen in hopes of satisfying the primary interpersonal need.

Finally, after meticulously tracing out his own inability to carry out the commands of the law in order to obtain the favor that he thinks that will provide, Paul cries out in anguish, "What a wretched man I am! Who will rescue me from this body that is subject to death?" (Romans 7:24, NIV). Then, in the very next verse, he answers his own question:

> Thank God! The answer is in Jesus Christ our Lord (Roman 7:25, NLT).

Most definitely! The answer of the Personhood of God was embodied in Jesus Christ, and it is in beginning a relationship with the PERSON that we begin to be delivered from the interpersonal and personal generation of shame.

> So now there is no condemnation for those who belong to Jesus Christ (Romans 8:1, NLT).

But *belonging* is much more than simply saying you belong to him—or doing things which say to others that you belong to him. Paul is still being subjected to the shame sendings—the scorn, hate, and disrespect—of shame-filled, sinful others.

Though we will probably never lose the fear that accompanies a physical threat, we will lose the fear—and the distress and the rage—which surrounds our efforts to utilize the seen to achieve favor and belonging. Paul clearly understands one important fact, however:

> I am convinced that nothing can ever separate us from God's love (Romans 8:38, NLT).

Indeed, just as nothing we *do* can totally eliminate the experience of shame in our lives, so can nothing prevent us from reaching out to him and beginning a personal relationship and reaping the total destruction of shame that it yields.

> The law of Moses was unable to save us because of the weakness of our sinful nature (Romans 8:3, NLT).

Actually, the law of Moses was never intended to "save" us.

> That's why those who are still under the control of their sinful nature can never please God (Romans 8:8, NLT).

Our *problem* was started when shame became attributed to an event cause.

> For all who are led by the Spirit of God are Children of God (Romans 8:14, NLT).

We can only start becoming led by the spirit when we begin a personal relationship. We have had God's spirit since the garden. The experience of shame *is* a *spirit-ual* experience.

# SHAME

> We, too, wait with eager hope for the day when God will give us our full rights as his adopted children (Romans 8:23, NLT).

Our full rights as his adopted children are available to us now! Paul still hadn't figured it out. Paul knew that the answer lay in Christ, but he still had yet to figure out the proper question.

> We were given this hope when we were saved (Romans 8:24, NLT).

But our "being saved" is just the beginning of a process—a decision—which must then focus on the building of a personal relationship.

> Does it mean he no longer loves us if we have trouble or calamity, or are persecuted, or hungry, or destitute, or in danger, or threatened with death? (Romans 8:35).

Most of these experiences were previously seen—and still are largely seen by some—as *found* punishments from God for sin. But having these experiences in our lives has nothing to do with the presence or absence of God's love. Even though God has no real direct control over the act of persecution, he has direct and complete control over the feel of persecution (over the shame that has been determined to have no cause).

> He calls people, but not according to their good or bad works (Romans 9:12, NLT).

Correct! We can't *do-good-and-not-do-bad* our way unto an eradication of shame; we can't *do* our way to favor.

> But anyone who trusts in him will never be disgraced (Romans 9:33, NLT).

No, trusting him has no effect on being disgraced, but once we get to know him, we'll no longer feel the shame when being disgraced.

> For Christ has already accomplished the purpose for which the law was given. As a result, all who believe in him are made right with God (Romans 10:4, NLT).

But David, Moses, and Jeremiah also believed and had faith in God. Faith and belief in Christ gets us no further toward the destruction of shame than did the faith and belief in God in previous generations.

> If you confess with your mouth that Jesus is Lord and believe in your heart that God raised him from the dead, you will be saved (Romans 10:9, NLT).

Whatever "saved" actually means, it means nothing unless it destroys the feel of condemnation. All this "confessing" and "believing" really gets us nowhere.

> So this is the situation: Most of the people of Israel have not found the favor of

# SHAME

God they are looking for so earnestly (Romans 11:7, NLT).

But material comfort has nothing to do with having God's favor. The problem with seeing material comfort—as well as positions of respect, fame, and power—as a blessing from God are the alternate perceptions: if you don't have physical comfort then you haven't found favor with God, and when you *lose* material comfort you have fallen out of favor with God. I am amazed by how deeply many still believe in this today, even though it's been four thousand years since Job! The acquisition of wealth, position, fame, and power are nothing more than shame minimization tactics that were wrongly discerned as positions of favor from God. These misperceptions resulted because of the linking of shame and sin to an action cause . . . the linking which has now finally been severed!

> For God has imprisoned everyone in disobedience so he could have mercy on everyone (Romans 11:32, NLT).

No, God has not imprisoned us in shame just so he could have mercy on us! Internalized shame is not the result of *disobedience*.

In Romans 12, Paul addresses the kind of shame sendings determined to have no cause. It had previously been believed that it was okay to return the shame to where it came from when it came without cause (the eye-for-eye principle). These verses indicate that not only is Paul still battling shame himself but he is also making suggestions to others for the defusing of shame that is perceived sent without cause. These tactics are not much different than those advocated by Solomon hundreds of years earlier:

> Wish good for those who cause you shame without cause. Don't return the shame that is sent without cause. Wish for them that God eliminates the shame from occurring in their lives as he has begun doing in your own life (Romans 12:14, paraphrase).
> Never shame those who shame you (Romans 12:17, paraphrase).
> Dear Friends, never take revenge (Romans 12:19, paraphrase).

Since positions of authority are so relatively free of incidental shame, they were perceived to be positions of favor granted by God for obedience. It was therefore believed to be a sin against God to shame those in authority by defying them, mocking them, or in some general way disrespecting them. In Romans 13, Paul addresses the believers and makes some suggestions for dealing with the shame that often arises from interaction with those in authority. This, however, is essentially nothing more than a shame control tactic.

> So you must submit to them, not only to avoid punishment, but to also keep a clear conscience (Romans 13:5, NLT).

The New Living Translation captions Romans 14 as "The Danger of Criticism." I would paraphrase this chapter as "The Dangers of Sending Shame to Others." When we criticize

## SHAME

someone, we are essentially more than likely shaming them. It is the shame in a criticism that actually causes the desired changes in the one criticized. But it is only to the degree that someone is important in our lives—that we give them authority—that we give power to their criticism. The problem is that once someone gains importance in our lives—whenever their attention gives us hope of interpersonal completion—their criticism or condemnation is often unconsciously used as a mechanism to transfer their own shame, under the guise of their *caring*. Even in situations where they are sincerely trying to correct our *bad*, *wrong*, or *sinful* behaviors, they more often than not purposely wrap it in shame in order to make it more effective. The mental health community has long recognized the inherent difficulties of addressing "bad" behaviors without causing someone to feel like a "bad" person.

At some level Paul also recognizes the havoc shame can have on someone when they are criticized by others. Paul is trying to explain the seriousness of criticizing someone, particularly when the reasons are largely just a matter of preference—that which one believes is either *right* or *wrong*. *Actually, shame should never be purposely or inadvertently wielded, no matter what the reason.*

>  Accept other believers who are weak
>  in faith, and don't argue with them about what
>  they think is right or wrong (Romans 14:1, NLT),

I would rather that Paul had said, "Accept everyone, and never enter into a discussion with someone about that which *either of you* believes is *right or wrong, good or evil,* or *sinful or not.*" Such discussions are really only relevant when they are applicable to our basic survival. Whenever we try to apply such differentiations toward gaining a sense of belonging in the world, we create shame and then often end up passing it to others.

> For instance, one person believes it's all right to eat anything. But another believer with a sensitive conscience will eat only vegetables (Romans 14:2, NLT).

During our efforts to find favor by combating shame, we used the same good/bad differentiations as we did during our efforts to survive. Though these efforts worked well for our survival, they didn't work at all towards the elimination of shame. We assumed the problem might be resolved by applying the "good/bad" differentiations more broadly and deeply. We then tried eliminating the "bad" delineations using physical punishment. But the harder we tried, and continue to try, the worse things got, and continue to get. And the worse things get, the more this fuels the belief that there is some malevolent, evil other that prevents us from reaching that place of inner peace we so desperately seek.

> Those who feel free to eat anything must not look down on those who don't. And those who don't eat certain foods must not condemn those who do (Romans 14:3, NLT).

We each have our own particular beliefs concerning the pursuit of favor and a sense of interpersonal completion. What causes shame for me might not cause shame for you.

# SHAME

Since it appears that *our way* of eliminating shame is successful to us, we feel that if everyone would adopt *our way*, we would all then get there at last! But it is impossible for everyone to be completely obedient to everyone's interpersonal expectations.

> So who are you to mock, criticize or condemn those who don't follow your way of trying to find favor and belonging? Let God decide if what they are doing is right or wrong. With God's help they will come into a Right Relationship, but it still might not *look* like your own Right Relationship with God (Romans 14:4, paraphrase).

It is not an easy task for us to move beyond the action-oriented, do/don't manner we once used to try and find favor, for it is not actually a *task* per se.

> So why do you condemn another believer? Why do you look down on another believer? (Romans 14:10, NLT).

We condemn others because it causes us to feel better about ourselves!

> So let's stop condemning each other. Decide instead to live in such a way that will not cause another believer to stumble and fall (Romans 14:13, NLT).

This is a lot easier said than done. There is essentially

no *real* difference between the *expression of condemnation* toward someone and the *feel of condemnation* toward someone in the heart. It is admirable that Paul is at least trying to slow shame's seemingly ceaseless generation and transfer, but he still hasn't made the vital connection between the generation of shame and the PERSON. Paul still perceives that shame has an action cause. He doesn't yet have even the slightest idea that it is *only* the personal relationship with the PERSON that will completely destroy the feel of shame.

We know that the experience of shame is relative to each self. The particular actions which cause one person shame might not be replicated in someone else. Paul has some amazing revelations concerning this relative aspect of shame generation.

> I know and am convinced on the authority of the Lord Jesus Christ that no food, in and of itself, is wrong to eat. But if someone believes it is wrong then for that person it is wrong (Romans 14:14, NLT),
>
> If you do anything you believe is not right you shame yourself (Romans 14:23, paraphrase).

The subjective experience of shame derived from each of our efforts toward favor and belonging is clearly evident here. And though Paul consciously thinks this is only in reference to the eating of pork chops, the concept is *now* to be extrapolated much more broadly, with a more encompassing view of the sky.

With the exception of violating our written code of laws, everything else is *now* a matter of choice and preference. We must *now* be allowed to pursue a sense of belonging and interpersonal completion wherever we each believe it lies, as long as it doesn't *directly* infringe upon someone else's pursuit of the same. In order for us to be completely done with effort and action, we have to have done most of what that we believed would satisfy our primary interpersonal need but still have found ourselves in want. *I believe that the finding of relational union is vitally dependent upon our recognition of interpersonal powerlessness.*

> For the Kingdom of God is not a matter of what we do, but of living a life in Relational Union (Romans 14:17, paraphrase).

However, just as we are *now* permitted to do whatever we want towards interpersonal wholeness, we need to also now be cognizant of others' beliefs that what we are doing is *not okay* to them. In other words, don't throw it in the faces of others when you know that what you are doing will cause them to *stumble*.

> You may believe there is nothing wrong with what you are doing, but keep it between yourself and God. Blessed are those who don't feel guilty for doing something they have decided is right (Romans 14:22, NLT),

and,

> It is better not to eat meat or drink wine or do anything else if it makes another person stumble (Romans 14:21, NLT),

and,

> We who are no longer experiencing shame must also be aware of, and considerate of, the ways we might be inducing shame in others (Romans 15:1, 2, paraphrase).

Jesus taught and acted in such ways that were totally devoid of causing others to feel disrespected, defective, sinful, or worse. However, he was really *only* able to do this because he was totally devoid of shame himself.

**Paul and the Gentiles: The Letters to the Church in Corinth**
While the group of believers in the city of Rome was probably comprised mostly of Jews, the church in the city of Corinth was definitely comprised mostly of gentiles. In other words, this letter is largely to a people who probably had little to no previous knowledge of the religious beliefs or cultural heritage of the Jews.

The city of Corinth controlled a short section of land that connected the Corinthian Gulf to the Saronic Gulf. Much of the trade between Rome and Asia was taken off ships, transported over this short piece of land, and loaded once again on other ships. Not surprisingly, by the time Paul arrived there during his missionary tours of the mid-first century AD, the city was awash with newly found wealth. For all intents and purposes, the city of Corinth was at this time what many cities in twenty-first century America are fast becoming: a population high in religious, socioeconomic, and ethnic diversity.

Consequently, Paul's approach to the people in the church of Corinth would differ from that he used when speaking

# SHAME

to Jewish converts. It is also worthwhile here to note that this letter to the Corinthians may have been written only a year or so prior to the writing of his letter to the group of believers in Rome. While Judaism was very attractive to many non-Jewish people in the first century, because of its strong moral and ethical teachings and its ancient heritage, Greek thought and Greek mystery religion were also very prominent among the backgrounds of the Corinthian believers. Fortunately, Paul's well-rounded education equipped him to approach these people largely on their own terms.

He begins his letter by announcing something that the Corinthians would have been pleased to hear:

> To the people of the church in Corinth who have now been called by God to be His people, along with everyone everywhere who calls on him as He was revealed in Union with Jesus Christ, who is now the one we follow (1 Corinthians 1:2, paraphrase).

Paul immediately includes these predominantly gentile believers among those *chosen*—some would use the theological term "elected"—by God. However, just because the gentiles were now chosen, it doesn't mean they were all chosen for relationship, for we have all been both chosen and Chosen, but not everyone is being chosen for relationship.

Without the need of overcoming perceptions about the Jewish law and its view of sin, punishment, and atonement, Paul moves directly into explaining their sanctification—the process of growing toward union with the PERSON. The following chart may help to visualize the differences between the process for

*Paul the Apostle and His Long Journey toward Understanding*

Jewish believers and that for gentiles:

| Jewish Conversion | Gentile Conversation |
|---|---|
| Election | (chosen by God) |
| ↓ | |
| Justification | *These intermediate steps were not pertinent to the gentiles, for they weren't down the rabbit hole—though both groups were currently suffering internalized shame equally.* |
| ↓ | |
| Propitiation (Atonement) | |
| ↓ | |
| Redemption | |
| ↓ | |
| Sanctification | (the process of building a personal relationship) |
| ↓ | |
| Glorification | (relational union) |

With these recently chosen believers, it was not essential—nor applicable—for Paul to explain how "God has now made us right in his sight" (justification), how "God has now removed our deservedness of punishment" (propitiation or atonement), and how "Christ has now paid all our sin debt by dying as a sacrifice unto God" (redemption). All that these intermediate steps really did was to get the Jews up and out of the rabbit hole. In other words, the concepts of justification, propitiation, and redemption are really nothing more than the

# SHAME

means of clearing away the misperceptions derived from the belief that obedience to the law was the means to favor and the elimination of shame.

Simply, the Old Testament takes us down the rabbit hole of the sin/shame bind, while the New Testament, generally, takes us out and then up. Paul's letter to the Romans starts down in the hole and then brings us out and up (the anonymous epistle Hebrews does much the same). Paul's letters to the Eastern churches—mostly gentile in makeup—largely start us at ground level and then take us up.

By the way, this is why, for those who feel they may be in the category of "chosen for relationship" and are thinking about starting a relationship with the PERSON, I'd suggest you stay away from the Old Testament for a while. I'd further recommend staying away from Romans and Hebrews, at least initially. Further, while building your relationship, please stay away, as best you can, from anybody who tries to take you down the rabbit hole by telling you that you must first admit that you're a sinner, that Jesus died for your sins, that Jesus was God's Son, or that Adam and Eve brought sin into the world.

> Now you have every spiritual gift you need as you eagerly wait for the return of our Lord Jesus Christ. He will keep you strong to the end so that you will be free from all blame on the day when our Lord Jesus Christ returns (1 Corinthians 1:7–8, NLT).

Paul indicates in these verses that he is clearly waiting for some future event—the second coming—to provide him with something he did not yet have and saw no way to get. Paul doesn't yet realize that he and his readers could be completely free of all shame *right now*. However, Paul's point here was for them to try as hard as they could to be blameless (remain "strong") so that when Jesus returns they will be awarded with a life in a kingdom which was totally devoid of all shame. To his credit, Paul sees the Person and his attendant spiritual gifts as helping them to remain free of sin and deserved shame . . . but he didn't see a way out of shame being sent by shame-filled, sinful others unless Jesus returned. In other words, though the believers of Corinth were not officially under law, he was still expecting them to be blameless—undeserving of shame for cause. Paul was not yet able to see that all shame had an interpersonal expectation cause and that this expectation cause arose because of a *still-unsatisfied* primary interpersonal need. Paul has yet to recognize that the development of the relationship itself would destroy all forms of shame production.

**Speaking of the Second Coming . . .**
We looked earlier at Jesus' prayer for future believers (John 17). Jesus' primary hope was for all his followers—including you and me—to find our way to complete union. It is then in the eternal moment with him that we discover eternal life and become totally immune to all forms of shame generation, regardless of what anybody else says or does; we will no longer be looking externally in an effort to satisfy the primary interpersonal need.

Therefore, there is really no reason why Jesus *has* to return again; there is no unfinished business he has to now yet come to accomplish. The kingdom is available for each of us *right now* when we reach out to where he is and begin a relationship. His kingdom was ushered in the moment they discovered him, after, the disappearance of his body. His *return* is accomplished when we each come to complete unity. It is then here within each of us where his kingdom lies.

As mentioned earlier, the endpoint of the sanctification process is glorification—relational union, the culmination of building a relationship. Accordingly, we neither have to die nor wait for his return in order to experience a life that is entirely free of all shame. Glorification is now available for each and every one of us who are chosen for relationship.

However, Paul rightly points out to the Corinthians that just because we may have been called—chosen—for relational union, we won't ever get there unless we continually grow in knowledge of him by experiencing the deepening of the personal relationship. It is a constant process that can be symbolically represented by the Christian concept of communion; it is as though we eat of him and drink of him. It is the consistent personal relationship that is all-important:

> But for all who are Chosen by God for Relational Union, whether they be Jew or Gentile, it is the Relationship itself which is the power and the wisdom (1 Corinthians 1:24, paraphrase).

### *Paul and Resurrection*

It is entirely possible that the Jewish idea of an afterlife was inherited from the Egyptians. After all, they spent centuries as a part-Egyptian society, and the Egyptian belief in and fascination with the afterlife is well documented by archaeology and other scholarship.

It is also interesting that the Pharisees, the sect of Judaism that Paul belonged to before becoming a follower of Jesus, were distinguished by their belief in the resurrection of the dead. Some, in fact, have traced the name "Pharisee" to a root word that might be translated as "Persianizers," underlining the belief that the Pharisees' insistence on resurrection was somehow borrowed from Persian thought, such as that in Zoroastrianism, which posits a bodily resurrection of "the righteous" at some point in the future.

However we explain it, it is clear in most of Paul's epistles that he holds out great hopes for the events following Jesus' second coming, including a bodily resurrection of all believers. He spends a significant amount of time talking about it in 1 Corinthians 15. I think it's important to understand why Paul places such emphasis on these ideas, since, as mentioned earlier, an understanding of true relational union with the PERSON removes the necessity for any future hope in some apocalyptic "second coming."

I hope it is becoming more obvious that Paul still suffers from shame without cause. I hope it is equally apparent that Paul perceives that believers can combat the shame-sendings of others by isolating themselves. It should also be rather apparent that Paul is still trying to combat shame using effort and action.

But the Jews had tried these isolationist, do/don't tactics for over 1,400 years, to no avail! I believe Paul recognized the ultimate failure of this maneuver, and that is why he latched hold of the necessity for Christ's physical return and the bodily resurrection of believers. Essentially, Paul believes that we will be rewarded later on for our endurance of shame right now.

Paul states, "But if it is preached that Christ has been

raised from the dead, how can some of you say that there is no resurrection of the dead?" (1 Corinthians 15:12, NIV). However, the true meaning behind Christ's resurrection was not that *we* would rise similarly. It is understandable why Paul would want to grab hold of the idea of another body experience; he simply saw no other way out of his continuing exposure to shame-sending others. Furthermore, I don't totally discount the possibility that there may be another bodily experience after this one. What I object to is the reasoning that Paul believes there *has* to be another body experience. He uses Christ's *finding* after his departure as symbolic for another life that we too will get to experience—a life that will be absolutely devoid of the ravages of shame.

Consider that when Jesus told us that he would give us "eternal life" he didn't mean that he would be giving us another bodily experience from which we would never physically die. The everlasting life that the relationship provides is in reference to the eternal life we discover through the building of a relationship with him now; it is the PERSON that is eternal life. Jesus' disappearance and finding, then, were done in such a way that would cause us to turn to the unseen him and seek him there. If Christ had stayed dead in the tomb, nobody would have turned to the unseen. Instead, he had to be perceived to have risen from the dead; his body *had* to disappear. Then, by seeking him in the unseen and entering into a personal relationship, we ourselves are resurrected from the *living dead*.

However, Paul does not yet understand that the relationship itself *is* the resurrection:

> If there is no resurrection of the dead, then not even Christ has been raised. And if

> Christ has not been raised, our preaching is useless and so is your faith (1 Corinthians 15:13–14, NIV).

The good news is, of course, that there is indeed a resurrection of the walking dead—all of us who are trudging through life with internalized shame. Jesus *never* told us that he was sent so that we would now live forever. *Besides, the idea of an eternal punishment was largely adopted as a desperate, last-minute weapon in the Israelites' war with shame.* Instead, he was sent to show us the way to life in this eternal moment. He is here, he is alive, and he is available for personal knowing. A certain amount of faith is required for us to reach out to where he is, but once we get to know him there will no longer be any guilt, for we will no longer be trying to find favor externally. As Paul says,

> So you see, just as death came into the world through a man, now the resurrection from the dead has begun through another man (1 Corinthians 15:21, NLT).

Just as Adam showed the way *to* spiritual death by using sight, effort, and action, Jesus showed the way *out* of spiritual death by using non-sight, non-effort, and non-action.

### Paul and Suffering

In several of his epistles, Paul discusses a topic that his readers, whether Jew or gentile, could appreciate: suffering. There are two distinct forms of suffering: physical and emotional. One is in

# SHAME

response to the body's will to survive, while the other seems to result from my efforts to find belonging and feel interpersonally complete.

I wish Paul had been a little more careful in delineating these two forms of suffering. While it is true, as Paul states, that "God is our merciful Father and the source of all comfort" (2 Corinthians 1:3, NLT), since the fear, distress, and rage that accompany my efforts to find favor will be eradicated in the relationship, it's also true that I'll never find my way to an elimination of the suffering due to a broken leg, a severe case of poison ivy, or a heroin withdrawal by looking to God.

Paul says in the next verse,

> He comforts us in all our troubles so that we can comfort others. When they are troubled, we will be able to give them the same comfort God has given us (2 Corinthians 1:4, NLT).

Unfortunately, I can find less to agree with here. There is nothing I can do to relieve the suffering that arises in someone else's pursuit of interpersonal wholeness. I may indeed be able to provide comfort for their physical pain—our medical profession does a fantastic job at doing just that—but there is really nothing I can do to eradicate the emotional pain someone feels when a spouse has just had an affair, for example. If they can't change the way they feel, then I surely can't change the way they feel. After all, I'm powerless over my own subjection to shame's onslaught, much less someone else's! I can indeed show compassion for their emotional suffering, but I am powerless over their feelings of humiliation, embarrassment, distress, and rage.

## Paul the Apostle and His Long Journey toward Understanding

> We are confident that as you share in our sufferings, you will also share in the comfort God gives us (2 Corinthians 1:7, NLT).

Notwithstanding Paul's encouragement and admonition, learning to endure emotional suffering requires that we learn how to *not* react to emotional pain. It may make us more patient and brave, and it may even win us the admiration of millions, but it is still a shame-defending strategy. Better, in my opinion, to pursue the relationship and put an end to shame once and for all! In fact, when Paul states in 2 Corinthians 4:10 (NLT), "Through suffering, our bodies continue to share in the death of Jesus so that the life of Jesus may also be seen in our bodies," it becomes even more apparent that his thinking does not encompass relational union. Is Paul really trying to tell us, for example, that through physical suffering we can be like Jesus? Is Paul implying that if we die like Christ, we'll rise like Christ? (In fact, he does assert this, in almost these exact words, in several places in his writings.)

However, physical suffering does nothing to contribute to the elimination of shame. As a matter of fact, it can actually be a hindrance to the needed recognition that action and effort are useless toward a sense of interpersonal completion. It is only when our basic needs are fairly well satisfied that we then begin attending the higher interpersonal needs—though this is also when we begin encountering shame. It is extremely difficult for us to realize our inability to find interpersonal completion while we're locked below the shame generation threshold. Physical suffering can be a powerful distraction to the realization that we're out of looking places. The fact is we can only become like Jesus when we get to know him as Jesus knew him. Physical suffering is actually a hindrance to the finding of relational union.

# SHAME

> So we live in the face of death, but this has resulted in eternal life for you (2 Corinthians 4:12, NLT).

I will forever stand in awe of Paul's determination to spread the good news. But I stand in stark opposition to his innuendo that his own suffering has led to the eternal life of others. Let me say it again: physical suffering is not the means to a non-shameful end; an intimate personal relationship is both the means and the end. When we are in the relationship we are in eternal life, and our physical circumstances no longer have any bearing on the matter.

> We know that God, who raised the Lord Jesus, will also raise us with Jesus and present us to himself together with you (2 Corinthians 4:14, NLT).

Regardless of whether this will or won't one day happen misses the point of Jesus the Christ. That which seems to be blocking Paul—and many of us—from the ultimate realization is the all-pervasive perception that all our needs are constrained by action and time. The primary interpersonal need is not the kind of need that takes *action* to be met at some future time. Way too many of Paul's teachings are action- and goal-oriented for some future place and time. The primary interpersonal need is only satisfied in the now.

**Paul and His Authority**

Paul had shamed—corrected—a number of Corinthian

believers in his earlier letter because of some behaviors they were exhibiting, and also because many were questioning Paul's authority to advise them on how to live. Remember that once authority is established, shame becomes an effective means to control behavior. Since authority was still seen as given by God, the wielding of shame was thus seen as a God-approved mechanism for teaching obedience to others by shaming them. As we will see, Paul was certainly not far enough along the relational union continuum to be able to avoid the use of shaming others, if that was what he thought was necessary to get them to do what he thought was right.

> I am asking you to respond as if you were my own children (2 Corinthians 6:13, NLT).

Thus having established himself as an authority figure (e.g., father/children) Paul now perceives that he has been given the right to wield shame for God. Authority positions by their very nature are often shame-inducing for others. Paul still believes shame to be sent by God in consequence to sinful behavior. Paul still believes that God uses those *given* authority as conduits for the transfer of shame to those whose behavior is considered sinful.

> Now I am glad I sent [the letter], not because it hurt you, but because the pain caused you to repent and change your ways. It was the kind of sorrow God wants his people to have, so you were not harmed by us in anyway (2 Corinthians 7:9, NLT).

# SHAME

The pain caused by Paul's condemnation was thus seen as having the backing of God. The experience of shame—through a correction—authenticated the act deemed sinful by the person in authority. When Paul caused someone to experience shame by correcting him or her, it gave the appearance of God's backing to whatever Paul said was sinful.

But shame is not the kind of sorrow God *wants* us to experience. Shame is not the result of any specific action, but the result of actions generally; it arises from the expectation of finding interpersonal completion in that which we see. Shame is meant to turn us away from each other and to redirect us toward him. However, Paul seems to intend for his readers to be looking to him (Paul) for some sort of direction—for obedience to him, if you will:

> And after you have become fully obedient, we will punish everyone who remains disobedient (2 Corinthians 10:6, NLT).

I'm out of expletives! What we have here is a total regression to Old Testament perceptions and beliefs. There is no place deeper down the rabbit hole than this!

And then, as if to prove the point, Paul says,

> I may seem to be boasting too much about the authority given to me by the Lord. But our authority builds you up; it doesn't tear you down. So I will not be ashamed of using my authority (2 Corinthians 10:8, NLT).

Too much boasting, indeed! But the question of boasting

is really a distraction for his real intent here—to establish his authority. Paul is willing to concede his vanity for boasting *about the authority given to him by the Lord.*

Paul perceives the authority given to him by the Lord as also an authority to wield shame on God's behalf. It is especially difficult to manage a position of authority without also using it as a place to slough off one's own shame. Paul was still heavily influenced by the ways and workings of shame; he still very much viewed authority as a sign of sinlessness and favor from God.

Regardless of what Paul says, shame never builds; it always tears down. *There is never a good justification for purposely causing someone to feel deficient, defective, bad, nasty, sinful, or worse.* More often than not the person in authority has no conscious awareness that a shame transfer is taking place—the person perceives that the condemnation and/or punishment is for the other person's ultimate good.

Authoritative arrangements are great for corporations, militaries, and governments, but not for organizing the kingdom, where we are all supposed to be just brothers and sisters. As Jesus stated, anyone who wants to be the "greatest" in the kingdom must be the servant of all (Mark 9:35, NIV)!

I commend Paul's concern for peace and harmony amongst the believers, but I believe he should have used a different approach. "Or else!" tactics not only have a high potential to induce shame in others, but they also often incite anger and rage responses—more shame-defending strategies to unlearn!

### Paul and the Pursuit of Relational Union

I hope that I don't leave the impression that I have anything other

# SHAME

than the deepest respect for the Apostle Paul. While I disagree with many of his teachings pertaining to the relationship and shame, I readily recognize that he was devoted to the cause of spreading the word about Jesus Christ throughout the entire world of his day, regardless of what it cost him personally. I further note that he worked at a trade—tentmaking—and supported himself financially in these efforts: a marked difference from the typical televangelists of our own day, who seem to constantly be asking their viewers to send in money for the support of their work. I don't question for a moment that Paul's motives were pure or that he did his utmost to live the way he believed God wanted him to.

As a matter of fact, I can trace a distinct development in Paul's attitudes and teachings as he continued to mature and develop his own relationship with the person. I see this most remarkably displayed in the epistles he wrote closer to the end of his life, especially in those letters written while he was a prisoner of the Roman Empire—the body of letters often known as the prison epistles. For the purposes of this book, I especially want to highlight Paul's Epistle to the Church in Philippi, or Philippians, as it is more commonly called.

Paul had been a prisoner for at least four years when he wrote this letter. Therefore, it had probably been at least four and a half years since Paul wrote his last letter to the believers in Corinth. Close to the beginning of Philippians, Paul says,

> And I am certain that God, who began a good work within you, will continue his work until it is finally finished on the day when Christ Jesus returns (Philippians 1:6, NLT).

My, my, my! What a change this is from the threatening—"or else"—Paul we last saw in 2 Corinthians! Where Paul once thought that sin had to be addressed through effort and action—and shame wielded by someone in authority—he now realizes that the process takes place solely from within and is brought about by the person.

On the other hand, though Paul obviously now understands that the destruction of shame involves a process initiated and pursued by God, he still hasn't fully realized that the process endpoint doesn't have to wait on Jesus' return.

Nevertheless, this is actually a very different Paul than the one we saw in earlier letters. For one thing, his incarceration has greatly hindered his ability to do the things he once thought he *had to do* in order to find favor with God, and thereby free himself from the effects of shame. Simply, Paul's *busy-ness* for God had actually been a hindrance to the development of relational union. Paul has apparently begun to realize that effort and action are relatively useless towards shame's destruction. All of this has resulted because of the exceptional amount of time that Paul has now been able to devote to the building of the *personal relationship*—though I doubt Paul has consciously realized that it is the building of the *relationship itself* that is the source of these changes in perception.

He says, "We put no confidence in human effort . . ." (Philippians 3:3, NLT). This is a Paul far distanced from the one with the endless litany of need-to's, ought-to's, musts, and shoulds. This is a far different Paul than the person who viewed authority as a place of favor awarded by God. Jail has interrupted his action-based pursuit of belonging in the world, as well as everything else concerning his defense of shame. Indeed, I can personally attest to the salutary effects the forced

## SHAME

inactivity of incarceration can have on one's ability to be still, let go, and focus on the unseen.

> Yes, everything else is worthless when compared with the infinite value of knowing Christ Jesus my Lord. For his sake I have discarded everything else, counting it all as garbage, so that I could gain Christ and become one with him (Philippians 3:8–9, NLT).

Yes! I suppose it could be said that Paul is finally getting rid of his religion. And in fact, there is really nobody less "religious" than somebody who has found their way to union; there was nobody less "religious" than Jesus. Or, as Paul puts it,

> I no longer have any faith in my ability to *do-don't* my way into freedom from shame. I become free of shame through faith in Him (Philippians 3:9, paraphrase).

But then he goes on to say,

> I want to know Christ and experience the mighty power that raised him from the dead. I want to suffer with him, sharing in his death, so that one way or another I will experience the resurrection from the dead! (Philippians 3:10–11, NLT).

Poor Paul! He still believes that if he suffers like Christ, he will not only possibly know Christ better, but he then might also share in a similar resurrection from the dead. Though at least now it is possible he has begun to doubt the possibility of a resurrection from physical death. When Paul says, "So that *one way or another* I will experience the resurrection from the dead," he could be suggesting that Jesus' resurrection was symbolic of the destruction of shame we can experience when we come to union. The point is, Paul's desire for *some type* of resurrection means he has yet to fully experience either. If he was experiencing complete freedom from shame he would no longer see any need for another bodily experience. Paul doesn't yet completely grasp that relational union *is* the resurrection.

> I don't mean to say that I have already achieved these things or that I have already reached perfection. But I press on to possess that perfection . . . (Philippians 3:12, NLT).

This, of course, is a major part of Paul's problem—the idea that perfection can be achieved or possessed, especially through effort and action. Still, there is hope:

> I am still not where I feel I need to be but I am trying as best I can to stay out of the past while simply looking forward to whatever comes next (Philippians 3:13, paraphrase).

Paul is definitely beginning to realize that the power lies in the *now*.

> Let all who are spiritually mature agree on these things. If you disagree on some

# SHAME

point, I believe God will make it plain to you (Philippians 3:15, NLT).

Gosh! Paul has even begun to recognize the ultimate worthlessness and vanity of human religious condemnational *instruction*! Absolutely! Everything *is indeed made clear* from within the relationship! Certainly, as Paul has been sitting in his prison cell, God has apparently been making many, many things clear to this man!

We have now come to the end of our lightning tour of the Bible as it records the history of God's millennia-spanning project to teach the human race about shame. While there is so much more in the Bible than I have even hinted at here, I believe that we have seen enough to get a sense of the grand sweep of biblical history, especially with regard to God, humans, shame, and the necessity of developing relational union with the PERSON in order to have our primary interpersonal need truly satisfied.

And now, as we move to the final section of this book, we will focus on the "so what": we will examine how each and every one of us has lying before us the opportunity of a lifetime—the opportunity of all eternity, in fact—to enter into the healing relationship that will at last completely free us from our most ancient enemy, shame.

# PART 3

## *Finding the Way of Redirection*

# CHAPTER 15

## So... Now What?

By now, we've been on quite a journey. We began by looking at what modern science has taught us about the origins, mechanisms, and effects of shame. We then embarked on a six-thousand-year tour through the pages of the Old and New Testaments, observing God's longstanding, patient, and unrelenting effort to demonstrate to humanity that its deepest interpersonal need cannot be satisfied in the seen—to redirect us toward the unseen, where we can at last find the kind of relationship that will completely satisfy our soul-deep ache for belonging and significance.

And now we come to the most brief and yet most important part of the book. In the pages that follow, you will learn how to begin your own journey toward an amazing sense of interpersonal completion. However, this passage is perhaps different than any trip, excursion, or voyage that you have ever undertaken. The central paradox of this journey is that you can't really "do" anything to begin, continue, or complete it. As I have said repeatedly throughout the book, any sort of action-, obedience-, or earning-based attempt or system toward favor is useless for satisfying the primary interpersonal need. Instead, you must be still and allow the PERSON to make himself available to you. Remember, God has promised that "those who seek shall find, and to those who knock, the door shall be opened" (Matthew 7:7).

Please understand that I know with absolute certainty that anyone can enter into the way of release from shame and its damaging effects. If someone who has been in some of the places I've been can find God—or, more accurately, be found by God—then it seems obvious to me that there's no one on earth beyond the reach of the Father who longs to be one with each of us. To prove my point, let me tell you a little more of my story.

### "Out of Looking Places"

I mentioned in the introduction that I was completely and utterly frustrated in my lifelong search for a place of lasting interpersonal satisfaction. I had repeatedly tried the so-called "straight" world, but it was the world of amphetamines that seemed to most provide me with that which I believed I needed: meaning, worth, purpose, relationship, incredible sex, and money.

The problem, of course, was that *my* world not only hinged upon an illegal substance, but that my position in that world was increasingly being demonized by the culture at large. It was one thing to be both a speed freak and a speed dealer, but another matter entirely to also be a speed cook. In the eyes of law enforcement—and increasingly so with everyone else—there was not much worse. (I would rationalize and justify my actions by telling myself that I wasn't doing anything that hadn't been done for decades by the chemists at Abbot Laboratories and Smith, Kline & French).

So, it was after a series of arrests resulting in the real

# SHAME

possibility that I now might die in prison that I finally became willing to look somewhere else for that which my heart so desperately seemed to need. At that point, having reached what was by any measure a dead end, I realized that I was truly, as I said in the introduction, "out of looking places."

In my despair and hopelessness, I remember uttering what could almost be thought of as a challenge to God: "If there is any such thing as truth, you need to show it to me. If you exist—prove it!" As I have already related, I began reading everything I could get my hands on that had to do with religion—any religion. I also studied sociology, psychology, and philosophy. I wasn't counting anything out. I had to get some kind of grip on whatever it was I was missing, or I was checking out—forever. I wasn't going to slowly die in prison, and die alone.

I've already described what it was like to read the Bible and Kaufman's *Shame: The Power of Caring*, allowing these two texts from opposite ends of the time spectrum to carry on a conversation in my mind. And now, I'd like to tell you about the day when I began to seriously think I had lost what few brain cells I believed I had left. You see, that was the day when everything began to change.

### *"Well, Just Do That"*

One of the benefits of being in and out of rehabs and prisons as many times as I have—not that I'm recommending shooting meth as a life strategy—is that you can acquire a decent variety of coping techniques from the various counselors, treatment professionals, and programs. At one long-term treatment facility I was in at Oklahoma City, the counselors had some of us write letters to God as a part of our treatment. When I was in jail in

## So... Now What?

Hopkinsville, Kentucky, I remembered this technique. Since I'm not much into TV or playing cards, I was desperate to find a lot of things to occupy my time—so I started writing daily letters to God. I figured that at the very least, there might be some kind of psychological benefits in doing such a daily exercise. I also started another counselor-mandated activity of writing a daily gratitude list (believe it or not, even when you're in jail, there are things you can be grateful for). I *knew* there were some psychological benefits in this exercise.

I'd been writing my letters nearly every day for about six months, and my entries pretty much amounted to a sort of glorified journal. I'd "tell God" about what was going on in jail, what I was reading, what I was thinking, and so on.

And then one day, God wrote back.

You may think this sounds crazy, and I can assure you, when it happened, I thought perhaps that I had suddenly lost my mind. It was just a normal day and a normal letter, when out of the blue while in the midst of writing some thoughts there came *another thought* from somewhere totally foreign: this *other* thought being expressed on the page as, "Well, just do that!"

I dropped the pencil as if it had suddenly become red-hot, and half expected it to keep moving and writing. It was then, of course, that I began believing that I was in the midst of some kind of psychological meltdown. I remember sitting there, immobile, for a few minutes, stealing glances around at my fifteen cellmates, but nobody was looking at me strangely. In fact, nobody was paying much attention to me at all. After a while, I decided I was okay.

It wasn't as if I had asked God some profound question and gotten an answer. "Well, just do that" wouldn't be my first pick of the phrases God would use to start altering the course of

# SHAME

someone's life. In fact, as I tell the story, it's kind of embarrassing. And yet, as I sat there in the cell, I knew that some unseen *other person* had somehow reached out to me in an amazing way, and I understood this other person as no other than God.

What I did the following day actually renewed the perception that I might not be well. I began entering into these extensive *make-believe* conversations on paper with God! For some reason I felt compelled to start doing this despite my perception of a deteriorating mind. I would pencil the word "me" on the paper and then starting writing something as usual. However, after reaching some stopping point, I would now write "God" in the margin, and immediately write down whatever came to mind as a response.

Though I kept thinking it was crazy, a daily confirmation that I was probably getting worse, I kept doing it anyway, day after day. It was as though I lost any and all will to resist; this further added to my perception of a worsening mental condition. This obviously caused me a lot of self consciousness, sitting at a table in a room full of inmates, carrying on "conversations with God." After a few weeks I began simply putting a "G" in the margin (if I got caught by someone I could explain away the "G" a lot easier than I could explain away "God").

I began wondering who it was I was actually communicating with. Was this person the Jewish God, Jehovah? Was he Brahma? Was he Allah? Jesus? Was *she* Jesus' mother Mary? (There has never been even the slightest indication of whether this person is male or female.) For whatever reason, this person never identified himself to me in any of these ways. (Today I simply refer to HIM as "Gee." I *know* he likes this *intimate* name I've given HIM. Coincidentally, "Gee" is remarkably gender-neutral.)

## So... Now What?

It was one day around a year and a half after I began these conversations that I heard a mention on the radio of a sixteenth-century—I think—Christian monk who advocated this exact same technique as a tool for not only building a personal relationship, but also for learning to discern his voice from ours! As soon as I realized what I had just heard, I erupted into a nearly violent fit of crying, more like wailing. It felt as if some inner dam had burst. I relaxed and let the wave of emotions take me, stunned by how little embarrassment I felt.

You see, this was the first real confirmation in over a year and a half that I might not be losing my mind, and I felt like screaming, "I'm not nuts, I'm not nuts. I'm not nuts, after all!" However, this would have revealed that my tears were ones of joy and relief, while my cellmates' tears had always been ones of sadness and despair. So I held back from shouting out the words and revealing my joy; it would have been disrespectful—shame inducing—if I had not done so.

As the months went by with these daily conversations, I started receiving this most fantastical picture of understanding. Over the course of the next year and a half I was taken on this most awe-inspiring journey of intellectual discovery. The experience far outstripped the type of excitement I had when I first began learning chemistry, physics, organic chemistry, electronics, digital electronics, microprocessors, calculus, computer programming, refrigeration, Adobe Illustrator, MS Access, MS Excel, and so on . . . Indeed, this journey of revelatory discovery continues to enthrall me these many years later, only now not so euphorically intense.

There was something about this captivating period of intellectual discovery that was way different than anything I had ever experienced before. It's actually pretty hard to describe.

# SHAME

I was as initially shocked by it as you may have been. I must have said to him a hundred times, "This can't be, Gee!" As the *image* developed more and more I began realizing how much it seemed to explain *everything*. Like a black hole, the *picture* continued expanding, capturing and explaining more and more.

I also began to suspect that I was being shown something that he hadn't shown—in toto—to anybody else before, and that scared me. "I ain't the one, Gee!" I remember saying. You see, for along with the revelation of this astounding picture came the clear indications that it wasn't for me alone. I remember going around and around with Gee regarding this; I recall using the argument that I wasn't "qualified to do this." Gee's *immediate* response was that he didn't "want somebody with qualifications." The consensus we finally agreed upon was for me to simply *describe* what I was being shown. I told him I could do *that*. It was in May of 2004 that I made Gee this promise. And now . . . here we are.

**Your Turn?**
If you've stayed with me this far, I can only conclude that you, like I once was, are longing for something different in your life. Perhaps you haven't reached the depths that were required for me to finally turn my search toward the unseen, but you still are longing for an end to the seemingly endless search for the kind of peace that goes all the way to the center of your being. The good news is that such peace really does exist. The even better news is that you can begin to experience it whenever you think you're ready.

I know how similar this sounds to what you hear from most religious pulpits, but it only sounds that way because I don't want you to change a thing in your daily life; I only want you to begin devoting some time to the building of a personal relationship.

I don't want you to start going to church or reading the Bible, if you're not already doing so! I'm not even going to ask that you stop drinking or drugging. I don't even care if you have a daily habit of a fifth of liquor, two bundles of heroin, or a gram of meth; you can even be spending a grand a week on crack!

## *Come One, Come All*

A convict isolated on death row can find her way to relational union . . . a paraplegic can find his way to relational union . . . a deaf and blind person can find her way to relational union. It seems that the best-kept secret on the planet is that we don't have to *do a thing* in order to enter God's kingdom.

For a long time I became furious whenever I thought of this truth; I used to think it was some sort of conspiracy by those running organized religion, a ploy to keep their flocks hungry and desperate for the answers that only *they* could provide. I now realize that *they* just don't know. Well, perhaps some do know, and shame on them if they do know!

When you begin to *know*, you also begin realizing that God's spirit teaches everything and leads you to everything you need to know, including the best way for you to live and to minister to, and help, others. Realize, however, that the ministry indicated by God may or may not include involvement in an organized religion.

You see, once you have begun a personal relationship with God and your primary interpersonal need is somewhat satisfied, you will increasingly be freed from the effects of

# SHAME

shame and can increasingly go anywhere without fear of slights, disrespects, or inattentions; shame's old weapons no longer have as deep of an effect on you. You'll increasingly discover that wherever you are, you *belong*. Suddenly the world begins expanding and the universe increasingly becomes yours—just as God always intended.

I don't believe there can be any real progress toward relational wholeness until you give up trying to *find* it. You have to go unseen. And in order for you to make that necessary daily commitment, you also must have reached a point where the diversionary interests, excitements, enjoyments, and pleasures are no longer working for you in the ways they once did. For me, that required hitting rock-bottom in a Kentucky jail cell facing the *real* possibility of dying alone in prison. I sincerely hope you don't have to go that far. There can't be any concerted effort to the building of a personal relationship without the significant devotion of one's time, at least initially.

*Shedding Shame*
It is this devotion to the building of a relationship that *will* one day result in the proof that he's not only real, but he is also very much alive. As the relationship develops further, you will begin noticing that you are no longer bothered as much by the things that once caused you to feel slighted or disrespected. Your *rights* will no longer seem so important. And not only will you begin gaining acceptance of others, but you will also begin gaining acceptance of yourself. Eventually, you will no longer wish that you had *done* things differently, because you'll come to realize that none of it would have *really* changed a thing. Your drive towards significance, favor, worth, and purpose becomes a mere walk.

## So...Now What?

As the relationship deepens even further, you will begin experiencing the world from an entirely different perspective. Where your relationships once contained the need for a certain degree of reciprocity, you will now be able to more *unconditionally* give and do for others, interpersonal expectations begin to lessen significantly.

The developing relational union may even cause you to have experiences that are startling and even frightening. I remember once looking at my hands and not recognizing them as my own; it was as if I were seeing them for the first time. Nobody, by the way, has described a characteristic of the union phenomenon more succinctly than the Apostle Paul when he wrote, "I, but not I" (see Galatians 2:20).

We eventually move into a realm with him where shame is hardly ever experienced. It will, then, no longer matter to us if we are favored, liked, or even respected. We will no longer be emotionally crippled by how others treat us. Even abuse itself will no longer carry the level of emotional devastation it once had. Fear, distress, and rage will almost completely disappear from experience. We will no longer even fear death; and never again will we question our place in the world. We will then have now moved from death into life. And it is a move that has required nothing from us—no *particular* effort or action—but only the abiding in the PERSON. It is the relationship itself that moves us from death to life—from the experience of shame to its total destruction.

It is in this unity that we recognize that he is in us and we are in him (or if you prefer, she in us and we in her). Though we will never lose our sense of self, neither will he. It is in this kingdom where he then manifests himself through us. It is in this *am-ness* where he then gets to experience his own creation *with us*.

Once we start coming to unity, we begin enjoying eternal life—everlasting life. It begins, ends, and has its meaning in this eternal moment; in this timeless state of being, the concepts of "past" and "future" have lost their meaning. Like God, we only experience the "now." Experiencing this moment with him where *he is* constitutes *the life* and *the kingdom*.

It seems that whenever I drift out of *now* toward some future concern or past regret, I leave him, and almost feel like I'm dying. These "out-of-him" moments are noticeably painful. But oh, how glorious it is when I bring myself back to where time disintegrates and I am in this *place of oneness with him*, and in *eternal life*.

Now, just in case you might be thinking something like, "There's no way God would ever choose to be in relationship with someone like me," or "I don't think I'm spiritual enough to do this," or some other phrase that indicates that you think you lack some sort of qualification or ability for entering union, let me assure you that in one way, you're right: No one is qualified! On the other hand, no one is unqualified. Remember this promise, made through Jesus Christ as he was in union with the Father:

> But to all who believed him and accepted him, he gave the right to become children of God (John 1:12, NLT).

In other words, the only requirements or qualifications are a willingness to begin a personal relationship. Notice, though, that *believing in* and *accepting* him merely gives us the *right* to become sons and daughters. In order for us to actually become his, we have to *get to know him personally*. We come into life through the establishment of a thriving and abiding *bi-*

*directional, interpersonal relationship.*

So, we must essentially allow him to enter into us, abide in him, and stay there! This process is begun and maintained through nothing more than the establishment and maintenance of the primary interpersonal relationship. I'll say it again: the destruction of shame is not contingent on *doing* or *not doing* anything; the destruction of shame is brought about solely through the establishment of an abiding primary interpersonal relationship.

**The Primary Interpersonal Relationship**

*Knowing* somebody—anybody—is not accomplished by reading something written about the person, or by what is said about the person by others. We get to *know* another person by *communicating directly and spending time* with him or her.

I have my own particular conceptualization of all this. I believe that the spirit—the receiver—has been with us since we first gained consciousness. I say this because I believe that as soon as we gained consciousness we also gained the ability to feel shame. I believe that it is at the level of this so-called permanently indwelling spirit that we feel shame.

By contrast, I don't believe animals feel shame—they survive. Thus, there is something uniquely human about the ability to feel shame (remember our example about the dogs in chapter five?). Something, then, about our ability to feel shame is connected to our uniquely human ability to experience relational union with the PERSON.

There are some who see this other as a self—even a higher self, or real self. Still others see the other as a higher mind or divine mind. This is all fine, really, because only a person possesses a mind: the same with a self. I believe this other within us is always facing God and receiving from him. I believe there is some sort of gap, synapse, or block that inhibits or prevents the *perception* of reception. The gap is bridged, the synapse is crossed, and the block is removed, through nothing more difficult—or simple—than the building of a primary relationship. The whole process is fueled and maintained relationally, with relational union being the final destination.

### *Our Opposing Inner Needs: Identification and Differentiation*

This looks like a perfect place to review the psychological concepts of identification and differentiation. The psycho-scientific community describes these two phenomena as the twin peaks—or the two poles—of our natures.

*Identification.* Since the father-son relationship was the primary model or metaphor used by Jesus to describe his relationship with God, let's consider identification in reference to the relationship between a young boy and his father. Kaufman says in *Shame: The Power of Caring*,

> [M]odeling is one vehicle through which such identification takes place. Modeling is observational learning (p. 38).

The son—both consciously and unconsciously—observes his father and emulates his behavior. Modeling is a behavioral trait recognized throughout the animal kingdom. However, we humans also possess the primary interpersonal need, and with the child this need has definitely not yet been satisfied (though with Jesus there are indications in scripture that this process was happening while he was quite young). So along with the instinctual need of learning how to survive, there is another motivation manifesting itself as the need of identification. The child's desires, whether he can articulate them or not, are to both learn how to survive as well as to no longer feel the effects of the non-satisfaction of this most primary interpersonal need. I believe it is one thing to observe so as to learn how to survive, but another matter entirely to seek to identify as a mechanism for completely ending that sometimes not-so-subtle feeling of aloneness and separateness.

While many have argued that it is the need to identify that has insured our ability to survive as a species, I think this can only be said true to a certain point. This rationale disintegrates completely in light of shame, for with the onset of shame, our ability to survive actually starts to become hindered. Look at what happened to the Israelites, as well as nearly every other great nation or civilization that began to deteriorate soon after reaching material success. Kaufman says,

> It is the awareness of separateness which in part, necessitates a striving to re-identify, to become one with. Phenomenologically, identification involves a merging with another, if only for a brief moment, of one's separate self (p. 38).

The reason we never outgrow the need to identify is because we can never find someone with whom this need is truly satisfied. Identification is the need that fuels our desire to find a relationship. We can feel absolutely safe and totally secure but still not lose the need to identify. In other words, it

# SHAME

is the son's seeking to identify with his father, so as to lose that subtle sense of separateness, which lays the groundwork for the generation of shame.

Remember: "We identify . . . to feel at-oneness or belonging with . . ." (p. 38). Thus, as we grow older, the need to feel at one with someone seems to change. However, the need itself doesn't change, but the places we next look toward in order to lose that sense of separateness do continue to change. Unlike the dogs in chapter five, we have begun the lifelong process of looking for a like kind with whom we can truly unite.

When we first began encountering the opposite sex we thought that here, at last, was what we'd been looking for. Up until that point, our families and our best friends couldn't quite get us where we needed to go. And when our girlfriends or boyfriends also soon came up short, we naturally assumed the problem was in our selection. We continued the endless search, always eventually feeling the need for something more, different, or deeper.

And throughout all this searching for someone to make us feel complete, we experience shame: sometimes lightly, sometimes severely. We have stepped onto the slippery slope of trying to earn favor as a mechanism to curb shame's onslaught—the *doing* and *giving* in order to get. We begin developing defenses and our hearts begin to harden. Some explained it as "losing our naiveté." And indeed, where once we rushed blindly into relationships, we now become much more cautious and calculating.

As a defense or compensatory mechanism, we often become increasingly involved in interests, excitements, enjoyments, and pleasures. We build impregnable bastions of comfortable numbness in order to prevent ourselves from ever getting hurt—shamed—ever again.

Some of us completely opt out of the pursuit of a primary relationship for the less risky art of busy-ness; we lose ourselves in our careers or our "good works." Whatever works at minimizing the possibility of shame ever occurring again and covering the seemingly growing hole within is all that matters.

And some of us have given up the interpersonal search entirely and have sought relational union with some object, experience, or substance. But until and unless we find a relationship with a person, our identification need will ultimately go unsatisfied.

*Differentiation.* The second peak, or pole, of our natures is the need to differentiate. Where identification is the need to "unite with" and lose our sense of separateness and loneliness, the need to differentiate is a need to "separate from" and manifest our own individual selves. As Kaufman reminds us, "Every individual needs to differentiate his own unique self . . ." (p. 61).

As you can probably already guess, our need to identify—to merge—one minute, while in the next wanting to separate, can cause a lot of confusion and anxiety for the self. This can also result in a lot of confusion and anxiety for the other with whom we seek to satisfy the identification need. The problem with these two poles within two different human selves is that they rarely will both want to identify or differentiate at the same time. I believe we men have driven our women half crazy with our ever-changing identification and differentiation needs (of course, we men could probably say the same with our women's ever-changing identifications and differentiations, but maybe not so much).

Though psychology recognizes the problem as trying

to identify and differentiate at the same time, I see it more as trying to do both, toward and from the same direction. We can become anxious and fearful, even angry, when trying to decide when it's appropriate to be with someone or to be by ourselves. We can feel shame for experiencing the need to separate while in "merge mode," or for experiencing the need to merge while in our "self manifestation mode." Meanwhile, the other person with whom we are in an external relationship with is going through the same confusing changes. Are you starting to see why trying to get our primary interpersonal need met by other humans is a recipe for failure?

As we have seen over and over throughout the book, it is our looking externally—to the seen—to "identify" that forms the basis for all shame creation. Differentiation does not in itself create the necessary backdrop for shame to occur unless it occurs from within the relationship that one is seeking completion from. In other words, the bite of the shame we feel from being condemned or criticized is significantly worse when it emanates from or occurs with someone with whom we externally identify. That's why to be cursed out by a special friend or family member is usually much more traumatic than when we are cursed out by a stranger. Remember the old song, "You Always Hurt the One You Love"? It's true, and the expectations we create because of the unsatisfied primary interpersonal need are the reason!

Thus, though science locates a cause of shame in trying to identify and differentiate at the same time, I see shame as arising as the result of trying to identify and differentiate toward and from the seen. Basically, when we seek to satisfy both needs externally, we will continue to suffer from shame. But when we seek to satisfy the identification need with the PERSON within us—and come to complete unity—we can then identify and differentiate at the same time without ever again experiencing shame.

A few comparisons may be of some help in seeing this more clearly. First, think of the self as the kind of prism that receives sunlight on one face, while from its other face it emits an incredible display of rainbow colors. The prism receives and emits from and towards different directions. The prism doesn't fulfill its created purpose by receiving and emitting only toward the direction of reception or only toward the direction of emission. We humans can currently be said to be rotating our receiving and emitting surfaces back and forth and around and around and around. *We are trying to fulfill our designed purpose by sending and receiving toward and from each other!* But we can't generate the type of light that we need to fulfill that purpose. The prism only works when it is not only receiving the light which it was designed to receive that is *always* available, but also when it at the same time remains at rest and "just is." In other words, the prism receives and sends effortlessly. Such effortless sending and receiving is a metaphor of relational union. Remember: Jesus spoke of his yoke as being easy and light.

Another analogy of the developing relational union can be found in learning to drive a car. Remember when you started learning to drive (especially if, like me, you're old enough to remember learning to operate a clutch). Each motion was something you had to think about carefully and control with your conscious mind: check the mirror, press the accelerator, check the mirror again, operate the turn signal, change lanes, press the brake, turn the steering wheel, check the mirror again . . . And then, after you'd been driving for a few weeks or a few months, you realized that you were doing many of these things without consciously thinking about them. You just—drove!

Similarly, the beginnings of the relationship are fully conscious, unseen, but still largely external. Because it is initially only fully conscious (not yet an abiding union), the relationship still presents some of the same symptoms of being singularly directional, external. But as the relationship grows, or as we become more familiar with "driving the car," it soon becomes more unconscious: abiding. We come to the realization that he's in us! Eventually, just as we are able to put our attention elsewhere while we drive, the relationship becomes a conscious/unconscious type of thing where we can receive and emit simultaneously (even while driving home as we Bluetooth a conversation on our cell phone!).

One more example: sometimes we hear athletes talk about being "in the zone." In other words, they are fully engaged in the moment: seeing, judging direction and velocity, making instantaneous adjustments to changing circumstances—all without being conscious of what they are doing. They simply "are."

Buddhism uses the term "mindfulness" to describe this bidirectional, conscious-unconscious phenomenon that happens "in the moment." For it is in a state of mindfulness in the moment that we are most open to the reception of the light. What I believe Buddhism doesn't fully realize is that this light—real self or divine mind—belongs to a person who wants a personal relationship. This doesn't mean that the relationship is never conscious, for the quality of mindfulness is vitally dependent on one's ability to stay open to where the mind is. Buddhism tries to keep the light entering the room by continuously cleaning the window through conscious practice while *true* Christianity does much the same thing through the establishment of a conscious relationship; the end result for both is the recognition that the window was never

## So... Now What?

there in the first place (i.e., that he has always been there within us). The problem with Buddhism is that it takes practice day after day after day to keep reminding us that the window isn't there. *I hope someday I'll hear from some true Buddhists and Hindus whether or not the states of Nirvana and moksha, respectively, are also completely destructive to the feel of shame.*

As suggested earlier, any professional athlete knows that the more he or she trains and practices the more the movements becomes automatic, unconscious. Similarly, the more the relationship is thriving, alive, and fully conscious—the more we "drive the car"—the greater will be our ability to always be always mindful of *him*. It is in mindfulness of him that he is then manifested in a glorious display of rainbow color. It is then in this mindfulness of him that the feel of all forms of shame is totally destroyed. In the final chapter, we'll explore some ways that this mindfulness can be fully appreciated, and some conditions that we can put in place to help us acquire the ability to cease doing/not-doing and simply *be*.

# CHAPTER 16

## The End of the Journey... and the Beginning

By now, I have just about finished telling you everything I've seen on my strange, other-worldly tour. I've basically described the "machine" that my extraterrestrial friend showed me, as described at the end of chapter five. In this final chapter, I hope to leave you with a bit more description of the friendship that alone can deliver you from the endless, spiraling, shame-filled, failed attempts to satisfy the primary interpersonal need. And then, it will be up to you to decide if this is the end of something, the beginning of something else . . . or both.

**What's the Point?**
Right now, it might be worthwhile to pose the question, "Does all this really matter? Can't I just keep on living my life the way I have?"

The answer is, of course you can. If your life is going pretty much the way you want and your days are full of a sense of accomplishment, fulfillment, and hope for the future, and if you have not yet begun to sense that there is something more, something vital that you're missing, then you may not have even

## The End of the Journey... and the Beginning

the slightest concern for anything I've said. Besides, if you are truly in a state of resting bliss, then why are you wasting your time reading this book?

However, maybe you have begun to suspect that, given how hard you have *worked* all this time—whether for the past few years or for decades—you should have by now acquired at least a minimal degree of resting contentment . . . but that sense of longed-for inner peace still eludes you. You may even have begun to feel that there is something "wrong" with you. You may have begun to question your ability to make the kind of changes that are needed to "achieve" the lasting contentment that you are so desperately searching for. Or, you may have even begun to suspect that *maybe it just isn't available*, or maybe that *this is all there is*; that no amount of respect—or being cared for, cared about, or loved —is really making all that much difference on the inside.

There were many, many times, as I was working on this book, when I too had thoughts similar to those expressed by Paul in Romans 3:1, when he starts wondering what value there was in "*doing*" all that he was *doing*." Yeah, I obviously knew I was writing a book . . . I knew it would be quite some time before I ever reaped any possible material or interpersonal rewards for my efforts. But even this intellectual reasoning didn't do much to stifle the occasional bursting forth of a desire for some kind of recognition from others right now! It seemed that *the harder I worked* the *more* I needed some kind of interpersonal reward for doing what I was doing. I can't tell you just how many times I finally sought someone out in order to tell them what I was doing! It seemed to fix me for a moment, but the need would always return . . . and on and on this went. It wasn't like I still needed some external confirmation for the significance or importance

# SHAME

of work, for I had received a more than adequate validation of the book months earlier from Dr. Albert Randall. But even this incredible praising seemed to have little effect on permanently eradicating an interpersonal need that continued to plague me. I found myself getting sick of myself for how interpersonally *neeeedddyy* I continually found myself. I couldn't figure out why I had to repeatedly tell someone about the book I was writing! This *sissyness* continued to torment me month after month after month . . . and then one day, finally, the revelation came. I suddenly realized that the interpersonal need that I sought to satisfy through selling meth was the same need that I was currently feeling as I wrote the book. I also realized that it had been months since I had really spent any quality conscious time with him! As soon as I returned to daily times with Gee, I noticed a nearly immediate and profound decrease in my neediness to tell others about the book. I then made the connection—that because nobody ever responded to me in a way that seemed to completely satisfy me—that it had *always* been my *doing to interpersonally get* that laid the groundwork for my ultimately feeling deficient, defective, or worse. And the harder I worked, the more this caused me to interpersonally expect! It had taken me years into this project to recognize just how deeply interpersonal expectations were tied to my efforts and actions.

Though I began this book exactly seven years ago, it has been these last three and a half years that have been the worst. These past few years have been a lot like having an addiction. In many ways it has actually been worse than an addiction; at least with an addiction you can periodically "forget." This hasn't been the case with the book; *the book is always there. I need to now detox.* I want this done . . . I'm tired . . . I *need* this over. The other day I would have shot it if it had been

## The End of the Journey... and the Beginning

a living thing and I had had a gun. But my point is that because of the recently restored daily time with him, I am now no longer being so deeply tormented by any interpersonal neediness concerning my efforts with the book. I want this book done for physical reasons, not interpersonal ones. I also recently discovered that as I leaned more and more into the PERSON each day I not only gained a lot of inner peace, but it seemed that the daily process itself—staying more in the moment—was now interpersonally providing me with all that I once hoped the end would provide. The process *in him* has become a kind of end, in and of itself. There is something *in the moment* that seems to give me everything I don't otherwise have.

    This peaceful sense of completion—of "enoughness"—has continued to permeate more and more of my life. Though I still obviously have to do things in order to survive—pay bills, keep a roof over my head, buy groceries—I am now seeing the depth of what you could actually say are *selfish* doings. Consequently, I am now being able to do things without so much concern with doing things to favorably affect the way I am responded to by others. I can now *do* without creating interpersonal expectations. I am now, finally, living a life that is much closer to the one God had always meant for me to live, regardless of whatever it is that I am doing.

    What I have learned, and what I have written in this book to help you learn, is that it is in this eternal moment where he is, that *we are*, that all our particular efforts and actions are actually useless toward the satisfaction of this utmost interpersonal need. It is then *here*, in this moment, that we can now live a life of astounding spontaneity, without the hopeful or fretful concerns about getting that "something" that we don't already have. We will no longer need to seek the *favor* of *anybody*. And we'll no longer need to run the slippery slope of feeling the need to give or do for others in order to get something in return—even as much as a "Thank You"!

You also need to understand another reason this is all pretty astounding to me: for most of my life, there was nothing I hated more than a writing assignment. I realize now, however, that most of this hate was actually fear for how my writing—indeed, all my efforts in life—would be perceived by others. I no longer have any such deep concerns. Once again, I simply *don't give a damn*—meaning that I no longer have hardly any interpersonal fears of what others think of me. And, when I do feel fear, I am now recognizing much more readily that it is the kind of interpersonal fear that stems from my efforts toward significance and belonging. I am so clearly seeing that one day—maybe soon!—I'll never again have an interaction with someone that causes me to feel less than, deficient, defective, or worse. Besides, I *know* this machine is going to work for you, *just as it worked for me.*

**Life with Wings**
As your own relationship develops, you may feel as if you have started growing wings—indeed, but you may have not even realized your wings have developed enough so you can now fly! So, for a time, you continue walking.

This principle applies to many of the habits we develop in response to shame. In response to shame, we "sin"; we start reaching for things as a means of coping with our bouts of loneliness and the responses of fear, distress, and rage we experience as we set about trying to no longer feel alone and separate. There is this incredible rearrangement, not only of

## The End of the Journey... and the Beginning

self-expectations but also of the expectations we hold towards others. Actually, it is more than a rearrangement; it is an outright destruction of the interpersonal expectations that caused us to either condemn our own behaviors or the behaviors of others. For once we are sufficiently in relational union—when we are no longer feeling so incomplete, and shame is no longer being as intensely generated—we will then have an ability to change our habits without realizing that we can. We will also be much more accepting of things about ourselves that we previously thought were barriers to the achievement of interpersonal completion. We find we love ourselves just the way we are. And we also realize that even if we had the ability to stop "sinning" that it would never have taken us to a place of interpersonal completion. We will realize, without ever consciously having willed it or sought it by any effort- or merit-based system, that we have acquired the ability to fly!

### Daily Life

Now, I don't want to give anyone the impression that I'm some kind of guru who is so deep into spiritual bliss that I never experience any kind of discomfort. Yes, I still suffer from occasional self-shaming experiences—the other day I momentarily tyrannized myself for forgetting to bring my five year old cactus in the house before the evening cool inflicted the plant with frostbite—but nowhere nearly as often or as deeply spiraling as before. I am no longer nearly as critical or condemnatory toward myself, and I am no longer nearly as critical or as condemnatory of others who hold perceptions that are vastly different than mine. I am also no longer nearly as affected by the sloughed-off shame of others.

# SHAME

I've been in this Relationship long enough that I can now clearly see where it's leading: a total eradication of shame! Unlike Paul, I have realized that I don't have to look to an afterlife before I no longer have to be subjected to the shame sendings of shame-filled, *sinful* others. And, when I do occasionally cause myself to feel deficient, defective, *sinful*, or worse, I am seeing ever more quickly and clearly how it has all resulted from the expectations—those musts, need-to's, ought's, and shoulds—that I have either created for myself, or have accepted from someone else. I now see most clearly how it all stemmed from my efforts to obtain the favorable attention of others, so I would feel that I belonged. These understandings, only made possible by the Relationship itself, have significantly reduced the intensity of shame as it happens—both the shame that occurs for some perceived cause and the shame that occurs when I feel disrespected: the shame that occurs for no deserved cause.

I have realized ever more clearly that it is when I seek to satisfy my primary interpersonal need through people that I begin creating unattainable expectations for others and for myself. I now see that it was my seeking of favorable attention from others that then created the performance expectations which I created for myself that I couldn't help but to ultimately violate…madness, madness, madness!

Little did I know—for over forty years—that nothing anybody did, and nothing I myself did, would ever cause me to feel interpersonally complete. Simply, I had created a perpetual shame-generating machine without ever realizing it. There was hardly a day where one of my personal/interpersonal expectations wasn't violated and caused me to feel "some kind of way." However, as the Relationship began developing, some

## The End of the Journey... and the Beginning

totally unsuspected things started to occur without my even trying. I first noticed a rising level of acceptance toward myself in my current situation, and I no longer had any deep regrets for my past.

I first mistook this new attitude as just not giving a damn anymore; in some ways, it felt as if I had given up caring about anything. But I then realized that this was definitely not the case. Now that the primary interpersonal need was finally being satisfied I no longer felt as pressured to act in certain kinds of ways so that others would give me their favorable attention. What was truly remarkable was how it no longer really mattered how anybody responded to me.

Oddly, there was a time, early on, when I was actually feeling guilty for this growing level of personal and interpersonal acceptance—for my "don't give-a-damn-ness." Eventually I did come to realize that I still deeply cared about myself and others, but it was now a kind of caring that I had never really experienced before. I saw that I was growing toward an unconditional acceptance of not only my past, but also toward my present. I now understood *the problem* in such a way that explained nearly everything that I had ever done. This understanding also explained many of the actions of others. I began having an especially deep compassion for the human predicament.

At the same time, I was also discovering an inner peace that was exceptionally free of any anger, fear, and worry. Regrets and resentments virtually disappeared. However, one of the most remarkable things I noticed was this: I had lived my life as a perfectionist of the worst kind and I was suddenly finding that however I was doing was *good enough*. However others were doing was good enough as well.

Now mind you, despite all this, there hasn't been even

the slightest decrease in my physical sufferings. I still get the occasional backache and headache. I got a blister on my hand one day from shoveling dirt, and three years ago I caught the flu. And I have no expectations that these sorts of sufferings will ever stop. But with respect to shame and its many heinous horsemen, well, I'm leaving them farther and farther behind. I am so looking forward to wherever this eternal moment takes me. In fact, my eager anticipation reminds me of some of Paul's words:

> We, too, wait with eager hope for the day when God will give us our full rights as his adopted children, including the new bodies he has promised us (Romans 8:23, NLT).

As I said before, I don't necessarily accept Paul's vision of any coming bodily resurrection, but I absolutely believe we will have new minds—mine is getting a complete overhaul, day by day! Besides, aren't we all really God's children already? The idea that we have to become "special" is just another of the many paths that we once believed would lead us to favor in world, or favor from God. We've got to trash these favor-achieving concepts from our minds and vocabularies. But this, too, will come about effortlessly as we come to unity.

I have also learned that whenever I look towards tomorrow, it often concerns a desire to escape the way I feel at this moment. This in itself often induces shame. It is only in the now where he is, devoid of these sorts of time-induced shaming experiences, where past regrets and future concerns can melt away in the brilliant light of the eternal now.

# The End of the Journey... and the Beginning

**Being Chosen**

Throughout the book, we have met various individuals and groups of people who were, in some sense, chosen. In the beginning, Adam and Eve were chosen as the beginning point of God's long redirection strategy for the human race. Later, the Israelites were chosen to embody, as a nation, the inevitable result of efforts to earn our way out of shame. Finally, Jesus Christ, the anointed one, was chosen to display union with the PERSON in living form, for humanity to see.

But we have also learned that since we have all had experiences with guilt, embarrassment, humiliation, shame, condemnation, and resentment, it means that we have *all* been chosen. I was chosen when I was born and have lived in a state of chosen-ness my entire life. But if you were an external observer watching my life as it unfolded, you would more than likely say I was cursed. You see, God doesn't define "chosen" as man defines it. And he surely doesn't define chosenness for relationship as man would probably define it.

It seems that I was born with an insatiable thirst of some kind. This thirst was characterized by a higher degree of restlessness and discontentment that relentlessly drove me to search for ultimate satisfaction and completion. I believe this more intensely manifested thirst has made me extra sensitive to shame. This heightened sensitivity then caused me to be more reactive to shame's onslaught, to react to shame much more boldly. I would do almost anything to no longer feel the effects of the unmet primary interpersonal need. As I've related above, I left nothing out of the quest, hoping that each new situation might interpersonally complete me at last. The consequentially heightened affect of shame would then cause me to be more fervid toward distractions. But nothing and nobody I could

# SHAME

see could *keep* me satisfied. Each time, I soon became bored and then wanted more or something different. I climbed into a squirrel cage of ever-changing people, excitements, interests, enjoyments, and pleasures, and eventually I couldn't find my way out.

I now believe that this heightened restlessness and discontentment is in fact typical of chosenness for relationship. Even though this extra sensitivity to shame will most vividly result in the development of addictions, I believe that the heightened, unquenchable thirst is in fact an indication of God calling us for relationship. I believe it is these extra-restless searchers to whom Jesus was referring in his Sermon on the Mount—the ones who *hunger and thirst after righteousness*—who suffer the most from chosenness for relationship. In other words, people chosen for relationship have an exceptionally high degree of dissatisfaction with the way things are; the *blessed* have a heightened sensitivity to shame due to a heightened thirst. I feel really *blessed* that I finally ran out of looking places before dying. And by sharing with you the insights I've been granted, I hope that I can afford you the opportunity to learn, as I did, that only when you turn from the seen can you begin to arrive at the end of your long, weary journey.

### Not There Yet, but On the Way

In Philippians 3, Paul said, "Not that I have already obtained all this, or have already arrived at my goal, but . . . I press on toward the goal to win the prize for which God has called me heavenward in Christ Jesus." Like Paul, I am not yet where I know this relationship is taking me, but I do know *where* it is taking me. Unlike Paul, I more quickly realized that *where* it is

## The End of the Journey... and the Beginning

taking me is independent of what I do.

I believe that I have been blessed with these realizations largely because of the work of Tomkins when he recognized that embarrassment, shyness, guilt, and shame were all still just shame under different guises. This of course led to my own understanding that the consistent occurrence of shame in my own life has resulted because of the heightened interpersonal expectations I've created for both myself and others, all of this being fueled by a heightened manifestation of the primary interpersonal need.

More pieces came together when in my developing relationship I noticed a remarkable increase in both my self-acceptance and my unconditional acceptance of others. As I said, I also noticed a decrease in my fear, distress, and worry. It was then that I came to realize the profound depth of my social fears. Through the continuing development of my relationship, the remaining pieces fell quickly into place. I began reading the Bible from a totally different perspective.

**Getting Started**

All it takes is a mustard seed of faith. You begin by acting as if he's there—then continue in the belief that he is. At first, you may feel as I did in that jail cell in Kentucky: you may think you're acting like someone who is delusional. It will all feel like foolishness. At first it may seem one-sided, but sooner or later, I promise, he will respond in a way that proves he's there. When he does respond, it will be in a "voice" that is distinctly not your own. And it'll be in the "kind of voice" that we saw exemplified in Jesus Christ. At that point, you'll be well on your way to developing relationship, and in the eternal now of relational

# SHAME

union, shame will begin to retreat from your life.

All it takes is a little bit of hope that he just might be there, waiting to answer your hesitant call. If you have even that much faith, act on it. Of course, it is probably helpful to know something about him—such as seeing how he was in the relational union with Jesus—so that when we yell through the doorway, "Is anybody home?" we'll recognize his voice more quickly when he does respond.

But all that you really have to know now is that shame is the way of interpersonal redirection and that the depth of the shame that we experience is inversely proportional to the depth of our personal relationship with God.

Remember: our lives were not given as some kind of endurance test, so that if we learn to patiently suffer—as Jesus suffered—we would be awarded a more glorious life in the hereafter. Instead, when Jesus said he was going to prepare us a place in his father's house, he was referring to the place where we would find him: living in the eternal now of relational union.

### *A One-Year Plan towards Union*

I extensively pondered whether or not to include some kind of *plan* in this book. For one thing, I didn't want this to suddenly become just another of the seemingly infinite number of "self-help" and "how to" books printed in the last few decades, religious or otherwise. Basically, all how-to and self-help plans are ultimately worthless for providing satisfaction of the primary interpersonal need, because anything that depends on effort and action has no real direct affect on our finding our way unto relational union.

## The End of the Journey ... and the Beginning

For example: have you ever wondered why there are so many Christian denominations? The problem with each denomination, as well as the many different plans of action advocated by those at the pulpit, is their advocating the need for a certain course of action, often comprised of the necessity of holding certain beliefs. One believes that you've got to do *this* to "be saved," while another believes that you've got to do *that*.

However, Jesus never asked or required anybody to first "do this" or "believe that" before he healed them. He never said they had to believe he was the Son of God before he healed them! All, however, did believe he was the "sent one." *Though there were a couple of occasions where even that wasn't required, or possible.* So, it is not essential that we believe Jesus was the *Son of God*, even today! All that we *now* need to believe is that he came to show us the way out of shame.

So, there is no need to follow some preacher's do/don't, action/belief system. In fact, most such systems of belief and action can actually be a hindrance to our ability to find our way to relational union. The primary focus should always be on the personal relationship with the PERSON.

Also, the finding of our way to union is not a process that necessarily requires a lifetime. Whenever I hear or see preachers whom I immediately recognize as being in union, they occasionally mention how long ago it was when they first "got saved": twenty, thirty, even forty years! The idea that it has taken someone like Charles Stanley fifty-plus years to be where he is can be extremely intimidating for someone who is just beginning the journey toward relational union.

But there is nothing further from the truth than the assumption that it takes decades to find such a place of interpersonal completion. As I now look back over those first few years, I am astounded at just how quickly and deeply everything changed. There was a paradigm shift in my perceptions the likes of which I didn't know was even possible.

So, after giving it some careful thought, I put together a plan that I really believe can be used as a way to get launched and headed in the right direction—maybe even more quickly than I was able to go. The thing you need to keep in mind, however, is the same thing I've been saying throughout this book: Neither d*oing* nor *not-doing*—even this plan!—will get you to relational union. What this plan does is help you cultivate the ability to simply be—to arrive at the place where the PERSON's voice can be heard, and where the realization of relational union can begin. So, let's get started . . .

**Written Conversations**

If you guessed that the plan would involve letters to Gee . . . well, you guessed correctly. First, I believe an hour of writing is as much as ten times more effective toward building a personal relationship than an hour of prayer—particularly if you're writing *conversations*. Unlike traditional prayer, writing includes more of the body—more of the entire self. And the conversations more closely mimic relational union than prayer. In fact, I believe that written conversations are like adding three feet of leverage and WD-40 to the loosening of an old and rusted nut! I have no doubt whatsoever that if Jesus had had the paper, pencils, and desks we have today, he too would have been having these written conversations with his Father.

For the first three months I'd suggest that you simply write personal letters. I'd recommend that you spend at least thirty minutes each day writing him, *or her*. I would also suggest

## The End of the Journey... and the Beginning

that you address the letters in whatever manner you feel most comfortable: Holy Father, Great Spirit, God, Jehovah, Allah, Brahma . . . and so on. "Jesus" is better, but not absolutely necessary. It would probably be best to break your daily writing session in half, say once in the morning and once in the evening. And no, don't use a computer and keyboard; use a pen and paper—involve the body as much as possible. And then on a day when you're off work, do at least a one-hour letter.

Don't ask for anything! I repeat . . . don't ever ask for anything! This is not to be a written prayer; this is all about the establishment of a personal relationship, an intimate, individual bond with the PERSON. You would never talk to someone you just met and wanted to get to know by asking him to provide a girlfriend, a spouse, a certain career, freedom, or anything else! Besides, *material* prayers don't work anyway. I asked for a couple things at the beginning and quickly realized that it created a lot of confusion, emotional pain, and turmoil. It's not that things don't change and happen, but it all occurs as a consequence of the developing primary personal relationship. Consequently, I haven't asked Gee for anything in years. The only way God works on a personal level—on a micro level—is in the destruction of shame. The only goal of these first few months of writing is the gaining of a sense that he is really there and somehow, really listening.

During the second three months, writing times should be increased 150 percent—after all, there will now be another person's response! Daily devotion time should total forty to fifty minutes, and around an hour and a half on your day off work. I also suggest that you decide on a more personable name for him, or her. If you are already using the name Jesus, continue using the name Jesus. If you are using Mary, continue using

# SHAME

Mary. But if you are using God, Allah, Jehovah, Brahma, Holy Father, Father, Lord, and so on, give him your own personal name: Gee, Betty, Harry, or whatever. Betty is a perfect name for insuring that this relationship is kept both casual and personal. Remember that last night when Jesus made the point to the apostles that he now considered them *friends*? *It is critically important that this developing relationship be as casual and intimate as possible!*

Simply alternate "me" (you, the person holding the pen) with the personal name in the left margin. Try not to think too much when writing his response. The goal here is to try and get yourself out of the way of his or her response. As soon as you write the other's name in the margin, write a response. I'll say it once more: *be quick* when writing his responses.

**Journaling**

Months seven through nine will be the most time-consuming, because along with what you are already doing I want you to start keeping a daily journal. Spend ten to fifteen minutes each day writing to your "self." I also want you to spend about ten or fifteen minutes each day writing a personal letter to someone you know: your husband, your wife, a parent, or a friend. This can be an ongoing letter, and it can also be a letter that you never actually send. The point of all this is to learn where it is within our minds that he is—his frequency, so to speak—so that it will be more readily accessed as you begin to be weaned from these daily *written* conversations. You'll begin noticing a distinct compartmentalization within the mind when you are writing these three different kinds of letters.

You should be spending about ten hours a week with

these exercises. I know how hard it may be to find the time for such devotion, but it's only for three months. You may decide that you need to discontinue other religious observances in order to make time. If you don't have any religious observances you can give up, then you'll still have to find a way to make time. Oh, by the way, if you are presently doing time—in prison or jail—and on a twenty-three-hour lock down, I want all these times tripled! In other words, you should be spending close to thirty hours each week doing these exercises.

### *Taking off the Training Wheels*

During the final quarter you'll begin transitioning away from writing letters. You can stop the personal letters—to your wife friend or mother—altogether. Beginning at month ten you'll start doing only one journal entry each week. You can also discontinue the *daily* written conversations, but not the big one on your day off. The goal this quarter is to start transitioning away from the pencil and paper. Think of this as *removing the training wheels*. If you used to write "Good morning, Gee!" now start only saying it when you wake up—do the same thing in the evening when you're in bed. The goal here is to have a number of these conscious recognitions of the PERSON's presence every day. I know how ridiculous it may feel, but go ahead and start talking—out loud—to him during the day. You'll begin noticing that these conscious recognitions of him are at a place within the consciousness that is different than your normal thinking.

An exercise you might try in order to see this more clearly is to close your eyes and think of your wife, husband, or close friend. Then think of your own plan for your day: things you've got to do, or things you want to do that day. And

# SHAME

then when you think of him—kind of like saying "hello"—you'll actually feel and sense his presence. You may suddenly realize that he's been there all along, but you just didn't realize it. You'll also realize that he is always with you, and in you.

My hopes are that by the end of a year you'll have established an abiding conscious/unconscious awareness of him. It will be this experience of his "there-ness" that is completely destructive of that sense of aloneness and separateness; you'll feel interpersonally complete and whole.

It will also be from there that he begins living his life through you. He'll begin guiding you to where he wants to go and toward what he wants you to do. Realize that it all will happen from the moment—the eternal now. Remove all of the preconceptions of what you think he wants you to do, and definitely don't let anybody else decide what you should do. (For example, if I had listened to them, this book would have never been written.) If you are married and have kids, his ministry for you—his plan for you to help others—might go no further than your immediate, day-to-day relationship with others in your family.

After a year I believe it would be good practice to continue writing at least one lengthy conversation each week. It would also be good to continue doing at least one journal entry each week. As I am writing these final words, I have returned to my daily written conversations. I've been a little surprised at how good it feels to be back to doing these every day. It is probably good to return to your own daily written conversations from time to time.

## The End of the Journey... and the Beginning

**"The Kingdom of God Is within You"**
And now, visualize with me for a moment what the world would be like—right now!—if somehow every single human on the planet could be released from the harmful effects of shame. As John Lennon once sang, "Imagine . . ."

In a world without shame, when all of humanity is living in relational union, there would no longer be any need to seek power. In fact, people would more willing to share with each other whatever was needed to sustain life and health, since no one would feel the need to impress anyone by hoarding or controlling resources.

In a world without shame, while there might still be sickness because of the inevitable frailty of the biological body, there would always be those willing and able to provide comfort and nurture, since we would all be more accepting of each other without placing conditions on what we do or don't do for others.

In a world without shame, crime and war would fade like a bad dream as the relationship brings humankind into a "natural" compliance with moral and ethical laws: we would no longer require the imperatives that are presently necessary because of our selfish and even murderous behaviors in response to shame. When shame is totally eradicated from the planet, there will no longer be a need for "Thou shall not kill."

In a world without shame, each human being would become wondrously and blessedly free to develop deep spiritual awareness, free of hindrance from the expectations of others or those of the restless, unsatisfied former self. We would behave toward each other with unfailing graciousness, patience, and acceptance, because we would no longer be looking to each other to take care of the empty spaces in our souls.

Instead, the PERSON would be each man and woman's

# SHAME

most intimate, most accepting, most constant friend—as well as parent. In God we would each find an unlimited supply of that which we need most: oneness. We would finally realize the granting of the prayer that Jesus Christ prayed for us so many centuries ago: "That they each become one, as you and I are one."

It is an amazing, wonderful vision, isn't it? And would you like to know the best part? It is this: you are free to begin living it—right now. All you must do is enter the way of redirection.

# INDEX

**A**

Aaron, 124
Abishai, 162–165
Absalom, 162–167
abuse, 9, 72–75, 173–174
acceptance of others, 246–251, 303
action cause, 99–100, 181
action to eliminate shame, 95, 97, 99–100, 131–132, 184–185, 201
*Acts of the Apostles,* 225–226
Adam, 1–5, 94–103, 177, 201–202, 301
adaptation, 51–52
addiction, 9, 74–75, 193–194
adolescence, 24
affect blends, 42, 58–59, 67
affect-shame binds, 41–42, 177, 178
affect theory, 8–9, 37–38
Ai, 121
alcohol abuse, 74–75
anger, 19–20, 51, 58, 123–124, 171–172
Asa, 187
atonement, 233–235, 253–254
authority figures, 245, 262–265
author's experience, 273–278, 293–296, 297–303
autonomous shame, 12, 33, 41–49, 64, 111, 185–187, 196

**B**

Bathsheba, 154
"because... then" model, 103, 118, 184–185, 189–190, 194, 201
"being saved," 242–243, 305

belief in God, 227–232, 243, 259, 303–304
belief systems, 305
Benaiah, 170
the Bible. *See also specific names and events*
    compared to *Shame: The Power of Caring,* 1–3
blame, 22, 59–63, 78–79, 201
bloodshed, 108–109, 213, 233
bodily resurrection, 257, 300
Buddhism, 290–291
bullying, 23

## C

Cain, 101
Caleb, 112
causal action statements, 184–185
children and parents
    abuse, 72–74
    developmental sexual activities, 43
    differentiation-shame binds, 45–46
    generational transfer of shame, 72–74
    modeling behavior, 35–36, 66–68, 284
    relationships, 19–23
children of God, 217–218
chosen people, 301–302. *See also* Israelites; Jesus
*Chronicles,* Second Book, 185–187, 193
cleansing of the Israelites, 108–111, 113–115, 118–119
comparison making, 26, 155
competition, 27
compulsive disorders, 72–73
condemnation of others, 248–249
conformity, 28–29, 47–48
conservative ideology, 28
contempt, 58–59, 78–79, 171–172
conversations with God, 276–278, 306–308
conversion, 253

# *Index*

Corinth, letters to, 251–255
*Corinthians,* First Book, 252, 254, 256, 258–259
*Corinthians,* Second Book, 260–264
covetousness, 236
creation, 102. *See also* Garden of Eden
criticism of others, 245–246
cultural binds and norms, 25–32
Cyrus, 202–203

**D**
daily life, 297–300
David
    Absalom's rebellion, 162–167
    described, 152
    help sought from God, 156–161
    king favored by God, 148–151
    psalms expressing shame, 152–157, 159–161
    as shame transfer target, 167
death, spiritual, 98
defending ourselves
    adaptation, 51–52
    prevention of shame, 52–56
    transference of shame, 52–53, 56–63
Democratic Party, 28–29
depressive posture, 49, 70
*Deuteronomy,* 124, 126, 128–130
developmental sexual activities, 43
the devil, 102
diaper changing, 22
differentiation, 67, 287–289
differentiation-shame binds, 45–47
dignity, 8
discontent, 301–302
dissmell, 37, 58, 78, 171

divine shaming, 117
do/don't plans, 65, 129, 179, 193, 200, 211, 229, 305
drive-shame binds, 42–44, 178
drives and needs, 31, 66–67
drug abuse, 74–75

**E**
Eastern religions, 214–215
*Ecclesiastes,* 179–181
effort to eliminate shame, 95, 97, 99–100, 131–132, 184–185
Eli, 143–144
Elisha, 189–191
embarrassment, 75–76
emotional suffering, 259–262
emotions. *See also* affect blends; *specific types of emotion such as:* anger
  basic affects, 37–38
  expression of, 28–32
  internalizing shame, 36–40
  primacy of, 7
  rejection of, 66–67
entering God's kingdom, 279–280
envy, 155
eternal life, 258
Eve, 1–5, 94–103, 177, 201–202, 301
evil, 177–178
excellence, pursuit of, 43–44
*Exodus,* 108–109, 113–115, 124
extroversion, 51, 56, 62, 69–70
*Ezekiel,* 194–195, 198–200
*Ezra,* 196–197

# Index

## F
facial expressions, 22
faith in God, 227–232, 243, 259, 303–304
fall from grace, 146–151
families, dysfunctional, 8–9. See also children and parents
favor of God, 116–117, 141–149, 243–249
fear-shame binds, 41–42
female gender script, 28–29, 127, 178
*First Corinthians,* 252, 254, 256, 258–259
*First Kings,* 166, 169–170, 188
*First Samuel,* 142–148, 150
forgiveness, 124–125

## G
*Galatians,* 281
Garden of Eden, 1–5, 94–103, 177, 201–202, 301
gender roles, 28–32
generational transfer, 72–74
*Genesis,* 1–3, 82, 96–97, 99, 102–103
getting started, 303–310
glorification, 256
God. *See also* favor of God; redirecting toward the PERSON
   Adam and Eve and, 94–104
   children of, 217–218
   cleansing of the Israelites, 108–111, 113–115, 135–139
   David and, 148–151, 156–161
   endlessness of shame, 126–139
   forgiveness, 124–125
   humans, relationship with, 4–5, 82, 87–88, 301–302
   kingdom of, 279–280, 311–312
   letters to, 274–278, 306–308
   personhood of, 240. *See also* the PERSON
   punishment from, 116–118, 242
   shame mitigation, 122–124

shaming of offenders, 116–118
"voice" of, 303–304
grace, 100, 146–151
guilt/shame dynamic, 75–79

# H
*Habakkuk,* 194
Hannah, 142–144
Hebrew nation. *See* Israelites
hiding from shame, 1–7, 11, 75, 96, 98
hierarchy of needs, 90–95, 110, 201
homosexual acts, 110
*Hosea,* 188
humans
   God and, 4–5, 82, 87–88, 301–302
   as images of God, 82
humiliation, 23–24

# I
identification, 284–287
identification image, 66–68
identification need, 34–36, 82–85
identification-shame binds, 44–45
identity, 8, 12
"if...then." *See* "because... then" model
incest, 73–74
independence, 28, 47–48, 67–68
inherited shame, 196
inner peace, 293, 299
intellectual discovery, 277–278
intentional shame inducement, 21–22
intergalactic tour analogy, 87–88
internal representative, 66–68
internal shame spiral, 49

# Index

internal transfer, 36
internalizing shame
  autonomy, 33–34
  disobedience and, 244
  emotions, memory and behavior, 36–40
  identification need, 34–36
  Israelites, 111–113, 185
  outgrowths of, 49–50, 187–188
  shame binds, 40–48
interpersonal bridges, 13–16, 45, 174
interpersonal completion, 214, 217, 272–273, 278–279. *See also* relational union
interpersonal need, 4–5, 17–19, 29, 44, 47, 79–82, 183, 201–202
interpersonal redirection, 4–5, 95, 108, 120, 122. *See also* redirecting toward THE PERSON
intimacy, 16
introversion, 51, 56, 62, 69–70
*Isaiah,* 188–189, 191–192, 198–200, 206
Israelites
  cleansing of, 108–119, 213
  defined by shame, 120–139
  internalizing shame, 111–113, 185
  kingdom divided, 183–201
  kings, 142, 144–148. *See also* David; Saul; Solomon
  moral code, 141
  peace and prosperity, 175–176, 200
  personal shame, 141–144

## J

jealousy, 155
*Jeremiah,* 194–200
Jeroboam, 185–186
Jesus. *See also* relational union

God, relationship to, 209–214, 305
kingdom of God, 214–218
the Messiah, 205–209
mission and message, 221–224
model of relational union, 211–219
prays for us, 219–221
second coming of, 255–266
Sermon on the Mount, 302
unconditional love, 233
"voice" of, 303–304
Jews. *See* Israelites
Joab, 164
*John,* 116, 206–219, 222, 223, 282
*Joshua,* 112, 115, 121–123, 133–134, 137
journaling, 275, 308–310
Judah, 186–187, 192–202, 233
Judas Maccabeus, 204–205
justification, 253–254

# K

karmic model, 190
Kaufman, Gershen
   on affect theory, 38
   on blame, 60–61, 61–62
   on bullying, 23–24
   on contempt, 59
   on cultural norm-enforcing, 30–31
   on cultural scripts, 27, 29
   on defenses, 51
   on definition of shame, 10–11
   on differentiation, 46–48, 287
   on disowning of self, 65
   on emotion, primacy of, 7
   on exposure, 14, 50, 147

## Index

on extroversion, 56
on the guilt/shame dynamic, 75–79
on identification, 34, 35–36, 47–48, 66, 285
on internalized shame, 48–49, 58, 187
on introversion, 56
on modeling, 284
on mutuality of response, 14–15
on paranoia, 70–71
on parent-child relationships, 20–21
on peers, 24
on performance expectations, 23
on personal worth, 12
on schizoid posture, 69
on sexual abuse, 73–74
on shame, a new perspective, 8
on shame-based identity, 68–69
on shame binds, 40
kingdom of God, 279–280, 311–312
kings. *See* David; Saul; Solomon
*Kings,* First Book, 166, 169–170, 188
*Kings,* Second Book, 189–190

## L

law of Moses. *See* Mosaic law
letters to God, 274–278, 306–308
letters to others, 308–309
Lucifer, 102
*Luke,* 206–207

## M

*Malachi,* 195, 203, 205
male gender script, 28, 127, 178
manna, 113–115
*Mark,* 206

Maslow, Abraham, 91
material prayers, 307
*Matthew,* 206, 273
Mechanism of Interpersonal Redirection, 108
memory, 38–39
Menasseh, 193, 233
Messiah. *See also* Jesus
   names for, 206–209
   prophesies of, 205–206
mindfulness, 290–291
mockers, 171–173
modeling behavior, 35–36, 66–68, 284
moral code, 141
Mosaic law
   consequences of, 128–133
   obedience to, 119, 227–233
   shame increases, 118–119, 140–141
   shame mitigation and, 122–124
   sin and, 235–239
Moses, 113–114, 134–136

## N
name for the PERSON, 307–308
need-shame binds, 44–47, 47–48, 178
needs, hierarchy of, 90–95, 110, 201
needs and drives, 31, 66–67
*Nehemiah,* 137
*Numbers,* 112, 114–115, 134

## O
*Obadiah,* 184
one-year plan toward union, 304–306
oneness. *See* relational union
original sin, 101–104

# Index

**P**

paranoia, 70–72
parents. *See* children and parents
Paul the Apostle
   authority, 245, 262–265
   on bodily resurrection, 300
   conversion of, 226
   early life of, 225–226
   epistles of, 227–229
   Gentiles and, 251–255
   inner struggle of, 235–251
   law and obedience, 119, 227–229, 229–233, 235–239
   relational union pursuit, 265–270
   on relationship with God, 302–303
   resurrection of the dead, 256–259, 269
   sin and atonement, 233–235
   sin/shame paradigm, 105–108
   suffering, 259–262
peers, 23–24
Peninnah, 142
people needs, 15
perfection, pursuing, 53–55
performance expectations, 22–23, 43
the PERSON. *See also* God; redirecting toward THE PERSON; relational union
   identification need satisfied by, 288–289
   indwelling spirit of, 223
   name for, 307–308
   relationship with, 283–284, 290
   satisfies interpersonal need, 202
   talking to, 309–310
personal shame, 141–144
Pharisees, 210–215, 257
*Philippians,* 266–270, 302
physical abuse, 72–74

physical suffering, 259–262
the point, 292–296
popularity, 28–29
postures, 49, 69–72
power, striving for, 53
powerlessness, 116–117
prayer, 307
prevention of shame, 52–56
primary interpersonal need, 4–5, 17–19, 29, 44, 47, 79–82, 183, 201–202
primary interpersonal relationship, 283–284
progressive ideology, 28–29
prophesies of Messiah, 205–206
prophets, 188–191
*Proverbs,* 171–179
*Psalms,* 152–157, 159–161, 194, 196
psychological syndromes, 69–72
psychotherapy, 39
punishment from God, 116–118, 242, 259

**R**
rage, 13, 24, 57–58, 191
Rahab, 197–200
Randall, Albert, 294
rape, 73–74
redemption, 253–254
redirecting toward THE PERSON
    cleansing of the Israelites, 108, 120, 122
    David and, 159
    Garden of Eden and, 4–5, 95
    shame's purpose, 202, 223
Rehoboam, 185–187
relational union
    developing, 279–283

*Index*

    getting started, 303–306
    interpersonal powerlessness and, 250
    Jesus as model of, 211–219
    shame binds, cause of, 47
    unconditional love and, 233
relationship with God, 301–302
relationships
    disturbed, 8–9
    expectations of, 17–18
    failed, 80–82
    parent and child, 19–23
    shame's effect on, 11–12, 286–288
religion
Republican Party, 28
resentment, 50
restlessness, 301–302
resurrection of the body, 300
resurrection of the dead, 256–259, 269
retaliation, 156, 190
revenge, 24
*Romans,* 106–107, 227–232, 234–251, 300

## S

*Samuel,* First Book, 142–148, 150
*Samuel,* Second Book, 162–165
sanctification, 252–254
Satan, 102, 177
Saul, 146–151
Saul of Tarsus. *See* Paul the Apostle
"saved," 242–243, 305
schizoid posture, 69–70
school and peers, 23
scripts
    cultural, 27–32

# SHAME

gender, 28–29, 127
interpreting emotional cues, 38
*Second Chronicles,* 185–187, 193
second coming, 255–266
*Second Corinthians,* 260–264
*Second Kings,* 189–190
*Second Samuel,* 162–165
Seleucids, 204–205
self
   disowning, 64–72
   division of, 183–201
   shame and, 11–12
self-acceptance, 303
self-actualization, 92–93
self-blame, 78–79
self-consciousness, 75–76
self-esteem, 8, 92
self-shaming, 22, 155
self-sufficiency, 28
self-talk, 12
Sermon on the Mount, 302
serpent in the Garden of Eden, 4, 97, 102–103
sex-shame binds, 42–43
sexual abuse, 72–74
shame. *See also* internalizing shame
   avoiding, 5
   effort to eliminate, 95, 97, 99–100, 131–132, 184–185
   endless nature of, 126–139
   genesis of, 9–11
   others and, 13–16
   reactions to, 113
   tenacity of, 201
   understanding, 6–9
   a world without, 311–312
*Shame: The Power of Caring. See also* Kaufman, Gershen

## *Index*

    compared to the Bible, 1–3
    Tomkins on, 7
shame-based identity, 68–72
shame binds, 40–48, 177, 178
shame-defending strategies, 78
shame-expression, 12–13
shame-free life, steps to, 175–176
shame inducement, 21–22
shame-sending, 189–191, 245–251, 257
shame/sin link, 117–118
shame spirals, 49
shame transfer. *See* transference of shame
shedding shame, 280–283
Shimei, 162–166, 168–171
shyness, 75–76, 77
sickness of the soul, 98
sight, effort, and action, 95, 97, 99–100, 131–132, 178, 179, 184–185, 201
sin, sinning, and sinners
    of Adam and Eve, 177
    David, 154–155, 159
    disowning, 185
    escalation of shame, 57, 117–118
    original sin, 101–104
    shame *vs.*, 85–87
sin and atonement, 233–235, 253–254
sin-shame tie, 229, 230
"since...then." *See* "because... then" model
slavery in Egypt, 110–111
snowballing, 49
Solomon
    as David's heir, 166
    described, 168
    despair, 176–178
    hope, 179

Proverbs, 171–179
Shimei's curse, 168–171
steps to a shame-free life, 175–176
tongue taming, 173–174
speech and transfer of shame, 173–174, 190
speech-binding effects, 75
spirit, 283–284
spiritual death, 98, 176, 259
Stanley, Charles, 305
success ethic, 27–28
suffering, 259–262, 300
syndromes, 69–72, 72–75


**T**
tail-spinning, 49
talking to the PERSON, 309–310
temperament, 69–70
temple in Jerusalem, 167, 171, 202–203
*Titus,* 206
Tomkins, Silvan
   on affect theory, 37–38
   on autonomic differences, development of, 30
   on emotions, study of, 6–11
   on the guilt/shame dynamic, 75–79
   on the guises of shame, 303
   on postures, 69–72
   on powerlessness, 116
   on shame described, 10
   on sickness of the soul, 98
tongue and transfer of shame, 173–174
transference of shame
   blood of enemies, 109
   defending ourselves, 52–53, 56–63
   Garden of Eden truths, 201

*Index*

    generational, 72–74
    internal, 36
    verbal, 173–174, 190
tree of life, 122, 136
trust, 45

**U**
unconditional love, 233

**V**
verbal transfer of shame, 173–174, 190
"voice," 303–304

**W**
wings, life with, 296–297
withdrawal, internal, 56
work environments, 25–26
world without shame, 311–312
written conversations with God, 274–278, 306–308